Boston Marriages

Boston Marriages

Romantic but asexual relationships among contemporary lesbians

*Edited by Esther D. Rothblum
and Kathleen A. Brehony*

The University of Massachusetts Press
Amherst

Library of Congress
Cataloging-in-Publication Data
Boston marriages : romantic but asexual relationships
among contemporary lesbians / edited by Esther D. Rothblum,
Kathleen A. Brehony.
p.   cm.
Includes bibliographical references.
ISBN 0-87023-875-2 (alk. paper). — ISBN 0-87023-876-0 (pbk. : alk. paper)
1. Lesbian couples — United States.   2. Platonic love.
I. Rothblum, Esther D.   II. Brehony, Kathleen A.   III. Title:
Asexual relationships among contemporary lesbians.
HQ75.6.U5B62   1993
306.84 — dc20   93-4281

British Library Cataloguing in Publication data are available.

Contents

Introduction: Why focus on romantic but asexual relationships among lesbians? *Esther D. Rothblum and Kathleen A. Brehony*　3

Early memories, current realities　*Esther D. Rothblum*　14

Coming to consciousness: Some reflections on the Boston marriage　*Kathleen A. Brehony*　19

THEORETICAL ARTICLES

Nineteenth-century Boston marriage as a possible lesson for today　*Lillian Faderman*　29

"Why limit me to ecstasy?" Toward a positive model of genital incidentalism among friends and other lovers　*Marny Hall*　43

Celibacy　*JoAnn Loulan*　62

Lesbian courtship scripts　*Suzanna Rose, Debra Zand, and Marie A. Cini*　70

The Boston marriage in the therapy office　*Laura S. Brown*　86

PERSONAL STORIES

What's sex got to do with it?　*Leslie Raymer*　99

When we were whatever we were: Whatever it was that we had　*Laura Moxie*　109

She will never have the access to the total person that I have　*Elizabeth*　124

We've had a lot of history under our belts
Part I: Angie   132
Part II: Cedar   138

Cast of Characters   *Pat*   141

"I think it has to do with the fact that I love her"   *Janet and
Marty*   148

We have bliss   *Ruth and Iris*   157

A Boston engagement   *Sarah*   164

Television and books and just people talking make it seem that
there is more sex going on than there really is!
Maria Briani and Kathleen O'Reilly   174

DISCUSSANTS

Is sex a natural function? Implications for sex therapy
Ellen Cole   187

A matter of language   *Marcia Hill*   194

So what is a "Boston marriage" anyway?   *Oliva M. Espin*   202

Notes on contributors   209

Boston Marriages

Introduction: Why focus on romantic but asexual relationships among lesbians?

Esther D. Rothblum and Kathleen A. Brehony

If you live long enough, the culture will find the truth of your
eccentricity and embrace it. — Clarissa Pinkham Estes

THE IDEA for this book germinated when one of us (Esther) received a letter from Charles Silverstein, author of the book *The Joy
of Gay Sex*, and so the first pages of this account will be in her words.
Silverstein was planning an edited book for lesbian and gay male psycho-
therapists that would be a compilation of case studies. In his letter, he
stressed the fact that gay and lesbian therapists had extensive knowledge
of issues facing gays and lesbians in U.S. society today, but that these
issues were rarely published. As an example, he listed the topic of "compulsive sex" among gay men.

When I read the letter, it was this example that caught my attention. It
reminded me of an anecdote I had heard at a lesbian psychology conference. The lesbian speaker told us she and a gay male friend had shared
their sexual fantasies. Hers was being seduced by an unknown woman
and murmuring, "I love you." Her gay friend said his fantasy was being
in a room filled with floating penises.

What could be further from the reality of most lesbians I knew than
engaging in frequent and often anonymous sexual activity? When my
lesbian friends and acquaintances discussed sex, it was indirect, in the
context of the relationship. We discussed whether to enter, stay in, or
leave partnered relationships. I listened to lesbians recount flirtations,
declarations of love, arguments with partners, advice from ex-lovers.

These stories were full of detail, and we analyzed, empathized, gave advice. What we never did was talk about sex. We assumed that couples were sexual. Most of my friends celebrated the anniversary of their relationship on the date they first had sex. Many women broke up with their lovers when they or their lovers had sex with someone else. So sex was mentioned, but it was definitional. In contrast to the enormous amount of information I had about my friends' relationships, I knew next to nothing about their sexual activity.

A major survey conducted in the early 1980s found lesbian couples to report having sex less frequently than did married heterosexual, cohabiting heterosexual, or gay male couples. The survey's authors, Philip Blumstein and Pepper Schwartz, studied the relationships of over 12,000 people and published their results in 1983 in the book *American Couples*. In 1988, JoAnn Loulan published the results of her interviews with over 1,500 lesbians and found a significant percentage — 78% — to have been celibate for some period of time. Although the majority had been celibate for under one year, 35% were celibate from one to five years, and 8% had been celibate for six years or more. As Marilyn Frye (1990) has said: "Whatever it is that lesbians do that (for a lack of a better word) might be called 'sex' we apparently do damned little of it" (p. 305).

These data, particularly the first survey which was widely publicized in the media, caused great anger and disbelief among lesbians. Lesbians in my community indicated that they and their friends did have sex, and frequently. They challenged the researchers' definitions of "sex." Added to their arguments was the concern that any negative findings about lesbians would further stigmatize an already oppressed group.

Unlike my friends, I believed the findings of these surveys. But I also believed that lesbians were tremendously involved in relationships and had romantic, erotic, passionate feelings for other women (usually for one other woman). There were some women in my lesbian community who lived together and shared long histories together. Sometimes they had been sexual in the past, sometimes they had never had sex with each other. Sometimes they were ex-lovers, both now involved with other women, but there was still a connection that made newcomers to the community assume they were the couple. I knew women married to men who talked about their best female friend in terms that could only be described as romantic. Lesbians who had been in the convent described the tremendous passion that some nuns had for each other, despite celibacy. I decided to write about these women, although I had only a vague sense of how to define this kind of relationship.

I responded to Charles Silverstein, indicating that I would like to write a chapter about *asexual,* but romantic, relationships among lesbians. I stated that my idea might be rather controversial, but added that it would make an interesting contrast to the proposed chapter on compulsive sex among gay men. Charles encouraged my idea, but said he thought the concept wasn't new at all; I was describing what used to be termed a "Boston marriage" when he was young. He also urged me to write the chapter with a therapist, and I phoned Kathy. We will now speak in both voices.

The term "Boston marriage" referred to unmarried women who lived together in past decades. These women were presumed to be asexual (thus the name "Boston," which probably referred to the Puritan and asexual nature of the relationship). Lillian Faderman has vividly described these relationships in her book *Surpassing the Love of Men* (1981). In the past century and beginning of the 20th century, women were not expected to want genital sex, and thus the women in Boston marriages were free to express their emotional intimacy and passionate love for each other openly. The women lived conventional, respected lives as "spinsters" or they married men while continuing to express their love through letters and shared activities.

The assumption by lesbians today is that women in these Boston marriages were in fact sexual with each other. Lesbian fiction such as *Patience and Sarah* (Miller, 1969) and *The Ladies* (Grumbach, 1984) is based on historical descriptions of women who lived together, and the authors have introduced a sexual component into the lives of the characters. There is no record of whether these relationships were sexual, and if they were, the women would have kept the fact of their sexuality a secret.

We decided to reclaim the term "Boston marriage" to describe the concept of romantic but asexual relationships between lesbians today. We were interested in describing lesbians who were couples in every way except that they were not currently sexually involved with each other (and might never have been sexually involved with each other). They were neither friends nor ex-lovers. (See Carol Becker's book *Lesbian Ex-Lovers,* 1988, for a discussion of the ex-lovers in the lesbian community.) We expected that these women, in contrast to couples in Boston marriages of past decades, kept knowledge of their *asexuality* hidden from their community.

As we began to discuss romantic but asexual relationships among lesbians, we quickly realized the difficulty of defining a relationship that lacked the presence of sex. When heterosexuals marry, their relationship is defined as a marriage until they obtain a legal divorce. It does not require the presence of sexual activity to be considered a relationship. In fact, married couples are considered married even when they are celibate or when they are having sex with other people. However, for all other couples (lesbians, gay men, and cohabiting heterosexuals), their relationships are defined by the presence of sexual activity. This definition of a relationship indicates the salience of genital sex in our society. If sex determines whether two people are in a couple, then sex takes on tremendous symbolic importance aside from sexual pleasure in its own right. Naomi McCormick has referred to this as "genital proof." She states:

Because women's sexuality is socially constructed by men, contemporary sexologists are inclined to demand genital proof of sexual orientation. Before labelling her as bisexual or lesbian, most sex researchers expect a woman to have had genital relationships with other women. Feminists have pointed out some serious shortcomings with this assumption. Female bisexuality and lesbianism may be more a matter of loving other women than of achieving orgasm through genital contact. It is entirely possible that many passionate female friendships enjoyed by our foremothers excluded the mutual genital stimulation that people in our time expect before categorizing a relationship as sexual or erotic. The absence of genital juxtaposition hardly drains a relationship of passion or importance. (p. 2)

The lesbian community shares this genital view of what constitutes a couple. Despite the focus on intimacy and relationships, lesbians are defined as a couple if they are having sex with each other. This becomes problematic if we believe the survey data that lesbians have sex less frequently than do other couples. Then lesbians, no matter how passionate and close their relationships, will not view themselves as a couple when sex is not present.

Components of a Boston marriage

When an intimate relationship lacks the presence of sex, it becomes difficult to define its components. Our conversations were sometimes heated and often humorous as we argued our points of view. Our consensus was that romantic but asexual relationships between lesbians have a wide latitude, but typically include the following components (see Rothblum & Brehony, 1991, pp. 215–216):

1. The two members of the Boston marriage are not currently engaged in a sexual relationship with each other. They may never have had sex with each other, but, more typically, had a short period in which they were lovers.

2. One or both of the members are still sexually attracted to the other. In this regard, at least for one of the partners, the Boston marriage is different from a friendship.

3. With the exception of the lack of sexual activity, all other aspects of the Boston marriage are indistinguishable from many lesbian lover relationships. The two members may refer to each other in public or private as lovers and be physically affectionate in public or private social situations. They will engage in shared activities (rearing children, buying property, making out wills) that are rarely done by friends (or, if done by friends, are done for a specific and nonromantic reason).

4. The lesbian community is generally unaware that the two members are nonsexual and views them as a couple. Often, the romantic nature of their relationship makes them role models for other lesbian couples to emulate, and there may be some social pressure on the two members not to break up. When the lesbian community is aware that the two are *not* lovers, they will not be viewed as a couple.

5. Both members of the Boston marriage have typically had no, or limited, sexual experiences prior to the Boston marriage.

6. Both members of the Boston marriage are likely to be closeted to some degree in their place of employment, with their family, and in their town. If one or both members of the Boston marriage are extremely closeted or only marginally involved in the lesbian community, then they are less likely to refer to one another as lovers.

7. The two members of the Boston marriage usually have little or no direct communication about the lack of sexual activity in their relationship and the nature of their relationship.

Interview participants

When we had completed our list of components for the Boston marriage, we felt somewhat shy discussing these with other lesbians. We were not sure how others would react to our assertion that some lesbian couples in our communities may be asexual. Our imposter feelings increased when most lesbians expressed ignorance of the term "Boston marriage."

Our original criteria for and description of the Boston marriage had been for a book of case studies for lesbian and gay therapists. In fact, the fictional case we had developed, a composite of romantic but asexual relationships we knew, had been of two women who were in distress because the relationship was terminating. Although it is difficult to know when an asexual couple is "breaking up" (again reflecting the salience of genital sex in initiating a relationship and its absence in terminating a relationship), we had developed a case of two women who had been in an intimate relationship for 15 years but had been sexual for the first year only. When one member of this Boston marriage became sexually attracted to a woman outside the couple, she shrugged off the former relationship as being celibate anyway. This redefinition of a long-term relationship caused tremendous anguish to her former partner.

The case study we had developed was in many ways typical of couples that seek therapy, that is, their relationship is terminating or has terminated and they are distressed about this. As therapists read our chapter, they often asked for additional copies to distribute to clients who they realized met our criteria.

Thus heartened, we decided to edit a book about the modern-day Boston marriage. We knew that our "composite" case description was only one of the myriad of shapes that Boston marriages can have. We began to spread the word that we were interested in the stories of lesbians involved in romantic but asexual relationships. We presented a workshop on this topic at the National Lesbian Conference in Atlanta in 1991, entitled "Is It a Relationship if We're Not Having Sex?" About 30 women attended the workshop and many indicated that they were in some form of a Boston marriage. Most of the women in the interviews that follow came to this workshop. Others are women referred to us by friends of friends during conversations. None is from our own communities.

The respondents vary widely in age, from their early twenties to their sixties. All are living in the United States, and only one is a woman of color. They live in the Northeast, the South, the Midwest, the North, and the West.

We interviewed women in person and over the telephone. The conversations were transcribed and sent back to the respondents for their comments and additions. One woman wrote her own story and two women conducted their own interview and sent us the transcribed conversation. In all cases, we asked the women just to tell us the story of their relationship. We had no prepared questions or expectations.

Almost immediately, we found that our respondents challenged much of our original framework of the Boston marriage. The criteria we had developed for a Boston marriage did not always describe the women who were telling us their stories. Some of our criteria were met in that all respondents were currently asexual and most, but not all, had been sexual for a short period in the past. Except for women who were describing a relationship that had terminated, all were still sexually attracted to their partners. And with the exception of the lack of current sexual activity, their relationships were indistinguishable from lesbian lover relationships (or had been, if they had terminated).

On the other hand, we were surprised that not all the couples kept the knowledge of their asexuality hidden from the lesbian community. Several couples were quite open about their asexuality, although there was some variation in whom they told and in how supportive the community was about this knowledge. Quite in contrast to our criterion that the members of the Boston marriage had no, or limited, sexual experience prior to the Boston marriage, most of the respondents had a number of previous lesbian relationships that were sexual. Also surprising to us was that most of the couples were extremely "out" as lesbians in their communities and places of employment. Several indicated that they were leaders in their communities, or that their relationship was viewed as a model by others. Finally, the level of direct communication between the members of the couple about their lack of current sexual activity varied widely.

Thus, we found that our respondents in many ways negated all but the first three criteria we had developed about the modern-day Boston marriage. Interestingly, these are the criteria that are phrased most positively; the last four criteria indicated more secretiveness and less sexual experience. In looking over our original criteria, we realized that we had conceptualized a Boston marriage as somehow less mature or less "out" than a lesbian relationship. This reflected our own biases.

We must keep in mind that all the women we interviewed were contacted through lesbian workshops and through contacts in the lesbian community. What we don't have reflected here are women who are homophobic and who may avoid a sexual relationship in order to avoid sex with women. There are women who are married to men and who acknowledge sexual passion for a woman, although they are afraid of initiating a sexual relationship with her. There are women who live together as friends, who may each feel passion for the other, but who have never broached this topic out of fear of being lesbians. Women in the military are routinely discharged for any hints of same-sex activity. Women who live in small towns or in conservative parts of the country may fear public scrutiny. Religious women may fear excommunication. These women live in great pain, even if they are not always aware of the source of their pain. They may not even seek help from feminist therapists because they are extremely frightened of the stigma of lesbianism. We cannot lose sight of the biases in our sample.

We also found a number of other themes in the stories of our respondents. Many women wondered, what *is* sex? This question has the potential to be tremendously important in defining a lesbian relationship. Some women have redefined what sex is, or concur that their relationship defines sex differently than does the lesbian community. When the two members of a couple disagree on what constitutes sex, they may also disagree on whether they are in fact a couple. When a couple's definition of sex differs from that of the lesbian community, their relationship may be invalidated by current friends or by future lovers.

The stories that follow also indicate the difficulty many women have initiating sexual activity. Both Blumstein and Schwartz (1983) and Loulan (1988) cited women's socialization not to initiate sex as a reason for lesbians' lower level of sexual activity. In addition, the respondents struggled with whether or not to include sex with other people in the context of their Boston marriage. Some respondents were "monogamous" (another term that is difficult to use in an asexual relationship), some had sex with men or with other women, some were looking for sexual partners. Our respondents also differed in the words they used to describe their partner in the Boston marriage. Most agreed that the word "lover" was not appropriate given the lack of sex, but there were few alternatives in our current language.

One of the most fascinating, and unexpected, findings in the interviews was how many women described an extremely close relationship with a sibling, usually a sister. These siblings were described as their closest friends and soul mates. It is interesting to speculate whether intimate early friendships with siblings become the model for asexual but passionate relationships later on. So many people find intimacy through sex; their friends are all past lovers. But forming an early close bond with a sibling may serve as an ideal for friendships and romantic relationships that don't need sex to create intimacy.

Many of the women mentioned being in therapy, although their therapists differed in how supportive they were of the Boston marriage. One woman had not told her therapist that her relationship was asexual, and another emphasized that her reasons for going to therapy were not because of her Boston marriage. Studies have shown that lesbians are more likely to seek counseling than are heterosexual women (Morgan, 1992). A recent article by Kris Morgan and Michele Eliason (1992) discusses interviews with lesbians in therapy and lesbians who had never sought therapy regarding why lesbians are more likely to seek therapy. Their results indicate the willingness of lesbians to be introspective and to place high value on interpersonal growth.

In addition to hearing the personal stories of lesbians involved in Boston marriages, we invited well-known authors in the area of lesbian relationships to contribute theoretical articles about the Boston marriage. Lillian Faderman contrasts her research on 19th-century Boston marriages with lesbian relationships today. She describes the pressure for lesbians to be sexual today, and states: "Same-sex love that was purely platonic had become as unimaginable as intense platonic heterosexual love, a contradiction in terms" (p. 36).

Marnie Hall discusses the enormous significance of orgasms as defining relationships. She argues that women's sexuality is multidimensional, and that language needs to reflect the multifaceted nature of lesbians' relationships.

JoAnn Loulan's chapter focuses on celibacy among lesbians and the reasons for celibacy in lesbians' lives. She states that we are socialized to equate sex with intercourse, so that adolescents who have engaged in a variety of sexual activities, but not intercourse, will say that they haven't "gone all the way." This has implications for attitudes toward sexual activity among lesbians who are not engaging in genital sex.

Suzanna Rose, Debra Zand, and Marie Cini have conducted surveys on what constitutes "dating" among lesbians. Their chapter on lesbian courtship scripts indicates that the concept of "dating" is poorly defined in the lesbian community. As a result, lesbians move quickly from casual sex to instant merger.

Laura Brown writes about the Boston marriage in the therapist's office. Her question, "Is there a primary relationship present, or just two good friends in denial?" is one that intrigues many therapists when they hear about the Boston marriage. She describes how the therapists' own homophobia and ambivalence about sexuality have a major influence on their interpretation of the Boston marriage and whether it will be viewed as a "real" relationship.

How do we, the editors, conceptualize the Boston marriage? From the beginning, our views were divergent, with Esther tending to idealize the Boston marriage and Kathy viewing it as more problematic. We would like to elaborate on our own perspectives in the chapters that immediately follow. We decided to begin this discussion by sharing some of our own personal experiences in romantic but asexual relationships, since our own stories seem to influence our theories about the Boston marriage.

In sum, as Sarah Hoagland (1991) has stated in her book *An Intimate Wilderness: Lesbian Writers on Sexuality:*

We need new language and new meaning to develop our lesbian desire, especially as we explore and develop what draws us, where our attraction comes from, what we want to keep, what we want to change and why, how our attractions vary, how our desires change over time, and so on. And this is an interactive, not an introspective, matter. We need a lot more discussion and exploration among ourselves in something like consciousness-raising groups, certainly among intimates — lovers and friends — to develop the meaning of lesbian desire, and to heal our fragmentation. (p. 168)

We hope that readers will be challenged to reconsider the very basis of what constitutes a lesbian relationship. Our lesbian communities need to redefine our terminology and move away from sex as the focal point of "legalizing" a relationship. We invite readers to contact us with their own experiences and opinions of ways of relating among lesbians.

References

Becker, C. S. (1988). *Lesbian ex-lovers.* Boston: Alyson Publications, Inc.

Blumstein, P., & Schwartz, P. (1983). *American couples.* New York: William Morrow and Co.

Elgin, S. H. (1985). *Native tongue.* London: The Women's Press.

Estes, C. P. (Speaker). (Fall 1989). *Women who run with wolves.* (Cassette Recording No. 1-56455-082-6). Boulder, CO: Sounds True.

Faderman, L. (1981). *Surpassing the love of men.* New York: William Morrow and Co.

Frye, M. (1990). Lesbian "sex." In J. Allen (Ed.), *Lesbian philosophies and cultures.* Albany: State University of New York Press.

Grumbach, D. (1984). *The ladies.* New York: Fawcett Crest.

Loulan, J. (1988). Research on the sex practices of 1566 lesbians and the clinical applications. *Women and Therapy, 7,* 221–234.

McCormick, N. B. (in press). Lesbian and bisexual identities. Ch. 4 in *Sexual salvation: Affirming women's sexual rights and pleasures.* New York: Praeger Publishing Co.

Miller, I. (1969). *Patience and Sarah.* New York: McGraw-Hill.

Morgan, K. S. (1992). Caucasian lesbians' use of psychotherapy: A matter of attitude? *Psychology of Women Quarterly, 16,* 127–130.

Morgan, K. S., & Eliason, M. J. (1992). The role of psychotherapy in Caucasian lesbians' lives. *Women and Therapy, 13,* 27–52.

Rothblum, E. D., & Brehony, K. A. (1991). The Boston marriage today: Romantic but asexual relationships among lesbians. In C. Silverstein (Ed.), *Gays, lesbians, and their therapists.* New York: W. W. Norton & Co.

Early memories, current realities

———

Esther D. Rothblum

I wrote her name on my note-pad / And inked it on my dress
And I etched it on my locker / And I carved it on my desk
— Meg Christian, "Ode to a Gym Teacher," 1974

How DID I come to be fascinated with lesbian relationships that are romantic and erotic, but that don't include sexual activity? My earliest memories are of being in love with or attracted to other girls — "real" sex came much later.

I was four years old and my family was on vacation. We stopped at a motel for the night. As evening approached, I went to the motel's playground. Although I was normally an extremely overprotected child, I have no memory of other adults around. But another small girl was there, about my age, and I immediately fell in love with her. We played together on the swings and in the sandbox until my parents called me back for dinner. This image is the more surprising because as a child I was painfully shy — I never talked to anyone outside my immediate family. As soon as dinner was over, I ran back outside. The girl — my instant love — was still there. I ran towards her with outstretched arms, and she too held out her arms so that we fell into an embrace. I can still recall that feeling of complete and uncomplicated love, with the secure knowledge that it would be reciprocated by that other little girl.

Two years later, I was in first grade. My family lived in the country, and school was an hour away. I was one of the first children on the school bus in the morning. After a while, two older girls got on the bus. (At the time, I thought they were college students, but in retrospect I suspect they were in fourth grade.) They always sat on both sides of me, all three of us squeezed together on the narrow bus seat. Each day, they put their arms around me and exclaimed how sweet I was. I luxuriated in their affection and at night fantasized that they were making love to me. I can't remember the details of that fantasy, but I do remember that my feelings were sexual and erotic, not merely thoughts of love and affection.

Surely these stories aren't unusual, although we don't have a name for such early sexual or romantic experiences. I know that I didn't tell my parents or friends about these experiences at the time. Did I suspect that they might disapprove? While the names and identities of my earliest friends have become memorialized through letters and photographs, the names of my first loves are gone.

My family strongly emphasized the importance of close friendships. I'm always surprised to hear lesbian friends tell me that their only friends are past and present lovers. In my case, it was the other way around. I fell in love with my friends.

When I was 11, Piera moved next door. She had long black braids similar to my short braids and was plump like me. In those years before weight loss became a societal obsession, we weighed ourselves periodically and it was the thinner one's responsibility to gain a pound or two to match the heavier one's weight. Piera was also a tomboy, and we shared our T–shirts and shorts. My passion, besides sports, was dolls, and Piera was crazy about horses. She had a dozen plastic horses, which she dressed in dolls' clothes. We matched them up with my Barbie dolls, so that for a long time her favorite filly, Jet Star, was having an affair with Ken. We talked about sex, but didn't know what it meant. It was my first experience of spending the night at someone else's house, and we spent each weekend in her bed together, mostly playing with toys. But we also played a game in which we took off our pajamas and took turns running our fingers down each other's spines. The trick was to make the other person move first, by finding places that tickled. I was extremely turned on.

When my family moved, I skipped a grade, and the other girls in eighth grade were adolescents while I still looked like a child. My only comfort was my crush on Dawn, a girl who struck me as the most sophisticated young woman I had ever met. She was even dating a ninth-grade boy. I was in love with her outfits. I drew pictures of each one and then tore them up in case anyone recognized that I was making drawings of Dawn's clothes. I was old enough to realize that crushes on girls were not okay. I didn't even tell Dawn how I felt about her, but instead did her homework for her so that she would want to be around me. When the annual school ski trip drew near, I had my leg in a cast, so I asked Dawn to spend the night. That night my parents got a call that my brother had broken his leg skiing. They left, and Dawn and I were alone. She asked me for a back rub, told me to watch her take a shower, and then asked if she could count the moles on my back. I made us hot chocolate and showed her my books; I was a little taken aback by her behavior, which so closely matched my fantasies of her.

It is remarkable to me that the sexual and loving feelings I had for these friends were never verbalized or acted out. I am quite certain that if anyone had found out about my sexual feelings for Piera or Dawn, I would have been forbidden to spend time with them. I might have been sent to a therapist for treatment of these "deviant" feelings. I would probably have been punished by my parents. And I would have been watched closely for signs of further attraction to girls.

How typical are such early passionate experiences with friends? We have no terms for early crushes on friends, and we do not celebrate the anniversary of when we first became "best friends." Lillian Rubin (1985) has touched on this phenomenon briefly in her book *Just Friends* (an appropriate title, because it illustrates how we devalue friendships in our society). She likens best friends to "new loves" and states: "I say 'a new love' because, irrespective of the sexual orientation of the girls involved, these friendships share many of the characteristics of a love affair, so obsessively are the friends entwined" (p. 113).

Two professors at Simmons College, Laurie Crumpacker and Eleonor Vander Haegen (in press), conducted a study in which they tried to develop classroom assignments for female students that would decrease their homophobia and distancing from the lesbian experience. They asked these students to read accounts of 19th-century Boston marriages and to write about intimate, nonsexual relationships with their own friends. The instructors were taken aback by the intensity of the students' accounts of their own friendships. They state:

We were unprepared, however, for the heartbreak of lost friendships, sometimes so painful that the student vowed never to open up again. These last accounts were not written in the heat of first rejection; rather they sometimes came from older students, and the vows have been in effect for many years. (p. 2)

As these examples illustrate, it is not only lesbians who struggle with passion in nontraditional relationships. In 1990, Ann Landers asked if married couples enjoyed "a full life without sex." She was flooded with over 35,000 responses from people of all ages who had no or little sex and didn't miss it. Women were more likely to be disinterested in sex than were men. Catherine Whitney (1990) interviewed heterosexual women married to gay men. She found that women in these marriages separated love from sex, and were often asexual. Interestingly, I have found little reference to asexuality among men, heterosexual or gay. Marilyn Frye (1990) describes her surprise at reading a book about gay male sexuality:

It was astounding to me for one thing in particular, namely, that its pages constituted a huge lexicon of *words:* words for acts and activities, their sub-acts, preludes and denouements, their stylistic variation, their sequences. Gay male sex, I realized then, is *articulate.* It is articulate to a degree that, in my world, lesbian "sex" does not remotely approach. Lesbian "sex" as I have known it, most of the time I have known it, is utterly *in*articulate. Most of my lifetime, most of my experience in the realms commonly designated as "sexual" has been pre-linguistic, non-cognitive. I have, in effect, no linguistic community, no language, and therefore in one important sense, no knowledge. (pp. 310–311)

At a recent workshop, Marnie Hall (1991a) described the reason sex remains the defining variable in lesbian relationships. According to her, lesbians have little external validation of our relationships; when we don't have sex, our internal validation is taken away as well. She recommended that lesbians throw away our "Cliff Notes" of relationships and write our own story, which would be an intimacy narrative rather than a sex narrative. If the patriarchy feels that a good relationship includes sex, then it's important to subvert sex. She stated: "There is no such thing as sex. There is romance and fantasy and orgasm but no IT. The closest thing to IT is male erection. We need to take an oath to stop trying." Hall has also quoted a client in therapy as saying (1991b): "I wanted to have a sex life of abandon, so I said, okay, just abandon your sex life."

In the book *Native Tongue* (Elgin, 1985), a group of women develops a secret language to liberate themselves from male oppression. The language is based on women's experience, and includes words for terms that are complicated to explain in male-made languages, such as the love felt for a friend versus the love for a lover. My own interest in editing the present volume is to describe romantic but asexual relationships among lesbians, as a way of naming a phenomenon that I used to think was true only for me.

References

Christian, M. (1974). "Ode to a gym teacher." Song from record album *I know you know*. Oakland, CA: Olivia Records.

Crumpacker, L., & Vander Haegen, E. (in press). Pedagogy and prejudice: Teaching about homophobia and gay experience. *Women's Studies Quarterly*.

Elgin, S. H. (1985). *Native tongue*. London: The Women's Press.

Frye, M. (1990). Lesbian "sex." In J. Allen (Ed.), *Lesbian philosophies and cultures*. Albany, NY: State University of New York Press.

Hall, M. (1991a October). Lesbian sex: Sapphic sizzle or phallocentric fizzle. Workshop presented at the Feminist Therapy Institute, Berkeley, California.

Hall, M. (1991b). Ex-therapy to sex-therapy: Notes from the margin. In C. Silverstein (Ed.), *Gays, lesbians, and their therapists*. New York: W. W. Norton & Co.

Landers, A. (1990 June 25). Sex among married couples: The thrill is gone, but love isn't. *The Burlington* (Vermont) *Free Press*, pp. 5A, 8A.

Rubin, L. (1985). *Just friends: The role of friendship in our lives*. New York: Harper & Row.

Whitney, C. (1990). *Uncommon lives: Gay men and straight women*. New York: Penguin Books.

Coming to consciousness: Some reflections on the Boston marriage

Kathleen A. Brehony

I WAS IN a relationship with a woman for almost five years but never knew how to describe it to anyone. I felt like I was in love with her but we never discussed it. I felt jealous and hurt when she would date men but we never discussed it. We owned a home together, moved together, shared expenses, acquired several pets together, slept in the same bed, but never discussed exactly what it was that we were to each other. We were never sexual with each other but we kissed once and that led to a frantic phone call to my therapist and a swooning spell that put her in the emergency room. But we never discussed any of that. I know that when she left me I was devastated and depressed.

Although a lot of time has passed since then, I occasionally hear a song that reminds me of her. As it turns out, it's Barry Manilow music that triggers these memories, and unless I'm trapped in an elevator by an easy listening station, I can pretty much live without any reflections on this time in my life. But I'm not sure that's good. Perhaps I need to remember her and some of the experiences of the earlier part of my journey.

In thinking about writing this chapter, I realized that my thoughts were shooting out in all directions and that I would have to be inspired (or lucky) in order to pull my thoughts together and make any kind of cogent point about the Boston marriage. My thinking seemed to focus on two issues: What is the meaning of the term "relationship"? and What is central to women's (and lesbian women's in particular) sexuality?

I felt that if I could address these two primary issues then I could clarify my perceptions of Boston marriages and, thus, add to the reader's understanding of this complex issue.

What is a "relationship" anyway?

There are many forms of relationship. For example, I have relationships with my mother, father, brother, colleagues, my yellow lab. I have
relationships with friends, but these don't all feel the same to me. I treat
some friends as family. They are the people I connect with when something great has happened in my life and we celebrate together. I share
my greatest disappointments with them and we grieve together. Other
friends are people that I enjoy being with, playing tennis with, going to
movies with. And although we are usually there for one another in some
ways, if one of us were to move away I'm sure that we would replace each
other relatively quickly. My closest, dearest friends are in my heart, and
no matter how the miles might conspire against us, that is where they
will forever remain. It seems linguistically inaccurate to use the same
word, "friend," to describe people whose souls are somehow attached to
my own as well as people with whom I simply enjoy some activities.
Nevertheless, we can explain the feelings, connections, behaviors, expectations in these diverse relationships by using adjectives and other
qualifying language: best friend, good friend, casual friend, my friend
from work, my friend in the neighborhood, and so forth.

We are infinitely restricted by a language system that has precious few
resources to describe the multilayered, complex, unique relationships
among people. This restriction points to the limited importance placed
upon human relationships in our culture. People who study such things
often note how cultures devise language precisely to describe things that
are important to them. That's why Eskimo cultures have so many different words for snow, I suppose.

It is not surprising that in a culture that has far more words for describing warfare than relationships among people, there is a failure of
language to define the central realities of those relationships. In Sanskrit,
the basis for Persian and many Middle-Eastern languages, there are 96
words for the English word, "love." I can't imagine that with 96 words
for this basic human expression, there is not some clear distinction between the friends held for life and those of a more transitory, superficial
kind.

This failure of language is even more pronounced as we consider gay
and lesbian culture. Think of the choices we have when we look for the
word to best describe the person with whom we share our love, our

life, our home, our bed, our deepest secrets, our sexuality. "Significant Other" sounds like a census questionnaire definition to me. "Partner" — someone I'm in business with. "Mate" — we pull the sails on the boat together. "Lover" — we spend most of the day in bed together. "Gal-Pal" — used by the tabloids to describe Martina Navratilova and her "friends" — too funny!

Not that the language for heterosexual relationships is really much of an improvement: husband, wife, spouse. But the difference seems to lie in the cultural understanding of the terms. If one is married there is a legal and common understanding about the nature of the relationship. One is a "spouse" to so-and-so whether one is currently involved in a sexual relationship or not. One is still the "spouse" even if the other "spouse" is having a sexual relationship with someone else. In fact, the person with whom one's spouse is having sex is usually referred to as his or her "lover." The word most widely used by gay men and lesbians to refer to one's primary emotional and sexual partner is the same word that usually describes the illegal — and oftentimes considered immoral — relationship with someone else's "spouse." No wonder we're confused.

To complicate matters even more, most lesbian relationships seem to be built upon this model of heterosexual, monogamous marriages. But since the legal role of "spouse" is unavailable to lesbians and gay men in the United States (and throughout most of the world) we have settled, by and large, for the role of "lover." And the word seems to imply that a fundamental aspect of the relationship is sexual.

What, then, is the nature of the "lover" relationship if there is no sexual relating? Is it a relationship if the partners are not having sex? How much sexual activity is necessary to qualify a relationship as one between lovers? What exactly was that relationship that I described earlier? We weren't "lovers" since we really never had sex. I don't think we were friends. I have never felt jealous or upset because a friend was dating someone else. In fact, I'm generally happy for friends who are dating someone who seems to make them happy. Why, then, was I so miserable when she left me? It felt just like being dumped by my boyfriend in college. Only worse.

Perhaps we are so limited by language that we will never come to any precise way to categorize any relationship. How do we go about defining a "lesbian relationship"?

What are our alternatives? First, we can accept that no system of language will ever adequately describe the complexity of human feelings involved in our relationship to another human being. While some languages clearly do a better job than others, none can ever do justice to the feelings in our heart and soul. Perhaps that is because emotions and language come from fundamentally different places within us. Second, we can develop a language of our own that at least comes closer to describing feelings than our current language. Many groups — from professional organizations to hi-fi enthusiasts — use language systems that describe their common interests. For example, I recently read a compilation of terms used by surfers to describe a variety of ocean conditions and people on the beach. It was quite an estoric language, but well understood by the members of that particular subculture. Perhaps it is time for the gay and lesbian culture to develop our own language to describe our realities instead of waiting for the mainstream culture to provide it for us.

The term "Boston marriage" is an attempt to create language for a reality of lesbian culture. As we are using it here, it simply means a romantic but asexual relationship between women. In order to understand it further, it is necessary to look at the nature of romantic and sexual feelings among women.

What is the nature of sexuality?

I believe that sexual expression is part of our very nature as human beings. This instinct that draws us into connection with other human beings is as real and as powerful as our need for food and water. But in patriarchal cultures, sexuality, especially for women, has been split off from the rest of life. As women, we have endured being cut off from our own natures. We have delineated sexuality into what Germaine Greer has referred to as the "Madonna/Whore" dichotomy. Most important, sexuality has been detached from our own spirituality. There was a time in the history of our species when sexuality and spirituality were more connected.

We have lived in a masculine consciousness for so long that most of us only have vague archetypal memories of that long-lost feminine energy. The split is so profound in so many women that many of us are largely unconscious of our own sexual and creative instincts. Our feminine energy is usually constellated around ideas of nurturance, compassion, connectedness. While the feminine is all of those, we often forget that she embraces passionate, fiery forces as well. She is the gentle summer rain that renews the fields, but she is also a lightning bolt. Patriarchy has all but obliterated this aspect of the feminine.

Nancy Qualls-Corbett (1988) has described this process in her excellent book *The Sacred Prostitute: Eternal Aspects of the Feminine*. She states:

In the ancient matriarchies, nature and fertility were the core of existence. The people lived close to nature, therefore their gods and goddesses were the nature divinities. Their deities ordered destiny by providing or denying abundance to the Earth. Inherent in the individual's human nature was erotic passion. Desire and sexual response experienced as a regenerative power were recognized as a gift or blessing from the divine. Man's and woman's sexual nature and their religious attitude were inseparable. In their praises of thanksgiving, in their supplications, they offered the sex act to the goddess revered for love and passion. It was an act, honorable and pious, pleasing to both the deity and the mortal alike. (p. 30)

This sexual/erotic aspect of the feminine was apparent in many ancient cultures — Sumerian, Babylonian, Persian, Egyptian. Qualls-Corbett described how this important aspect of women changed in more recent history: "There came a time when the goddess was no longer worshipped; then the physical and spiritual aspects of the feminine were declared evil." (pp. 40–41)

As patriarchal cultures continued their advances against the feminine-identified cultures, women's sexuality, which was once regarded as a gift from the heavens, became more and more split off from mortal women. Qualls-Corbett elaborates:

Roman law placed a woman under guardianship and stated that she was imbecilic. In Greece the laws of Solon gave her no rights at all. Hebrew law condemned a woman to death if she was not chaste at the time of marriage, and if she committed adultery she was stoned to death. A husband could take several wives but a woman's virtue, indeed her very identity, depended upon being married and faithful to her husband. . . . The laws of the Manu state "A woman assumes through legitimate marriage the very qualities of her husband like a river that loses itself in the ocean." Pythagoras wrote: "There is a good principle, which has created order, light and man; and a bad principle, which has created chaos, darkness and women." (pp. 45–46)

Sexuality in women was seen as part of that dark world energy. Women became dismembered, split apart from their bodies, from eroticism, from feeling in general. The feminine principle was elevated to a distinctly ethereal place, and those aspects of the goddess were spiritualized and attached by Christian theology to the Virgin Mary or were eliminated altogether. The split in the feminine became one of spiritual purity against evil. A split in women's nature occurred that has yet to be healed. This split is likely to be exacerbated in a relationship between two women. They have been profoundly affected by this split, even if unconsciously so. This becomes a central issue for women: How do we heal this duality in our lives, in our relationships, and in our own sensual way of relating to our lives? What happens to sexual energy when a couple is not relating sexually?

The women we interviewed for this book seemed truly to love each other. They reported feeling that they were in loving relationships. But in every case there was an absence of sexuality, of Eros. Indeed, our very definition of a Boston marriage is based upon the exclusion of sexuality from the relationship.

Adding to the problems caused by the cultural splitting of sexuality from life, many women have experienced sexual abuse. For those women, sex has been connected with violence at an early age, and sex and violence continue to be linked in adulthood. Sex has been used as a weapon, primarily by men against women. For a large number of women this occurs through personal experiences with sexual violence as women are the targets of rape, incest, sexual harassment, and battering, predominately by men. But for *all* women, this attempt to annihilate the feminine through sex occurs also more indirectly, as we watch sexual violence on television, read about its occurrence in our neighborhoods, and are warned to constrain our own behavior (walking alone at night, wearing certain clothes) in case we should "invite" sexual violence. In this way all women have had our sexuality curtailed.

It is not the case that there is only one legitimate way to make love and that all other ways are invalid. Sexuality is about physicality; about being in one's body. As our sexuality is taken away, so are almost all our other instincts. Many lesbians of our generation, free to pursue careers without the constraints of a heterosexual marriage, and often without children, have become our fathers' daughters. We have moved away from a woman's reality, away from instinct. It requires a great deal of insight and effort for women to reclaim the sexuality that has been taken away from us.

The drive for a sexual union in whatever form that takes is an instinct for most living beings. And that has been taken away from women. Women should not be blamed for this lack of sexuality, as if it reflects some kind of [personal] neurosis; it should not be pathologized. Nevertheless, it seems to me that our sexuality must be reclaimed. We serve ourselves when we "re-member" the goddess and the instinctive nature that is our birthright.

The Boston marriage

If you believe, as I do, that sexuality is a part of our human nature, then you must conclude that there is a certain energy attached to those instincts. Where does that energy go in a relationship without sexual expression? Does it become sublimated? Does it manifest itself in some addiction — drugs, alcohol, food, work? Many lesbians in relationships seem to channel unexpressed sexual energy into falling in love with women other than their lovers, thereby terminating the original relationship. The passion can be reignited, reawakened as it is transferred to another relationship. Often the relationships that are left behind were ones characterized by mutual responsibility, communication, trustworthiness, love — characteristics of relationships that many heterosexual women would covet.

There is a big difference between consciously rechanneling this instinctive energy into creative acts and unconsciously allowing it to drift or, worse still, drive us to unhealthy behaviors or decisions. Celibacy, for example, can be a perfectly fine and healthy way to live if it is a conscious choice. Women who are celibate and aware of the motivations behind that choice are making a conscious, volitional decision. Celibacy may be the preference for reasons of spirituality, health, or physical concerns, or it may reflect a decision to focus libido into creative pursuits. However, if there is not a conscious choice then the sexual energy will lack focus. Many lesbians blame their partner for her lack of interest, or they may feel guilt, or suffer low self-esteem based on their "lack of sexual attractiveness." Often they will not discuss the issue. Instead, the sexual aspect of the relationship just withers and dies, and both partners may come to wonder whether they are "lovers" or not.

The level of sexual activity and passion that is generally present in the beginning of a relationship is not usually present to the same degree as a relationship ages. Michael Liebowitz (1983) discusses the chemical, hormonal, and pheremonal variables that play a part in this initial attraction. In fact, this author compares the passion of a new relationship to an amphetamine-induced state! As a relationship matures, the level of sexual passion can be expected to wax and wane. Sometimes this may have to do with external events, but often it seems cyclical in and of itself. But each partner in a relationship has some threshold for, some expectations about, the acceptable level of sexual passion (even if this expectation is not to have sex). Relationships often break up when one partner feels her needs not being met even though she may never have discussed these needs with her lover.

In contemplating the Boston marriage among lesbians, we noticed that the women we interviewed differed in their level of happiness and acceptance of their relationships. In our original chapter, written for a case studies book for therapists, we described a couple that was breaking up and in distress. However, most of the women we interviewed for this book were, in fact, quite content with their relationships.

In reflecting on my own five-year Boston marriage I can only conclude that this was an unconscious, unhappy, unhealthy relationship for me. Now, many years later, I can see that my own insecurities, my homophobia, my need to feel connected to a partner, motivated me to stay in a relationship that was more often anxiety-producing, destructive, and sad rather than offering the good feelings and opportunities for self-growth that characterize healthy relationships.

A relationship is a relationship whether is has a collectively agreed-upon name or not. Our use of the term Boston marriage is not meant to further categorize or, in any way, pathologize any form of relationship. Rather, it is intended to expand the vocabulary of lesbian culture to incorporate relationships that have not been described by our language system but have nonetheless existed and continue to exist.

In my opinion, the relative desirability and healthiness of a Boston marriage (or any other type of relationship) comes down to consciousness. Is the individual in such a relationship aware of her own needs and motivations in not being sexual with her partner? Is she blocking her own instincts and nature? If so, in blocking her own sexual instinct is she blocking other instincts as well? Is she directing the energy attached to her erotic nature into other avenues? Are these good and healthy choices for her? Most important, does she know herself and are her choices made with self-knowledge and awareness?

References

Liebowitz, M. R. (1983). *The chemistry of love.* Boston: Little, Brown and Co.
Qualls-Corbett, N. (1988). *The sacred prostitute: Eternal aspects of the feminine.* Toronto: Inner City Books.

Theoretical Articles

Nineteenth-century Boston marriage as a possible lesson for today

Lillian Faderman

MARK DeWOLFE HOWE, a late 19th-century editor of *Atlantic Monthly*, numbered among his friends notable female pairs such as the writer Sarah Orne Jewett and Annie Fields. These women were usually feminists and almost always career women, or otherwise financially independent of men, and they tended to live in couples, in long-term, devoted relationships. From what Howe could see their relationships were marriages in every sense on which he dared speculate. The female pair was inseparable: they not only shared a home together, but they also had mutual friends, they vacationed together, they were totally involved in one another's lives and devoted to each other.

Whether they had a sexual relationship was not a question that bore examination, as far as Howe and his contemporaries were concerned. It was undoubtedly taken for granted (probably rightly in many cases) that the women, being respectable middle-class females who understood and internalized their society's strictures about sexual expression outside of duties to a husband and procreation, did not have sexual relations with each other. The inevitable individual differences with regard to sexual appetite were ignored. The assumption was that, as well-brought-up females, these women would have had no autonomous sexual drive but could only have been reactive to a male. Yet despite the apparent lack of sexual relations between such pairs, Howe could say of these relationships that they were "a union — there is no truer word for it" (H. Howe, 1965, p. 83).

The pervasiveness of such relationships in late 19th-century urban

America is attested to in Henry James's eponymous novel *The Bostonians* (1885), in which James presents a myriad of devoted women pairs. James characterized his novel as "a very *American* tale . . . [about] one of those friendships between women that are so common in New England" (Matthiessen and Murdock, 1947, p. 47). In fact, such relationships came to be called "Boston marriages." For the career woman of the late 19th century, a time when female same-sex relationships were not yet widely stigmatized as "lesbian," such "marriages" made wonderful sense. They afforded a woman companionship, nurturance, a communion of kindred spirits, romance (and undoubtedly, in some but not all such relation-ships, sex) — all the advantages of having a "significant other" in one's life and none of the burdens that were concomitant with heterosexuality, which would have made her life as a pioneering career woman impossi-ble. For many middle-class career women they have continued to make sense even a century later.

It was apparently not difficult for many people in the late 19th century to understand that if a woman was serious about working in one of the new careers that were then opening up for females, she could not tie herself to a situation that would obligate her to numerous pregnancies and the running of a large household. She had best remain a "spinster." As a spinster she was not permitted by the rules of morality to avoid loneliness through a heterosexual liaison, but there was no apparent reason to deny herself the companionship of a close female friend.[1]

Close female friendship has had a noble history in earlier eras. Else-where I trace the development in the West of the institution of romantic friendship, which dates back at least to the Renaissance.[2] Analogues of that Western institution may be found in the non-Western world as well — in, for example, China, India, and Africa.[3] Romantic friendship was possible and prevalent in other eras (and places) before Western sexologists defined into being the species of "lesbian" and disseminated their definition to popular consciousness. "Lesbian" signified a sexual identity that made the presumed and much admired "noble purity" of romantic friendship suspect. The emergence of the category "lesbian" also separated women who loved other women from the rest of female humanity, forcing them to accept the new classification of their affec-tions — and hence themselves — as abnormal.

But the evidence is overwhelming that intense female affection was not always seen in that light. Historically, young women were often permitted relationships with other females in which they might kiss, fondle each other, sleep together, utter expressions of overwhelming love and promises of eternal faithfulness. To what extent those relationships were actually sexual is impossible to determine definitively. Assuming a spectrum of individual sexual appetites, it is difficult to believe that none of them were genitally erotic, and the historical record confirms that some of them certainly were.[4] But my guess is that most of them were not, for the very reasons, suggested above, that the romantic friends' contemporaries believed they were not. Although biology accounts in a general way for the potential of sexual desire, the individual's interaction with her society and individual environments more often than not has determined the extent of its expression. For example, in the 1950s only 20% of the women Kinsey interviewed had had sexual intercourse by the age of 19. In 1971, the number in a comparable sample had risen to almost 50% (Kanter and Zelnik, 1972, pp. 9–19). What had changed, obviously, was not the biology of sexual desire, but the social mores that permitted (and sometimes even forced) more women to acknowledge desire and to act on it. A parallel may be drawn between heterosexual and homosexual behavior.

To an extent even greater than in the 1950s, women in the 19th century were encouraged to deny sexuality. They were brought up to believe that good women had no autonomous sexual drive — they merely did their duties to their conjugal bed and procreation. If they were not married, not pushed by considerations of a husband's needs, they were not sexual. Probably more women, whether heterosexually or homosexually inclined, internalized rather than fought those proscriptions on their sexuality. Thus, most women were socially constructed not to be very sexual.

From the vantage point of our very sexual era, it may be difficult to believe that women could have denied what we see as peremptory urges. But Kinsey's statistics demonstrate to what extent young women, even in the 1950s, were denying "sexual urges." The conclusion is almost tautological: in a society of sexual permissiveness, women tend to express themselves sexually (whether heterosexually or homosexually). In a society that is sexually repressive, women are more likely to internalize that repression and to have fewer sexual relations outside of marital *duties*.

Hence, 19th-century Boston marriages, and the romantic friendships that preceded them, were probably most often not genital in their expression.

But whether or not such relationships were usually sexual, it is clear that they were intensely passionate yet socially condoned. The published record of the romantic friendship of the late eighteenth-century French writer Mme. de Stael and her beloved Juliette Récamier, unselfconsciously preserved for posterity, illustrates that women took for granted the social permissibility of female-female passion. For example, Mme. de Stael wrote to Mme. Récamier at various times:

I love you with a love surpassing that of friendship. I go down on my knees to embrace you with all my heart.

You are in the forefront of my life. . . . It seemed to me when I saw you that to be loved by you would satisfy destiny. It would be enough, in fact, if I were to see you. . . . You are sovereign [in my heart], so tell me you will never give me pain; at this moment you have the power to do so terribly.

Adieu, my dear and adorable one. I press you to my heart. . . . My Angel, at the end of your letter say to me *I love you*. The emotion I will feel at those words will make me believe that I am holding you to my heart. (Levaillant, 1958, pp. 137, 182, 183–84)

Why were such relationships permissible in other eras and stigmatized in our own? Perhaps one answer is that for centuries men did not take them seriously — and not only because to do so would have violated an inviolable and universal male chauvinism that mandated the notion that women had no real existence apart from men. Romantic friendship was not considered threatening to the social fabric primarily because, in the middle and upper classes where it appears to have been the most common, it was generally assumed until the late 19th century that women had to marry for the sake of economic survival if for no other reason. In other words, such relationships were seen as temporary, or at least secondary to marriage.

And such relationships served a recognized social purpose as well. In the eras under consideration, it was incumbent upon the "decent" woman to have little to do with men outside of marriage. She had to be wary where she placed her affections lest she endanger her reputation. She could permit no imputations on her chastity. But it was unrealistic for society to demand that she love no one, feel no emotion or exaltation whatsoever, until she was carried away to her husband's home. Romantic friendship with another female could supply those needs and, as I have already suggested, was also presumed to be innocent and harmless. It was considered no threat to a young woman's virginity (which was generally deemed to be of great value), and it kept her out of trouble until her marriage. Henry Wadsworth Longfellow in his 1849 novel *Kavanagh* described such relations between young women as "a rehearsal in girlhood of the great drama of woman's life," that is, marriage. Similarly, Oliver Wendell Holmes observed, not without smugness, in his 1885 novel *A Mortal Antipathy*, "the friendships of young girls prefigure the closer relations which will one day come in and dissolve their earlier intimacies."

The sexologists' creation of the category "lesbian" began in the 1870s, simultaneously (and perhaps not entirely coincidentally) with the opening of possibilities of economic and social independence for women. For a period of several decades, middle-class women began to enter the work force, though not yet in threatening numbers. At this stage, the new sexologists' pronouncements had not yet become popular knowledge. Thus the "Boston marriage," a late 19th-century version of the earlier romantic friendship modified by the women's new economic independence, could develop and flourish for a period without stigmatization.

There is evidence that by the teens of the twentieth century the sexologists' categorization of love between women as abnormal had indeed infiltrated popular consciousness.[5] Intensely affectional relations between women were no longer socially condoned and accorded innocuous-seeming labels such as "romantic friendships" and "Boston marriage." Women who loved other women were generally forced to accept the label "lesbian." The tremendous alteration of the public's perception of women's relationships is well illustrated by Mark DeWolfe Howe, who observed and admired Boston marriages. As the friend of James Fields, an *Atlantic Monthly* editor, Howe befriended Fields's widow, Annie, and became her biographer and adviser. He knew that Fields, just before his death in 1881, considered Sarah Orne Jewett as the ideal friend to fill the impending gap in his much younger wife's life, and that Fields encouraged the relationship between the two women. Jewett and Annie Fields then lived together in Boston for almost 30 years, until Jewett's death in 1909. On occasion Jewett went off to Maine to write in isolation. But the two women kept up an amorous correspondence which they, like de Stael and Récamier and countless other female pairs, preserved for posterity, seeing no need to hide the expressions of their devotion and love:

Here I am at the desk again, all as natural as can be and writing a first letter to you with so much love, and remembering that this is the first morning in more than seven months that I haven't waked up to hear your dear voice and see your dear face. I do miss it very much, but I look forward to no long separation, which is a comfort.

I shall be with you tomorrow, your dear birthday. How I am looking forward to Thursday evening. I don't care whether there is starlight or a fog. Yes, dear, I will bring the last sketch and give it its last touches if you think I had better spend any more time on it. I want now to paint things, and drive things, and *kiss* things [italics are Jewett's]. . . . Good night, and God bless you, dear love. (Fields, 1911, pp. 16–18)

But consciousness was different in the 20th century from what it had been in the 19th century. In 1911, a couple of years after Sarah Orne Jewett's death, Annie confided to Howe that she wanted to publish a volume of Jewett's letters to her. Howe, reflecting on the incident in 1922, at the height of Freudian consciousness, claimed that he "laid a restraining editorial hand across [Annie's] enthusiasm" (M. Howe, 1922, p. 283). He suggested that Annie omit four-fifths of the indications of affection between the two women, "for the mere sake of the impression we want the book to make on readers who have no personal association with Miss Jewett. . . . I doubt . . . whether you will like to have all sorts of people reading them wrong" (H. Howe, 1965, p. 84). Clearly what had been considered perfectly common and appropriate behavior and affectional expression in the 19th century suddenly became abnormal in the context of the twentieth century, though nothing in the nature of the relationship had changed.

By the 1920s women no longer had the luxury (or rather the safety) of being able to call their relationship a "Boston marriage," even if it was as asexual as most people generally assumed 19th-century Boston marriage was. With the growing popularity of sexology in the 1920s (particularly through the fashionableness of Freud and psychoanalysis), as well as the publication of Radclyffe Hall's *succes de scandale, The Well of Loneliness* in 1928, and the emergence in the 1920s of a somewhat visible homosexual subculture in both Europe and America, it became virtually impossible for two women to enjoy intensely close relationships and not be sus-

pected of lesbianism. As Wanda Fraiken Neff observed in her 1928
novel, *We Sing Diana*, even on women's college campuses, which had
been little heavens of romantic friendships in the second half of the 19th
century, "intimacies between two girls were watched with keen, distrust-
ful eyes. Among one's classmates, one looked for the bisexual type, the
masculine girl searching for a feminine counterpart, and one ridiculed
their devotions." Terms such as "romantic friendship" and "Boston marriage" slipped out of the language to be replaced by terms such as "per-
version," "inversion," "homosexuality," and "lesbianism."

The change in attitudes cannot be explained by a growing awareness
of sexual possibility alone. By the 1920s the institution of female-female
relationships had become socially threatening as it could not have been
in earlier eras. The various successes of the feminist movement now
meant that many more women were in the work force and could be
economically independent. Legions of women, not just a pioneering few,
no longer had to marry for the sake of survival. If economics could not
lead women to marriage, and if they were perfectly fulfilled through
relations with other women, what would become of the beleaguered
institution of heterosexual marriage that had long borne the brunt of
feminist attack? The stigmatization of female-female relationships as
abnormal became a weapon of heterosexual defense.

The effect that stigmatization had on female-female relationships is
complex. On the one hand it was devastating, because it meant that
women who could not accept the stigmatizing label of "lesbian" had to
deny themselves the possibility of intense same-sex emotional involvement that females had enjoyed for centuries. If only *lesbians* loved other
women, and they themselves were not lesbians, then they had to repress
any intense feeling they might experience for another female. In that
sense, women of the 1920s and thereafter had far less latitude than their
earlier counterparts.

But on the other hand, the introduction of "lesbianism" gave women
far greater freedom to take their same-sex relationships seriously, since
they could now see them as potentially permanent. And if they were
willing to accept the label "lesbian" for themselves, they could build a
lifestyle and even a subculture out of their love for other women that was
generally impossible earlier.

However, once a woman accepted the label "lesbian" and took her
place in a lesbian subculture, she suffered other pressures connected

with her love for other females that had not existed earlier, pressures quite apart from having one's identity stigmatized. The new wisdom of the modern era was that everyone, even woman or child, was a sexual being (an idea that, as I've already suggested, would have been passionately contested in most earlier eras in Euro-America). Entirely inverse to the assumptions of the previous century and earlier, it was now widely presumed that the kind of relationship that would stimulate such passion as attested to in, for instance, the letters of Mme. de Stael or Sarah Orne Jewett must invariably have a sexual component. And, undoubtedly, that assumption was often made by the women involved, whether their own impulses led them in an erotic direction or not. That is, if they permitted themselves to experience an intense involvement with another female, they had to accept the label "lesbian"; and since "lesbian" implied female-female *sexual* relations, they were under an internalized pressure (even if only for the sake of seeing themselves as emotionally consistent) to perform.

Twentieth-century psychoanalytic theory, or its popular interpretation that suggested a universal sexuality, generally failed to acknowledge varying levels of erotic interest and drive in individuals. (In this sense it was as naive as the 19th-century view that similarly failed to acknowledge individual differences, assuming that all females other than prostitutes had little or no autonomous sexual drive [Faderman, 1981, 147–56]). Hence, "lesbians" were reduced to "women who are interested in having sex with other women." The categories that existed earlier such as "romantic friendships" or "Boston marriages" were no longer valid since intense female same-sex love that was purely platonic had become as unimaginable as intense platonic heterosexual love, a contradiction in terms.

Moreover, the "lesbian" who had little desire to be erotic now had to question her own "sexual repression," a concept that did not exist earlier: Perhaps she was not sexually driven because she had suffered some "trauma" that had "inhibited" her natural "sexual drive"! Were her sexual "repressions and inhibitions" making her "neurotic"? In astounding irony, society's attitude toward female sexuality had undergone a diametrical inversion. In earlier eras a woman had to worry that her sexual feelings were inappropriate and abnormal, and had to hide from everyone the fact of any sexual experience she might have had. In the post-sexologist era a woman has had to worry that her lack of sexual feelings is inappropriate and abnormal, and she must hide problems such as asexuality or "inhibited sexual response," another modern construct. In earlier eras a woman was educated to feel anxious and guilty if she indulged in nonmarital sexual relations. Women in more modern times have been made to feel anxious and guilty (at least toward themselves) — to feel that they have not expressed themselves fully, and that they are endangering their physical and mental health — if they do *not* indulge in sexual relations. In popular wisdom, sexual pleasure has become something of a medical necessity. In the modern era, the internal and external pressures on women to be sexual have been as insistent as the pressures to be asexual in other eras. And those pressures have been at least as strong for lesbians as for heterosexual women.

In fact, the pressures on lesbians to be sexual have been even stronger. For the 20th-century heterosexual woman, until the sexual revolution of the 1960s and 1970s, society delivered a dual message, as the Kinsey statistics cited above bear out. On the one hand, sexual repression was bad for you. But on the other hand, a "good girl" dared not express herself sexually lest she become a "bad girl." For the lesbian such a conflict did not exist. On the contrary, as Esther Newton (1984) has pointed out in her essay "The Mythic Mannish Lesbian," one benefit a woman could enjoy in becoming a lesbian was the privilege to "lay claim to her full sexuality" (pp. 7–25). That is, since it was believed that a lesbian was a man trapped in a woman's body, the lesbian had a kind of permission to claim for herself a sexual drive that was as strong as the male's. If she were not interested in laying such a claim, was she really a lesbian after all? To be a lesbian meant, and continues to mean, to feel permission, or pressure, to assert oneself sexually.

This permission has been wonderfully liberating for many women. For others, who see it less as permission than as pressure, it has been perplexing. It may be especially perplexing to those who identify themselves as being in a lesbian relationship but would prefer to have that term signify what "Boston marriage" meant in the 19th century. They value their relationships because they provide nurturance, companionship, practical financial and domestic arrangements, affection, tenderness — everything except genital sexuality. But despite the success of such relationships in so many areas, the women involved may feel something lacking because popular modern wisdom (inculcation of which one cannot escape) says that sex is central to everyone's well-being.

Perhaps such pressure can account for the often-observed phenomenon of serial monogamy among lesbians. The modern pattern tends to be that of two women who identify themselves as lesbian and form a relationship that is initially sexual. (That aspect is ineluctable since the label "lesbian," as they learn in the subculture, denotes sexual behavior.) They live together for a number of years, and the sexual contact almost invariably diminishes as the two women fuse emotionally and settle into a domestic routine. One of the women then becomes sexually involved elsewhere. The first relationship ends and a new monogamous one begins, the pattern being repeated. Implicit in the pattern is the assumption, often felt as a pressure, that "real" lesbian relationships must continue to be sexual through the years.

In reality they often are not. A study by Philip Blumstein and Pepper Schwartz published in 1983 indicated that only one-third of the lesbian couples in relationships of at least 2 years' duration had sex once a week or more (compared to two-thirds of their heterosexual counterparts). Even more striking is the statistic in this study that almost half the lesbians in long-term relationships of 10 years or more had sex *less than once a month* (compared to only 15% of their heterosexual counterparts) (p. 196). Whether because of biology or vestiges of a socialization process that has made many women ambivalent toward sex, or for any other of a myriad of possible reasons, the fact is, most woman-woman relationships tend to be less sexual than relationships in which a man is involved.

Those 1983 statistics are confirmed by a more recent study by Susan Johnson, *Staying Power: Long Term Lesbian Couples* (1990). Johnson found that 92.3% of her sample of couples who had been together for at least 10 years reported that the frequency of sexual contact decreased since the beginning of their relationship. Almost 60% of her sample had sex once a month or less, and almost 20% had had no sex whatsoever during the year in which they were interviewed (pp. 152, 159). Perhaps one secret of the "staying power" of these couples is that despite 20th-century pressures to be sexual, most of them have been able to satisfy themselves with a relationship that is as asexual as most 19th-century Boston marriages appear to have been.

There are numerous reasons why lesbians seem less able to sustain sexual activity within a long-term relationship than heterosexual couples. The most obvious is that there is no male (who has been trained to be sexually aggressive as part of his induction into manhood) present in a lesbian relationship. Women must consciously learn to be sexual initiators, and our society does little to assist with such lessons. The task is a difficult one, and once the impetus of initial passion disappears it is not easy for a woman to maintain her role as initiator. It is even more difficult because for women there are no undeniable signs of sexual arousal such as male tumesence. Hence, sexual desire that is less than full-blown is often not brought to a genital conclusion. After the first excitements of a sexual relationship have passed, it becomes easier to replace sexual activity with less energy-consuming cuddling.

These facts are not easy to face for lesbians who prize their hard-won rights to express their sexuality. Perhaps the resurgence in the 1980s of butch-femme relationships and the interest in lesbian s/m can be seen as attempts to overcome what has been called "lesbian bed death,"[6] that is, the disappearance of sex in long-term lesbian relationships. This "bed death" has been attributed to the tendency of lesbians to fuse with their partners and thereby destroy the barriers and differences that are often the most powerful stimulants to the sexual appetite. But there is no statistical evidence that these attempts have been successful.

Lesbians, perhaps like most women, often seem to crave two things that appear to be mutually exclusive: long-term monogamous relationships and satisfying, on-going sexual relations. But the statistics confirm that the combination is seldom possible, and lesbian relationships that last are generally those that do not make such a dual demand.

Nineteenth-century Boston marriages did not have to deal with those contradictory demands if the women most often assumed, as I suspect, that while cuddling and fondling and emotional support were essential to their relationships, sex was not. Perhaps that explains why serial monogamy appears to have been less prevalent in the 19th century: Most of the women involved in Boston marriages probably did not chase the elusive permanent passion. Thus they were freer than lesbians of our own age to cherish and maintain what was valuable in an emotional relationship that was not genital.

It has become extremely difficult in the late 20th century for women who love women to accept the fact that some contemporary female-female love relationships, like 19th-century Boston marriages, are not particularly genital. Ironically, in *Staying Power*, Susan Johnson shows that most of the women in her sample of long-term lesbian relationships are not very sexual; but even she has difficulty with the idea that genuine lesbian relationships do not always have some genital expression. She presents in the first chapter of her book two 93-year-old women who have been together for 65 years and are presently sharing a room in a nursing home. Throughout the years, they pooled their money, bought property together, took care of the invalid mother of one of them, shared daily tasks such as cooking and driving. They still talk about the love they have for each other and the "wonderful life" they have had together, and they cry at the thought of its coming to an end (Johnson, 1990, pp. 29–31).

Johnson claims, however, that theirs is not a lesbian relationship because they have never been sexual together. Yet many of the women in her sample of long-term lesbian relationships have not been sexual together for years, and some of them were barely sexual together even at the beginning of the relationship. Perhaps it is inaccurate to suggest that the sine qua non of a lesbian relationship is its genital sexuality if most long-term lesbian relationships (to which lesbians so frequently aspire) are so often barely sexual and may even be asexual. Perhaps we need to learn something from the 19th century that will help us broaden our concept of the meanings and structures of committed love between women.

It may be useful to resurrect from history the term "Boston marriage" as a description of long-lasting love relationships between women that are seldom or never sexual. That term might give women another way to look at their relationships that transcends 20th-century pressures to seek an elusive sexual passion, which often accounts for the breakup of a couple. The re-creation of that category would permit many women to explain their relationships to themselves and others not as problematic because they lack what has been socially constructed in more recent times to be seen as essential, but rather as viable unions with honorable histories.

Although it may be anachronistic to apply the term "lesbian" to women in 19th-century Boston marriages who had never heard that term, to call contemporary committed relationships that have ceased to be (or never were) sexual "neo-Boston marriages" has better justification. The phrase provides a category for lesbian relationships that are "unions," as Mark DeWolf Howe described them, in every sense but the sexual. It also recognizes such relationships as part of the spectrum of possibilities in lesbian life, and legitimizes a common form of relating within the lesbian community.

Notes

1. I discuss 19th-century Boston marriages at greater length in *Surpassing the Love of Men*, pt. IIA, chs. 4 and 5, and *Odd Girls and Twilight Lovers*, ch. 1.
2. See *Surpassing the Love of Men*.
3. Compare to romantic friendships the female relationships described in Gay; Oldenburg; and Sankar.
4. See *Surpassing the Love of Men*, p. 208, and *Odd Girls and Twilight Lovers*, pp. 31–36.
5. See *Surpassing the Love of Men*, pt. IIIA, ch. 1.
6. On lesbian fusion and "bed death" see Loulan; Krestan and Bepko; and Nichols.

References

Blumstein, P., & Schwartz, P. (1983). *American couples: Money, work, sex*. New York: William Morrow and Co.

Faderman, L. (1981). *Surpassing the love of men: Romantic friendship and love between women from the Renaissance to the present*. New York: William Morrow and Co.

Faderman, L. (1991). *Odd girls and twilight lovers: A history of lesbian life in twentieth-century America*. New York: Columbia University Press.

Fields, A. (Ed.). (1911). *Letters of Sarah Orne Jewett*. Boston: Houghton Mifflin.

Gay, J. (1985 Summer). "Mummies and babies" and friends and lovers in Lesotho. *Journal of Homosexuality*, 97–116.

Howe, H. H. (1965). *The gentle Americans: Biography of a breed*. New York: Harper and Row.

Howe, M. DeW. (1922). *Memories of a hostess: A chronicle of eminent friendship drawn chiefly from the diaries of Mrs. James T. Fields*. Boston: Atlantic Monthly Press.

Johnson, S. E. (1990). *Staying power: Long term lesbian couples*. Tallahassee, FL: Naiad Press.

Kantner, J., & Zelnik, M. (1972). Sexual experience of young unmarried women in the United States. *Family Planning Perspectives*, 4(4), 9–19.

Krestan, J. & Bepko, C. (1980). The problem of fusion in lesbian relationships. *Family Process*, 19, 227–89.

Levaillant, M. (1958). *The passionate exiles* (M. Barnes, Trans.). New York: Farrar, Straus, and Cudahy.

Loulan, J. (1985). *Lesbian Sex*. San Francisco: Spinsters Ink.

Matthiessen, F. O. & Murdock, K. R. (Eds.). (1947). *The notebooks of Henry James*. New York: Oxford University Press.

Newton, E. (1984). The mythic mannish lesbian. *Signs: Journal of Women in Culture and Society, 9* (4), 7–25.

Nichols, M. (1987). Lesbian sexuality: Issues and developing therapy. In Boston Lesbian Psychologies Collective (Ed.), *Lesbian psychologies: Explorations and challenges* (pp. 97–125). Chicago: University of Chicago Press.

Oldenburg, V. T. (1990). Lifestyle as resistance: The case of the courtesans of Lucknow, India. *Feminist Studies, 16*, 259–287.

Sankar, A. (1985 Summer). Sisters and brothers, lovers and enemies: Marriage resistance in southern Kwangtung. *Journal of Homosexuality*, 69–81.

"Why limit me to ecstasy?" Toward a positive model of genital incidentalism among friends and other lovers

Marny Hall

SANDWICHED between other musty tomes in the library stacks before me, *Psychopathia Sexualis* looked like an alchemical manual. The medieval impression was reinforced by the first paragraph I opened to:

> The sexual life of these homosexuals ... is entirely like that in normal heterosexual love; but since it is the exact opposite of the natural feeling, it becomes a caricature, and the more so as these individuals ... are subject to excessive sexual desire. (Krafft-Ebing, 1904, p. 240)

Scrawled in the margin next to the paragraph was "Ignorant and homophobic! Views have changed." At another objectionable point the irascible exegete had scribbled "Bullshit. Gays are as healthy and happy as anyone else!" The bravado of the scrawled sentiments seemed almost as quaint to me as the original text.

I was in the library looking for a way out of a clinical cul de sac — my inability to provide my couple-clients with solutions to their fugitive or mismatched sexual desires. Even before these scores of couples came to my office, many had already exhausted a variety of home remedies: ex-

NOTE: This chapter's title is a quote from Jane Heap, partner of Margaret Anderson. (Anderson, 1971, p. 232). Their lesbian literary capers are detailed in Anderson's autobiography *My Thirty Years War*, originally printed in 1930, reprinted in 1971, by Greenwood Press.

Heartfelt thanks to Jeanne Adleman, Liana Borghi, Nanette Gartrell, Richard Hall, Susan Kennedy, Diana Russell, and the women who were willing to be interviewed, for their contributions to this article.

otic vacations, erotic dates, electric toys; well-placed crystals, Kegel exercises, and chakra adjustments; and, finally, simply white-knuckling their way through disinclination.

I, too, had suggested remedies of various kinds for slumbering libidos. I had assigned sensual massages combined with communication exercises. I had challenged and provoked and supported. I had probed fears about the consequences of their impasse. I had ferreted out hidden power imbalances. I had traced the historical resistance, in each, to personal boundary dissolution. I had recommended individual therapy.

Some of these strategies worked — temporarily. For the most part, however, the incandescence of their first months returned briefly, only to vanish again.

The problem, I finally concluded, was not with relationships or desire, but with the phallocentrically based prescription of sexuality. Such a prescription also informs lesbian sex. To be sure, lesbians have transformed, elaborated upon, erotically mocked, and even zealously avoided the old phallocentric/coital model. We have, in short, done everything except totally discard it. If I could show that our attempts to perform or even to vary sex — a phallically inspired act — was actually a cognitive misadventure, based on a narrow, irrelevant model, perhaps I could begin to reconfigure touching, intimacy, and fun into new female pleasure forms. In this process, genital touching, instead of the primary signifier of intimacy, would become incidental. New forms of intimacy — playfulness, for example, or special rapport — might include genital touching, but then again they might not.

Getting rid of inappropriate notions of sexuality would also rehabilitate relationships deemed substandard because they were "sexless." I hoped, in this brave new world of intimacy, that genital access might be demoted as the index of all that was relationally significant between women. Such a recalibration would then allow other intimacy patterns, currently invisible, to emerge.

In order to achieve all this, I needed evidence. Having moved on from Krafft-Ebing in the library, I was browsing through a collection of gay documents when I came across the following account from a turn-of-the-century lesbian's diary:

While we did indulge in our sexual intercourse, that was never the thought uppermost in our minds. That was but an outlet for emotions which too long had been pent up in both our lives for the good of our health. We found ourselves far more fit for good work after having been thus relieved. We had seen evidences of overindulgence on the part of some of those with whom we came in contact, in loss of vitality and weakened health, ending in consumption. (Casal, 1983, p. 307)

Apparently for the diarist Mary Casal, sex was purely functional, a capacity for release which, underexercised or overused, might interfere with one's work or other "higher" aims. Was this, I mused on my way to the restroom, the smoking gun, the proof that sex — even among avowed lesbians — was entirely reflective of phallocentric reality? After all, Casal's account is saturated with the language and the norms that governed heterosexuality a century ago. One would be hard-pressed to find anything uniquely lesbian in her description of lesbian sex.

Once inside the restroom stall my eyes alighted on the following graffito: "Will one of you heterosexual nazis or homosexual elitist bigots please explain why anyone would give a shit who I — or anybody else for that matter — fuck?"

I felt a bit lightheaded, as though I had traveled through a century of change in a few minutes. Krafft-Ebing's disdainful "scientific" scrutiny of "these homosexuals" had melted into Casal's recipe for the "purest and most ideal of any type of union known" (Casal, p. 306), and had been replaced, in turn, by a postmodernist restroom proclamation of emancipation from all norms governing private, idiosyncratic expressions of desire. It was, I concluded, impossible to define lesbian sex independently of the discourses of any period. Even more compelling than this revelation, however, was my glimpse of the structure of change. I realized that what had happened to me in the library was, on a small scale, exactly what had happened in the century between Krafft-Ebing's pronouncements and the bathroom door proclamation. I had added my own mental notations about the commentary scrawled in the Krafft-Ebing margin. *Psychopathia Sexualis* was itself a notation on previous texts. I had become one among a legion of contributors to the fragmented, contrapuntal conversation between authors and readers, clients and therapists, the deviant and the "normal." Seeing the traces of information on the pages and in the margins, on restroom doors, and in my own ruminations, I realized that such fragments took decades, centuries to coalesce into paradigmatic shifts. Much as I would like to make a definitive statement about sex, I have to reconcile myself to recording a few observations that one day, I can only hope, will be part of a critical mass that culminates in a new female framework of intimacy.

Grand Central Genitalis

This incremental approach to sexual redefinitions makes sense for other reasons. How, after all, can I expect to make an end run around the importance of erotic passion — of sex — in my own life? Over the years, the most dramatic shifts in my identity, my habitation, my work have been, in large part, attributable to my attempts to be close to someone I was "in love with" at the time. Perhaps if I can identify how such passion has come to occupy such a privileged position in my life and memory, I may have more insight into the power of the phallocentric models of sex.

I can identify several elements, some neurological, some existential, some psychological, which, in combination, seem to account for the memorableness, the saliency, of sexual passion for me:

— Pleasure, often genitally focused, that I attribute to the enriched nerve endings which give Homo sapiens a reproductive edge (and sapient homos, an erotic one).

— Surprise that comes from the rupture in the ordinary. Events, sub- and extracutaneous, become unpredictable. I, too, am transformed in surprising ways by my lover's gaze.

— Excitement that seems to be a by-product of the anxiety about loving someone who because of gender or other circumstance is "off-limits."

— Intensity, which seems to come from a feeling of "oneness" with a partner. Perhaps because I am psychologically minded, such blissful moments seem to be reenactments of an early scene in my life — perhaps a reunion with a parent I thought had abandoned me, or just a repetition of infant-parent fusion;

— Satisfaction that comes from doing something that I feel "counts," as inscribed in a personal yet universal ledger.

Combining physiology and psychology so seamlessly, it is no wonder that sex is memorable. And why quibble about whether it is a phallic act if, in the course of doing something that approximates "it," I can heal ancient wounds, recalibrate my nervous system, reinvent lovers as goddesses, and transform my own fumbling into moments of grace. It is no wonder one client protested, when I insisted that she stop trying (and failing) to "do it," "You want me to abandon sex when all I want is a sex life of abandon." (Hall, 1991, p. 94)

Sex may be a phallic act; but it is also the code word for lesbian bliss.

Friends and other lovers

Any challenge to the power of sex to type and rank our relationships seems to depend on finding other forms of intimacy that, while perhaps not able to displace genital centrality, can engender comparable levels of stimulation, pleasure, and well-being. At first glance, it seems as though the bonds with good friends and ex-lovers might compete with genitally based intimacy. However, these relationships too seem structured by sex: no sex or ex-sex.

The most promising area for new intimacy forms would seem to reside in the borderland — within relationships not easily categorized as friend or lover or ex-lover, but which might have elements of each. In order to find such relationships, I began to quiz women I met socially about their intimate arrangements. I polled friends and friends of friends. Through this social scanning, I eventually found a handful of women whose intimacies defied simple categorization.

What was most striking about these relationships was the unselfconsciousness of the partners. I have often interviewed conventional lesbian couples. They are typically aware of the image they want to present and often make comments like, "We've learned and practiced so much that we're now at a stage where things actually work," or, "We still have our crises but we handle them differently." In contrast, the women I interviewed, since they hadn't viewed their affiliations as intimacies, were startled that their stories merited anyone's interest. One interviewee said, "The best of the relationship was that we improvised as we went along. Since we had no expectations, the relationship developed at its own pace without disappointments about how we weren't meeting each other's needs." By jumping the old definitional tracks, these women not only generated new forms of intimacy, but also escaped the orthodoxies, the "shoulds" that vitiate conventional intimacies.

Shinko and Trey: Affidamento[1]

Shinko and Trey have been intimates for 15 years. Their bond, though they are both lesbians, was never eroticized. Once they got drunk, kissed, and dissolved into giggles. Lovers have come and gone. Their current household consists of Trey's lover, Shinko's two-year-old child, a dog, and two cats. They met in a professional training course in 1975 and were drawn to one another. They careened in and out of each other's lives for several years, usually when one, needing refuge after a painful breakup, moved in temporarily with the other. Gradually, without realizing it, both became crucial to each other. Ten years ago they bought a house together. This was a turning point. Trey says, "Shinko put up more than twice what I contributed. She did it in a very trusting way . . . so different from what I had learned in my family. Her generosity blew me away."

Against all advice, the papers they drew up stated nothing about possible dissolution. It was understood that neither should have to move out of the house because of the other one. In case of death, the survivor would inherit the entire house.

TREY: Of course I love my lover but Shinko . . . well . . . I'm very proud of her. I idealize her. I'm proud to be known as her friend. It enhances me. She can be a bigger, stronger person when I'm tripping and can calm me down.

SHINKO: And I get unconditional love from you . . . well not unconditional, but as close as I can get. I can let you see aspects of me I wouldn't let other people see . . . you'll see the good part of it. . . . Because of you, I get pushed into projects I would never initiate. I wouldn't have bought a house on my own.

TREY: Because of Shinko, I got drawn into political activities, working on the battered women's center and on a lesbian custody battle.

Italian feminists call this kind of bond *affidamento*, or entrustment. The concept of a relationship built on entrustment differs from friendship or sexual bonding because it acknowledges and builds on inequalities that are customarily denied in women-women relationships.

Differences are not always complementary. Sometimes Trey and Shinko detest each other's choice of friends and lovers. They bicker regularly about differences in housekeeping styles. A crisis came two years after they'd moved in together. Because Trey felt Shinko could outtalk her, she took to leaving notes: "Please make sure when you do the dishes you wash the silverware. . . . I had to rewash five of your spoons."

SHINKO: Once after I'd dropped a few crumbs on the floor, and she looked at me with total disgust, I lost it.

TREY: You threw a knife.

SHINKO: It was a potholder.

TREY: It was a knife, but not at me.

Afterward they talked for hours. They never resolved the issue, but agreed to a new formula for fighting:

TREY: I agreed to stop writing notes.

SHINKO: She has held her own for a long time now.

Our conversation has not deterred Trey's lover, Shinko's child, a friend, a project collaborator, several animals, and a member of a child-care collective from ambling into the room to confer or simply to be stroked. Trey and Shinko's relationship is clearly one in an elaborate filigree of intimacies — overlapping, competing, and complementary, each with its distinct signature.

Pearl and Levelle: Computer jocks together

Both had checkered pasts. They had been married, divorced, worked as teachers, saleswomen, one hawking knife sets door-to-door and the other, stuffed animals on Telegraph Avenue in Berkeley. Along the way, they had each taken a couple of computer classes and parlayed them into jobs, Levelle teaching at junior college and Pearl working as a systems analyst at a corporation. They met at a women's computer organization, went out for lunch and, on a whim, decided to print some letterhead and offer their services as software training and development specialists. Pearl's contacts got them in the door at a major corporation and their company was born. They couldn't handle the volume of work and hired their lovers to help. Though Pearl and Lavelle are very contented with their lovers and they are now integral members of the company, they cannot, Pearl and Levelle claim, supply the magic connection the company's co-founders have with each other. Pearl says if she expected the same connection from her lover, she would be frustrated and upset. Levelle says Pearl supplies the stimulation that doesn't happen with her lover. They agree that there was a certain frisson between them at the beginning that could have developed erotically. It was almost as if they had something more precious and didn't want to jeopardize it.

PEARL: It's like finding a playmate who plays the same way you do and knows the same things you know.

LEVELLE: It is wonderful to be able to relate to each other in a way that we cannot relate to anyone else. . . . We know what we're going to say without finishing sentences . . . we make logical leaps that border on the telepathic.

This sort of attunement makes them resent any interruptions.

PEARL: We may be working on some esoteric puzzle for hours and hours. It's very exciting and relaxing at the same time. When I have other social commitments I hate to drag myself away. All other conversation pales by comparison. I'm bored until I get back to Levelle and the problem we're trying to solve.

This intimacy is reinforced by what they have to contend with in the corporate world.

LEVELLE: If you were black and fat and had breasts I thought corporations assumed you shouldn't be programming.

PEARL: I think sometimes that if I were a six-foot jock in these settings, I wouldn't constantly be worrying . . . about how my hair looks, if I'm going to trip in my heels or am about to pop a shirt button.

They dressed casually at first and then were told by their corporate contractors that they had to dress up. Their male counterparts receive no such directives. This has led them to devise a new plan. If they hire people to do the training — people for whom corporate interface is not so compromising — they can free themselves to pursue their real dream, the development of new software programs.

At one point during the discussion Levelle's lover knocks and comes in to confer about handouts. At another point, Pearl's partner, apologetic about interrupting, comes in to ask about mailing lists. The intimacy between Pearl and Levelle may be invisible and unacknowledged in the world at large. It is clear during these exchanges, however, that it is witnessed and respected by their lovers.

Pearl says they are always busy, almost too busy to really think about things. "This is why marriages stayed together in the old days," she says. "They worked so hard they didn't have time to think if they were happy or not."

Bejay and Jamie: Family improv

Bejay, 37, met Jamie, 1, at a party. Their rapport was immediate. Jamie's mother, who was heterosexual, began to talk about the burdens of single motherhood. Bejay managed, after a few calls, to convince Jamie's mother that her intentions were sincere — and that she had always been an "ace babysitter." Jamie was colicky and her mother was overwhelmed. After Bejay had demonstrated her usefulness and dedication for a year, Jamie's mother asked her to move in. They lived together for the next eight years, Jamie's mother providing the musical and academic training, and Bejay taking the "goofy" athletic approach. Bejay made it clear to prospective lovers that this was her "family," and whoever couldn't adapt to the unusual menage should go her way. When one lover stayed for a while, Jamie had three moms. Over and over, family and friends mistook Bejay and Jamie's mother as primary intimates. They were, in fact, at their closest merely cordial and respectful of each other, not even close friends. As Jamie got bigger, the house seemed to get smaller. Three years ago Bejay decided to get her own house, a few blocks away. Jamie comes over after school a few days a week, frequently stays over. They collaborate on homework, play catch and go to games together. Even at age 11, Jamie is still unselfconsciously affectionate, a gangly preteen who sprawls over Bejay, confides in her, teases, and in general, adores her. Since Jamie's mother has recently had surgery for breast cancer, the co-parenting arrangement has taken on even more significance. Bejay now has to consider the possibility of something she never aspired to — being a single parent herself. She will manage if she has to:

Parenting came very naturally to me. There were times when my patience and energy wore thin, but it never worried me. I always knew that I knew how to do it. Children are very demanding. They don't care "how you are," . . . they just want you to be with them.

Bejay tells me a little about her past. Her father was a good parent. "Whenever I'm in doubt, I do what he would have done. Invariably it works out." Her loss when he died was incalculable. The easy intimacy Bejay shares with Jamie echoes, to some extent, Bejay's own childhood idyll with her father. It is a form of intimacy with which lovers can't compete. "My relationship with Jamie," says Bejay, "is a much more satisfying relationship than any lover I have ever had."

Hannah and Maire: Aphrodite shrugged

Hannah and Maire have lived together for three years. They had sex once five years ago — a clandestine encounter when Hannah was living with another lover. Hannah remembers she had a delightful time, but when she moved in with Maire she elected to build the relationship on another basis:

Eros is all encompassing for me . . . the ocean of love. . . . Aphrodite coming out of the waves. At the moment I'm in transition. I'm using all that exuberant energy hiking, dancing, and socializing. No white heat, but I'm happy. I feel complete. I feel I am with Maire. We are "sleepers" . . . women who will fool everybody because we'll probably be together forever. It's a lover/nonlover relationship. I've had two or three other lovers in the last two years but I've been unwilling to leave the situation at home . . . because of Maire.

Hannah and Maire touch and kiss. They walk or talk or eat together every day. In contrast to previous lover relationships, in which Hannah says she was unable to work out being separate enough and together enough, they give each other enough support and separation. "We can each say, 'leave me alone, get off my back' without mortally wounding each other. I've never had that before."

During the interview, I had a live demonstration of this independence. Maire, who had been out biking, came in to change her clothes before going out again to meet a friend. After we were introduced, she went to her room. After some minutes of bustling, quite audible because the apartment was small, Hannah inquired if she would be much longer: "I can't continue all my private revelations as long as you're eavesdropping." Maire emerged, grinning and waving good-bye as she left.

Their dream is to be a nucleus of an ever-widening circle, a family of women — lovers and friends who cohere because of shared interests and values. Whatever happens, Hannah says, their center will hold as friends now, as well as past and perhaps future lovers.

Hannah's mother survived the holocaust because a friend hid her and gave her false I.D. papers. "I understand," says Hannah, "what it means to have to depend on people. This is what I've come to look for in people . . . the depth of goodness . . . I don't look for anything less. It's all that really matters in the end. Maire has it. She's a beautiful character. I love her."

THE INTERVIEWS are refreshing. They are also disappointing. I had hoped to find partnerships in which genitality was really incidental — nonsexually based associations in which (except for the adult-child relationship) partners might or might not choose to have genital contact.

Even though there is a passionate resonance among the partners I interviewed, sex is shadowy. Sometimes erotic connection gets a ceremonial nod, or has a possible future, but for the most part it remains unacknowledged and dormant. More significantly, all these women regularly or irregularly have other lovers. Their alternative intimacies may counterbalance primary connections, but they do not replace them. Had I asked the interviewees to describe their relationships with lovers, their stories might have sounded quite conventional.

I can't use the interviewees as the models I had hoped to find. In fact, what has been inadvertently illuminated is the importance of genitally based relationships even when other sorts of playmates, even soul mates, are available. What is unique about the women I interviewed is that they made room in their lives for more than one primary intimacy. Perhaps what these women can teach me is not about genital incidentalism, but about a sense of proportion. Most of the women I interviewed had, at one time or another, acquired lovers when the alternative intimacies they described were firmly established. When lovers came into their lives, the interviewees did not retreat into the romantic world characteristic of newly minted lesbian couples. Instead, their lovers became part of a stable or unstable triangle with the interviewees' significant others. Lovers competed with these alternative intimates for the role of "most significant other." Often, it was the lovers who bowed out of the relationship. Sometimes the interviewees' lovers shared "primariness" with the alternative intimates, or reached some mutually respectful truce.

It would seem that intense involvement of one sort balances other kinds of intimacy. Sexuality may not change between lovers, but the primacy of such experience as the measure of real closeness is challenged by the presence, in the interviewees' lives, of alternative intimacies. The interviewees' inclusion of two significant others in their lives would be labeled "triangulation" in standard couples' therapy and would be considered a condition to be "treated." Perhaps the interviewees are demonstrating a distinction between different kinds of triangulation. The sort that causes the trouble for which we seek professional help is episodic, hence, unpredictable and conflictual. Another kind of triangulation is structural—a permanent and normalized balance among intimates which we might designate "polyfidelity."[2] Perhaps instead of being automatically pathologized, polyfidelity is a state to be respected and cultivated.

The alternative forms of relationship the interviewees described may actually be more difficult to establish than sexual rapport. We are, therefore, more likely to base our intimacies on sex than on other forms of reciprocity. Still, most of us do have circumscribed or pocket intimacies — with friends or children, coworkers or relatives or pets — who may, collectively, counterbalance sexually based partnerships. Projects or groups may serve the same function. Giving such relationships or causes their due — noticing them, acknowledging their importance — is the first step toward challenging, not the genitally based model of intimacy but, rather, its hegemony in our lives.

(Un)doing "it": Serious fun

The interviewees' relationships flourished in an unnamed zone between or beyond the polarized categories of "friend" and "lover." Sex was not the index of these decidedly primary intimacies. I had hoped to find some examples of genital incidentalism, i.e., sex as an occasional byproduct of their intimacies. As unique as the interviewees' relationships were, however, their unconventionality did not extend to the rules typically surrounding sex. In this dimension, these intimates were definitely "friends." Blurring standard friend/lover distinctions in certain ways, then, does not necessarily challenge the ultimate power of sex to determine the "type" of relationship in which we are engaged. To accomplish this, it seems that we must reconceptualize sex itself. If we can redefine certain elements currently identified as sexual — play, fantasy, sensation, for example — and give each its separate due, we may be able to undermine our certainty about what comprises "it" and what does not. Perhaps, in the future, we may no longer be able to convincingly combine what we have come to perceive as disparate elements into one special act which can occur only in one special relationship.

A few lesbian theorists have already begun this redefinitional task. Marilyn Frye writes that we need to

> begin creating a vocabulary that elaborates and expands our meanings; we should adopt a very wide and general concept of "doing it." Let it be an open, generous, commodious concept encompassing all the acts and activities by which we generate with each other pleasures and thrills, tenderness and ecstasy, passages of passionate carnality of whatever duration or profundity. Everything from vanilla to licorice, from puce to chartreuse, from velvet to ice, from cuddles to cunts, from chortles to tears. (Allen, 1990, p. 314)

Teresa Corrigan also writes about a new language:

Maybe the secret is breaking down the behavior into its component parts — to really name what we do. . . . it might force us to really think about what we're doing, to expand the territories of sexual geography. . . . You could say to someone who attracts you, "Hi baby, I want to nuzzle your nape, blow on your belly and maybe more." Her mind will expand with creative possibilities. And if she turns you down, you can just say "Fuck it," secure in the knowledge that it was HER linguistic limitations, not your charming smile, that doused the flame." (1990)

The synchronized playfulness that is characteristic of Pearl and Levelle, the computer jocks, suggests a form of intimacy that is often replaced among conventional lesbian couples by genital contact. If such partners in the course of playing do anything that might be construed as sexual, the playfulness is remembered only as sex. Even in situations where playfulness is simply too predominant to disappear, it is never central to partners' description of themselves or their relationships. In therapy, playfulness comes up incidentally, when couples mimic conversations with their pets or relate how, after a fight, they played a "game" in which hands covered by improvised sock-puppets or bean bags or stuffed animals parody their recent altercation. Sometimes play, when acknowledged, registers only as shameful behavior. Certain clients after some time in therapy may "confess" sheepishly to "baby talk" and ask for ways to remedy it. What if instead of pathologizing or minimizing playfulness, we emphasize and affirm it?

Perhaps a way to render genitality incidental is simply to reverse the usual order of orgasm (goal) and play (fore). If the goal is play, not sex, then doing "it" can legitimately and exuberantly become the make-believe it has always been. Whether play includes genitals is incidental. Most significant are the cameo appearances of the usually exiled parts of ourselves. These may be summoned by pet names, special postures and pouts, raised eyebrows and modulated voices. Vampires and maidens, sirens and bullies may, for a few moments, displace the standard versions of ourselves as loyal mates and hard workers. We can be wanton or coy, absurd, awkward, tyrannical, or "out of control," and still be appreciated by the witness of our antics. The reciprocal invention of these alternative personae is a form of intimacy that breaks taboos, reworks childhood themes of dominance and submission, union, abandonment, and reunion.

There are formal ways of role-playing — at Halloween or Carnival, at butch/femme soirees or top/bottom scenes. I suspect that most of us share with our intimates idiosyncratic scripts which, retrieved from the shadows, validated and embellished, can subvert sex's authority. They provide not a new but a newly acknowledged staging area for intimacy. Oscar Wilde observed, that we are least candid when we are being "ourselves." Give us masks, he suggests, and we will tell the truth.[3]

(Un)doing "it": Genital conviviality

All the disparate elements that make sex so memorable seem to be harmonized and summed up by orgasms. The contractions that release us for a few seconds from volition, ordinary consciousness, and comportment are special events. All women are not among the orgasmically "chosen," and even those who are usually experience some uncertainty about strength, length, when, where, and how this minor miracle occurs. Each orgasm therefore seems to exemplify an exquisite blend of authorship, receptivity, and perceptivity. Special status is thus retroactively conferred on the stroking, gazing, whispering that preceded it. As well as enshrining our genital intimacy, orgasmic rituals seem to confirm our prowess as lovers. No wonder orgasms figure so prominently in sex-based intimacy.

This reinforcement power of orgasms probably accounts for much of sex's saliency. The same reinforcement, however, may also provide the antidote to the privileging of sex. I notice, after months or years with a lover, the prelude to orgasms becomes abbreviated and stylized. Our focus on orgasm is so single-minded that, over time, the rhythm of stroking changes from unpredictable, apparently magical sensuality to as-the-crow-flies genital directness, from exploration to goal-consciousness. The same is true for women who don't have orgasms. Partners who were lambently limerent in the beginning months become more and more clitorally focused and frustrated when one or the other doesn't come. This "death of passion" or "mechanical sex" is a common complaint of clients I see. When the mundane mechanics of orgasmic response become, through repetition, more obvious, it is difficult for partners to sustain the incomparable starbursts of the first months. Perhaps, during this shift, the knowledge that as lesbians we really can't do "it," or aren't doing "it," begins to emerge. Such decline of magic often accompanies other disillusionments and signals a turning point. Without any marker of significance in place besides the magically orgasmic, partners can only experience a less sexually exciting relationship as deficient, and, overlooking other forms of intimacy, yearn to recapture past glories.

What about another form of intimacy, one that lies somewhere between genital centrality and genital incidentalism? To establish such a framework — designated "genital conviviality" — we might begin to acknowledge the oxymoron that, as lesbians, we self-pleasure (masturbate) together. Anticipating the response (perhaps from our own interior monologist) that derides anything that is merely "mutual masturbation," we might point out that at least part of such stigmatizing of masturbation comes from the same Old Testament passages that condemn homosexuality. Testicular economies require that "seed" be saved for the propagation of offspring.

During the most recent wave of women's liberation, a number of radical feminists promoted masturbation as a form of psychological and physical emancipation. It seems as though this *esprit de clit* was co-opted by a patriarchal agenda aimed at helping previously "frigid women" find and stroke the fires presumably smoldering in Everywoman. Thus masturbation groups at the University of California Medical School in San Francisco, originally intended for women who did not have orgasms, were deemed insufficient by the program architects. So-called secondary preorgasmic groups were formed. In contrast to the original primary groups, these secondary groups were designed for women who were by now regularly or fitfully orgasmic. Through a series of "bridge maneuvers," these women were trained to teach their partners how to "pleasure" them. This impetus back to the couples was also, implicitly and sometimes explicitly, an impetus back toward intercourse.

So, the split between superior and inferior orgasms, i.e., the dividing of heterosexual intercourse from the "other" kind, of vaginal from clitoral, continues to prevail. Among lesbians this two-tiered division of orgasms into superior and inferior has resurfaced as the distinction between magic and mechanical orgasm. So-called mechanical orgasms are devalued because they suggest masturbation rather than "genuine sex."

This is borne out by many of my clients' unwillingness to masturbate under certain circumstances. When clients seem anxious that they cannot adequately stimulate or be stimulated by their partners, I have tried to relieve the pressure by suggesting that they masturbate with their partners nearby. I notice that the massive resistance that usually meets this proposal disappears when I ask them to masturbate out of range of their partners' awareness. Thus, it appears that masturbation is acceptable, if at all, as a solo act. When we masturbate under our partners' gazes, it becomes more difficult to maintain the dichotomy between "real sex" and masturbation, between loving conjugality and loneliness, between superior and inferior, between magic and mechanics. Convivial genitality would mean total rehabilitation of the lonely, inferior, "neural itch" version of masturbation. Such a reclamation has to include a credo that can compete with our faith in sex, our belief in its ability to blend two bodies into one seamless, transcendent whole.

The highly charged oppositeness of butch and femme roles may provide us with a partial model and solution to the problem of perceiving sex as real or unreal. The powerful pleasures of butch and femme roles are based on the fantasy of difference rather than sameness. Differences, however, need not be polar. The differences in our bodies, responses and touches, in our privacies (our unspoken fantasies), apparent in a context of mutual masturbation, can be as charged with meaning as the polarity of butch and femme. If our most compelling fantasy no longer depends on the denial of difference, if differences are, themselves, stimulating, then one partner need not expect herself to be so similar, so tuned in to her partner that she can effortlessly stimulate her to orgasm. This notion of difference could be the fantasy framework of mutual masturbation. In such a framework self-stimulation would shed its baggage of shame and inferiority, and other-stimulation would lose its halo. We would be as likely as our partners to touch our own genitals during sex. Perhaps our partners would not touch our genitals at all! We could notice our partners touching themselves and notice them noticing us when we touch ourselves. Thus self-stimulation, even perfunctory orgasms — rehabilitated as a demonstration of nuanced contrasts, as an exercise of personal agency — would be included as part of intimacy. Such a framework challenges the sex-as-magic-done-unto-me perspective and at the same time provides a legitimate post-romance pattern for touching and intimacy.

When I showed an earlier version of this paper to my brother, who is gay, he looked incredulously at me when he came to "convivial masturbation." "You mean," he said, "that women don't touch themselves as a matter of course during sex? Gay men almost always do." It was my turn to be incredulous. The enormity of gender differences, no matter how often I encounter it, never ceases to stun me. The revelation also demonstrated a paradox. In order to avoid dominant phallocentric discourse, it might be necessary to adapt rather than resist parts of it, to learn from rather than to reject male sexual practices.

A framework of convivial genitality that makes orgasm less important can, of course, simply result in easy orgasms with more lovers. It can also mean that specialness is less likely to be imputed, exclusively, to lovers over other kinds of intimates. Emancipated from the genital zone, certain emotional intensities are, at least theoretically, free to develop within alternative intimacies, to be expressed in alternative (non-genital) terms.

Additionally, a framework of genital conviviality can avoid or accommodate the inevitable change in orgasmic meaning in conventional lover relationships without disillusion or disappointment. Normalizing friendly, casual, even perfunctory orgasms would provide long-term lesbian partners with newly legitimized, valued, post honeymoon forms of eroticism. I suspect that women who claim they are having sex after a long period together have accepted a mutual masturbatory framework; they accept that they have established orgasmic habits with each other that are tried and true, even perfunctory, but are nonetheless meaningful. In conjunction with other intimacies, such genital conviviality can be a sustaining alternative to the overemphasis on a certain romantic brand of sex.

Conclusion

Frye writes, "I would not assume that 'doing it' either has or should have a particular connection with a lover, or that it hasn't or shouldn't have such a connection." (Allen, 1990, p. 314)

I haven't been able to melt down the lover/friend dichotomy entirely, to make genitality incidental in the way Frye describes. The women I interviewed, though coming close to occupying the borderland between friends and lovers, did not have sexual relationships with their friends/lovers. What if I myself audition for this particular social/sexual innovation? In my mind's eye I picture myself at a chum's house, pouring the tea or giving her a backrub or sympathizing about her latest setback. I, who am not even particularly comfortable hugging friends, shudder at the thought of cultivating orgasmic habits with them.

The interviews have not provided me with ready-made alternative models. They have, however, reoriented me. Sex has become less important, not because I can take it or leave it, do "it" with friends or lovers. Rather, it has become less significant because it has assumed its correct relation to other intimacies: one among several. In addition, reconfiguring genitality into playfulness and orgasmic habits desanctifies sex. And this is only the beginning. Perhaps there are other patterns of intimacy which, when noticed and acknowledged, can absorb elements of the previously overrated — and for lesbians the problematic — category of sex. Perhaps the day will come when, with the elements of currently monolithic sexual practices successfully redeployed, I can indeed have tea, sympathy *and* orgasms with my chum.

A NEW COUPLE comes in for counseling. They have not had sex in a year. They stopped when it got "too routine." Now their attempts to be erotic always seem to misfire. One partner wants to return to basics: to begin to set time aside for sexual intimacy, to talk about what each is feeling as they touch and explore. The other feels pressured by this proposal and wants to be seduced — "to be swept away by body language, not verbiage." Both are, in turn, distressed, angry, tearful.

I realize as they talk that I do, indeed, have a new map. I can chart the positions they are describing. I can also see other features, find orienting points previously invisible to me. I make a mental note to find out about the alternative intimacies that co-exist with their relationship and to explore the ways they play together. I decide, at that moment, to introduce the tenets of convivial genitality. As I start to rehabilitate the "rote sex" they have discounted, I notice that the partner who wants to be swept away clenches her jaw and crosses her arms over her chest. Body language, indeed! Map or no map, this isn't going to be easy.

I remember my through-the-looking-glass experience in the library and my insight about the actual slowness of apparently lightning fast paradigmatic changes. What I didn't consider at the library was that my own and my clients' internal shifts are, like macro-changes in the culture at large, sometimes a lurching but more often a creeping exchange between old categories and fresh distinctions. In order to be effective, my new map has to incorporate this syncopated rhythm of change.

I realize that I, too, have been tense. I sit back in my chair. "It seems as though I'm skipping over something important. Tell me," I say to the woman with the clenched jaw, "about the passion you used to feel when you first got together." Her eyes get a cloudy, faraway look as she begins to reminisce. Finally, she turns and, looking directly at me, announces, "I will never change."

This convulsive declaration is, of course, the first step. Now we can begin.

Notes

1. I found a description of *affidamento* in a review of *Sexual difference: A theory of social-symbolic practice* (1990), by the Milan Women's Bookstore Collective. The review (1991, June) was written by Maureen Lister and appeared in *The Women's Review of Books, 8*, 26.

2. According to Jeanne Adleman, the term "polyfidelity" was coined in the 1960s or 1970s by the founders of Kerista, an organization designed to promote and support alternative forms of intimacy.

3. Oscar Wilde's essay "The Critic as Artist" is quoted by Ronald Sharpe in his *Friendship and literature: Spirit and form* (Chapel Hill: Duke U Press), p. 80.

References

Casal, M. (1983). At last . . . I was not a creature apart. In J. Katz (Ed.), *Gay/lesbian almanac* (pp. 305–307). New York: Harper Colophon.

Corrigan, T. (1990). Untitled — for lack of better words. Unpublished paper.

Frye, M. (1990). Lesbian "sex." In J. Allen (Ed.), *Lesbian philosophies and cultures* (pp. 305–315). Albany: State University of New York Press.

Hall, M. (1991). Ex-therapy to sex therapy. In C. Silverstein (Ed.), *Gays, lesbians and their therapists.* (pp. 84–97). New York: W. W. Norton.

Krafft-Ebing, R. (1965). *Psychopathia sexualis*. London: Staples Press. (Original work published 1904).

Celibacy

JoAnn Loulan

To BE CELIBATE is to experience, by choice or circumstance, the absence of sexual contact and activity. As a lesbian sex educator, I think it is critical for us to understand what sex means to lesbians before we can appreciate the reasons for and significance of its absence in our lives. There are many forces in a culture that is informed by heterosexist and patriarchal assumptions that obscure our lesbian sexuality. Consequently, we cannot assume that we share a common understanding of what constitutes lesbian sex.

The word "sex" is generally used to mean genital contact, which *really* means penis-vagina intercourse. Vaginal intercourse in heterosexual relations is used to determine which side of virginity you are on and whether you are "having sex." Ask teenagers who have done everything but have intercourse and they will tell you they haven't "gone all the way." This construct, whether it is in fact even useful to heterosexual relations, is irrelevant when it comes to lesbian sexual relations. When lesbians use the word "sex" we are referring to a very different set of sexual activities that take place within a very unique context of social relations. Our experience and understanding of celibacy, which is a facet of our sexuality, is then uniquely lesbian in character.

Sex is part of our physiological, emotional, and social yearning for human connection. To seek that connection between women renders us outlaws and places us in many ways on the margins of society. Being lesbians in a hetero-patriarchal world gives us a collective identity as an

NOTE: This chapter was edited and encouraged by Laurie Bell, a lesbian mother, activist, musician, and writer in Toronto, Canada.

intergenerational, multiracial, cross-class, differently abled community of women. And so our intimacy needs are met in many and varied ways that are distinct to our lesbian community. We work on political and social projects together. We share lovers and friends and organizations with each other. We know who each other are whether we have ever met. We have hurt each other's feelings, we have held grudges for years, we have gossiped about one another. We have put aside differences, we have become lovers with our worst enemies. We can process endlessly with each other the latest chapter in our lives. We kiss and hold hands, dance close and trade clothes. We are the perpetual girlfriends endlessly talking on the phone after spending all day together at school. We have fought for our very lives, our right to exist, to love each other in corners and out on the streets. We have birthed our babies, buried our dead, and cradled our survivors. We have layers of connections and tenderness that do not always or exclusively include sex. Genital sex assumes a different place in this setting, where the intimate connections between women are so varied and deep.

An examination of lesbian celibacy is therefore no easy task. First, it has to do with sex, which we are not supposed to talk about. Then, it has to do with not having sex, and talking about that is even worse than talking about sex. Our lesbian sexuality, including practices and experiences, questions and issues, has suffered a privatization imposed by mainstream culture. If we are going to be doing "it," or not doing "it," we are expected at least to keep quiet about it. Lesbians have had to and must continue to struggle against the conspiracy of silence that surrounds our sexual lives.

I have had several extended periods of celibacy in my life, usually one or two years in duration. My definition of celibacy for myself is that I do not have sex with another woman (I never have sex with men, so that is not part of the consideration). I have had celibate periods during which I have also not masturbated, but that has been either during profound mourning, or before I discovered the joys of vibrators.

My celibate periods have been consciously chosen. I have often made time limits for myself, deciding that I would not have sex with another woman for a determined period of time. Setting a minimum time period has created room that allows me to move around and not be concerned with deciding when this period of abstinence is going to end.

Despite the focus on lesbian sex in my work, in my personal life I have found not having sex with another person to be a crucial part of my sexual identity. One of the tenets of sex education is that you cannot say "yes" to sex unless you are free and able to say "no." My celibate periods allow that "no" to resound clearly. You cannot really know how to be with another unless you know how to be with yourself. Celibacy allows me to be with myself so that whatever thoughts, doubts, peace, or turmoil I have, are about me. It is one joy to dance with another, to find rhythms with her, slow, sexy, fast, fun. It is another joy to dance alone, to find and weave my own rhythms. I have found these celibate periods of my life to be truly profound and quieting. I have cherished these rare opportunities that bring a certain stillness. Celibacy has been to my sexual life what rests are to music. They are the pauses that give the notation form.

Without the concerns that accompany sexual relationships — whether our expectations are the same, whether we are sexually compatible, whether the relationship is going to work, whether the relationship makes sense to my friends — I am free to focus on myself. This is a revolutionary act for us as women who are expected constantly to focus upon and care for others: our children, our parents, our partner, our neighborhood, our world. With the romantic food cleared from the table, the mind feasts upon other more solitary and self-defined concerns that invite me to nourish myself.

Periods of celibacy have also been important to me as a way to heal from a relationship that has ended. A period of time when I am not sexually active with another woman is part of the process of drawing to a close a sex affair, love affair, partnership, lovership, lesbian marriage. I do not do well moving from one relationship to another with no break, although I have certainly done so in my life. The loss, grief, and mourning are clearer without the presence of a new emotional and/or sexual connection.

Inevitably, celibacy also has its own difficulties. It can be particularly challenging to maintain one's self-esteem during celibate periods. So many of us have a fear of being alone that is cultivated by our society. The patriarchal, capitalist system has an investment in reinforcing the idea that we all need something more than ourselves to be worthwhile. That "more" can be money, possessions, power, or some other person who confirms to ourselves and the rest of the world that we are worth being with. We are bombarded with images of couples. Can we imagine an advertisement for a vacation paradise portraying a person alone?

The pairing imperative is a reflection of the terror of being alone. Anything but that. We will take drugs, watch television, read, shop, eat, gamble, or be with someone we don't want to be with, rather than feel what it's like to be alone. Anything but the sweetness of watching our own breath or listening to our own heartbeat. Anything but waking up, going to bed, waking up, going to bed, waking up once again with ourselves. What then to distract us from the existential dilemma presented by our ultimate aloneness?

Even though I believe that being celibate is powerful and important, the presence of doubt and fear is inescapable. It is precisely the opportunity and willingness to face these head-on that is the essence of celibacy. My own mind inevitably will allow to surface the self-doubt and fear that I usually attempt to hide and run away from. And then, most difficult of all, I must answer the voices that say, "You are not worthwhile." Or I rely on friends to say, "You are worthy, you are loved," but this isn't wholly satisfying because they do not love me "best," as a lover surely would. I must respond not only to the voices within but also to the voices around me that say, "If you were worthwhile, you would have a lover, a relationship that works."

We have been taught to believe that sex is the way to feel good about ourselves. When someone else enjoys our body, likes to kiss us, holds us when the lights are out, only then can we believe we have worth. But most of us have had the experience of feeling lonely even when we are being held by another. And many of us have felt completely secure even if there was not a sexual partner in our lives. Yet these real experiences in our own lives seem to disappear when we are lonely and wondering what celibacy is all about.

There are many reasons why women are celibate. Celibacy can be a rational reaction to a bizarre world; a way to protect ourselves; a choice to simplify life; a state we have slipped into unconsciously; a means of reclaiming ourselves. There can be a combination of reasons for being celibate. The situation may be complex or quite simple. We may go through the period of celibacy with great anxiety, or hardly notice it.

Lesbians choose celibacy for different reasons. There are women who choose celibacy in order to confront a sexual addiction in their life. There are lesbians who find that they have been jeopardizing their well-being by their behavior in sexual relationships. They have found their sexual obsessions and compulsions have put them in physical danger. Or they may have found that their inability to achieve autonomy in the realm of sex has compromised their quality of life. For these women, abstinence from sex is crucial to their emotional, spiritual, and sometimes physical, recovery.

The power of keeping one's own counsel in the carnal sense is beyond calculation. To allow one's body to be loved simply with one's own heart, mind, and hands with no self-doubt but rather with a mind that is open to the unknown. To explore this not just one night but night after night, day after day. A meditation that can be part of a spiritual journey unsurpassed.

When we are simply not having sex because we want to have time with ourselves, the experience can be inspiring. Yet the reactions from the world around us are often disturbing. Lesbianism is often defined by sexual activity or the presence of a partner relationship. The absence of these features in our lives can obscure our very lesbian identity. Straight friends and relatives may view our lack of sexual activity as a sign that we are no longer lesbians and perhaps there is still hope. Our lesbian friends may decide this is a perfect time to fix us up with that woman from work, killing two unattached birds with one stone. We can be a fifth wheel in a social environment designed for couples. Where will they seat us at the dinner table? There is often little support from those around us for our celibate state. Few people will let us know how wonderful it is that we are spending time with ourselves.

There can also be the opposite phenomenon: pressure from friends who think it would be good for us to be celibate, to take some time before we get involved with another woman. This may come because we have had a breakup, a sexual trauma, or a difficult time in our lives. We often succumb to this pressure to be celibate because we think it will make us a better person. I don't think so. Convincing ourselves to be celibate to please our mothers, friends, ex-lovers, the goddess, or our therapists is really just a road to resentment. Celibacy is a path that must be our own choice to travel.

A society that permits hatred of women, rape of young girls, and ignorance of lesbians provides many good reasons to be celibate. Our choice not to have sex in order to protect ourselves from negative memories, acts of violence perpetrated against us, or fear of the sex act itself is the result of living in a society that does not support or even respect our female or lesbian selves.

Choosing celibacy as part of the healing process is common. Many women feel it is crucial to take a rest from the anxiety caused by having sex with another. It can be easier to work through layers of denial about sexual abuse when one is not having to fulfill or even consider a partner's sexual needs. It is a time when there is no need to conquer ambivalence toward sex. Concerns about phobic reactions, attempts at counterphobic reactions, and analysis of every movement toward or away from a partner are not necessary while celibate. This can bring great relief and loving self-interest.

There is also a celibacy that comes as a result of terror. The terror of letting another in. The terror of reexperiencing an episode of sexual violence that is out of one's reach to heal. This is a celibacy that is not so much chosen as demanded by a mind, heart, and soul that cannot allow another transgression. Any sexual contact with another may seem to be a violation. This protection can be a comfort. It can be the only hope, the only possible choice, the only way to breathe. This is the celibacy that may feel like cotton batting, like sweet relief. For others it may be the kind of celibacy that feels more like something stolen, a tenderness ripped away, an emptiness that cannot be filled. There may be a bitter resentment that there seem to be such few choices, that every turn brings us to a wall, that all exploration seems to bring another raw sorrow. A period of celibacy may be the only remedy for a past filled with pain.

Celibacy can also be imposed upon us. It can be the consequence of an illness or an accident that prevents us from being sexually active. This can be a terrible loss, and we may have to deal with a bitterness or sorrow that accompanies such a restriction. Celibacy can be imposed upon us because we have a disability and we are not recognized as having a sexuality, much less a lesbian sexuality, much less a desire for actual sexual activity. As a result of a disability our freedom of movement and right to make our own choices, particularly about our sexuality, may be stripped from us, removing them from community and the natural opportunities to seek and engage in sexual relationships. This kind of celibacy is a violation of each woman's right to sexual freedom.

In addition, there is a celibacy that is a consequence of other choices we make for our lives. We may choose to live or work in a place that does not hold the opportunities to have sexual relationships. This is particularly true for lesbians, who cannot expect to find visible community in many places. Or we may not be willing to put our job, reputation, or physical safety on the line to engage in sexual relations.

There is also a passive celibacy which can evolve in varied and complex ways. Some women may not even notice that it's been months, maybe even years, since they had sex with anyone. With no conscious choice, no personal inventory, and no discussion, some women will find themselves being celibate. It may be that two women have been in a relationship for a long time and suddenly one of them tries to remember when it was that they last shared sexual intimacy.

Many of us are predictable in our sex drives. I wish that some lesbian would do research on lesbians, sex, and hormones. Hormones have so much to do with our sexual drive. Many women only want to masturbate or have partner sex during certain parts of their menstrual cycle. During new lust or love, hormones are released that enhance our excitement about sex.

Taking conscious stock of celibacy when it has been unconscious may be a valuable exercise. What is the reason for this celibacy? What is the purpose of this celibacy? Is this the path that is most meaningful at this time? Is this a true path, or one of least resistance? Is there healing going on? Is there fear built up? Sometimes this questioning is painful. There may be no apparent reason for having stopped engaging in sex. The thought of starting again may be overwhelming because overcoming sexual inertia can be difficult. Why tonight? Why change things? What will be gained from upsetting the apple cart? The important thing is to become aware and honest about the lack of attentiveness to one's sex life. No judgment, no inference that one is bad or this isn't right, just an openness to discover what it is all about. Was this what I intended to do? Is this the path I want to be on?

There is also a celibacy that comes from simply feeling that sex is not important. The choice to not have sex is not necessarily an outgrowth of some pathology or painful past experience. Not all women want to have sex. Some women hate sex. Others are totally indifferent to sex. Some find that there are many more interesting activities that take their time and interest. The state of celibacy does not have to be a soul-wrenching, spiritual journey. For some women it is more like a trip to the market.

As with most phenomena in lesbian culture, there is no one common way. Celibacy is yet another state of being, action, belief system that will have its unique aspects for every lesbian. There are groups of women that can stand together and say, "Yes, this is why we are celibate." However, even among these women, each will experience a celibacy with its own character.

Celibacy can be a way of life or a short passage within a life. It can be the focus of one's self, or an irrelevant detail on the periphery of identity. It can be the source of endless spiritual nourishment, or be useless to one's growth. It is as individual as the fingerprints on the hand that reaches toward another and within oneself to satisfy the yearning for connection.

Lesbian courtship scripts

Suzanna Rose, Debra Zand, and Marie A. Cini

L ESBIAN courtship — or the lack of it — is a topic that recently has captured the popular imagination of lesbians. Current accounts of lesbian dating etiquette (e.g., Sausser, 1986; Tessina, 1989; West, 1989) appear to have originated in response to the confusion surrounding just how two women select and couple with each other. That lesbian relationships typically lack a well-defined courtship stage has been captured in the joke: "Q: What do lesbians bring on a second date? A: A U-Haul." This humorous description of how quickly lesbians set up house together after meeting a potential partner suggests one of the major ways in which lesbian relationships tend to differ from heterosexual ones. It reflects the aptitude with which two women are able to establish intimacy and the quick merger into couple status that frequently occurs between lesbians.

Another unique characteristic of lesbian courtship has to do with the absence of sex-typed roles involved in the interaction. Freedom from constricted sex roles often is cited as an advantage of same-sex relationships, because individual talents determine who makes the initial approach, organizes and pays for any entertainment or other activity, and what level of sexual intimacy is expressed. However, it also frequently means that neither person is prepared to assume the traditional male role of initiator. Lesbians' notorious unwillingness to approach a prospective partner has been satirized as the lesbian "sheep" syndrome: Animal behaviorists have observed that female sheep signify sexual readiness by standing stock still in the pasture. A similar phenomenon is observable in lesbian bars. Women often signify sexual interest by avoiding all contact with those very women they are most attracted to.

This chapter will explore the scripts lesbians use in courtship. A script is a schema, or set of stereotypical actions, that is used to organize the world around us (Ginsberg, 1988, p. 28). Scripts serve as a guide for making decisions about what actions to take and for evaluating behaviors (Ginsburg, 1988). In courtship, scripts represent "blueprints" for how and with whom to express sexual desire and romantic interest (Gagnon, 1977, p. 6). The types of scripts lesbians use will be explored and categorized using popular and academic sources as well as our own research. The Boston marriage, representing one type of courtship script for lesbians, will be placed within this context. The term courtship was selected to describe the couple formation state of lesbian relationships because, despite its heterosexual connotations, sociologists define the courtship phase as being emotionally intimate, oriented toward a lasting commitment, and usually sexually exclusive (Laws & Schwartz, 1977, p. 105), characteristics that describe the early stages of many lesbian relationships. The term dating normally is used to refer to relationships having a less serious future orientation, or to the stage preceding courtship; however, as there often is little distinction between the two in practice, courtship and dating will be used interchangeably here.

In order to determine what courtship scripts were available to lesbians today, we examined a wide variety of materials, including lesbian romance novels, "how-to" books aimed at dating, mating, and improving the quality of a relationship, coming-out stories, first-person accounts of falling in love, and empirical research on lesbian courtship, sexuality, and relationships. From these we identified three basic scripts: the friendship script, the romance script, and the sexually explicit script. We regarded these scripts as distinct because they appeared to differ in four significant aspects: the level of emotional intimacy, the importance of sexuality, and the initiation and progress of the relationship.

The friendship script

The friendship script appeared to be the most common courtship script for lesbians (Peplau, 1982). Typically, the two women fall in love and become a couple during the course of a friendship. Emotional intimacy is the hallmark of the friendship script and is viewed as a primary means of developing and maintaining a love relationship. Sexuality often plays a less important role. For instance, physical attraction as a basis for the relationship tends to be downplayed. Even lesbians seeking partners through the personals columns tend to emphasize their hobbies and interests more than their own or a prospective partner's physical or sexual attributes, unlike gay men and heterosexual women and men (Deaux & Hanna, 1984). A friendship script also is compatible with the egalitarianism lesbians value and seek in relationships (e.g., Peplau & Amaro, 1982). Lesbians tend to choose lovers of similar social status, race, ethnicity, and age (Cotton, 1975), enhancing the likelihood that the common values, interests, and equality basic to friendships are present. Indeed, friends are so highly valued by lesbians that many indicate a reluctance to risk losing the friendship by becoming lovers (e.g., Vetere, 1982). One reason the friendship script may be so common is because, for many lesbians, the process of coming out is likely to occur within a friendship. For instance, Jeannine Gramick (1984) found that women most often develop a lesbian identity as a result of falling in love, often with a friend.

The friendship script provides no guidelines concerning how to initiate the relationship or how to signal friendly versus romantic interest. The progression of the relationship also may be unclear or confusing, especially if the two women perceive the relationship differently. The friendship script may be comfortable for lesbians partly because they are unfamiliar with assuming the role of initiator in a romantic relationship. In general, women have not been socialized to take the lead in courtship or to risk being rejected.

The ambiguity of friendship as a courtship script has both advantages and disadvantages. In a book of lesbian etiquette, Gail Sausser (1986) humorously extolled the advantages of the "fawning friendship" approach to a prospective partner as "often ineffective, but nearly always safe" (p. 85). Conversely, the "fawning friendship approach," referred to earlier as the lesbian "sheep" syndrome, has been lampooned frequently within the lesbian community. Writer Katie McCormick (personal communication, July 1991), has protested:

Personally, I don't think the sheep go far enough. When I feel attracted to someone, I don't just stand there [like sheep], I go out of my way to avoid her — LEST SHE THINK THAT I LIKE HER! I mean, what if she suspected? I could never go out in public again. This commitment to avoid anyone who is an object of my affection or could become such an object supersedes any desire on my part to find love, companionship, or even sex. . . . What I have found is that I have become so highly evolved, I can now have entire relationships without ever even speaking to the person.

Research by Debra Zand (1991) of courtship behaviors of eight white and four African-American lesbians, aged 21 to 32, indicates that the friendship script indeed often allows participants to avoid having to assume the initiator role, but also makes it difficult to know what type of relationship is being pursued or if a love interest is mutual. For example, many of the lesbians interviewed signaled their interest in both prospective friends and lovers using the same pursuit strategy. They spent time with the other person and had long conversations. However, interviewees did not interpret either of these behaviors as signs of romantic interest when they were on the receiving end. More direct signals were required for a participant to realize a woman was attracted to her as a potential lover rather than friend. Direct signals included initiating light physical contact such as briefly holding hands when talking, hugging tightly when greeting, or telling the participant directly of her interest. These results indicate that lesbians using a friendship script may send signals that they themselves would be unlikely to interpret as intended. However, it is possible that lesbians who have been "out" longer than the young women sampled by Zand would not be as confused by the indirect cues.

The friendship script allowed the women to be more reactive, if they so wished. One woman interviewed by Zand explained:

I'm uncomfortable initiating. It feels too vulnerable. I don't want to let any woman know I'm attracted to her unless she's attracted to me. I tend not to think so unless she's told me directly or someone else has. A person that I would be attracted to is often a person I'm very invested in a friendship with. I don't want to jeopardize the friendship. I'll do everything possible not to let them know. Only if it comes out in the open would I be direct.

However, when asked how they distinguished between a friendship and romantic relationship, most of the participants admitted to being confused by the ambiguous signals of the friendship script. Four reported that, unless told directly, they were never able to discern if a woman was interested in them romantically. For example, one woman reported: "I can't really tell. Only after they tell me they're interested do I get it. I've had several women tell me after the fact, but I really don't get it until someone's direct." Two other lesbians said they did not distinguish between friendships and romantic relationships; no clear boundaries between the two were discernible. One noted:

I am attracted to a lot of my women friends on some level. There aren't any lines or definitions. It is kind of nice, but kind of scary too. Being heterosexual is easier that way because the roles are so much more defined — the boundaries are clearer. Things are just not that way with lesbians. You need a strong sense of self to be able to know, . . . to feel comfortable with boundaries, and to decide where to draw them. I'm just not sure.

A few made some slight distinctions between friendship and romance. Four indicated that they would tend to disclose personal information more rapidly if they were romantically interested in a woman than they would if pursuing a friendship. Another common distinction involved feeling less self-conscious with potential friends than lovers. As one woman related:

I'm not as delicate with my interactions with friends. I'm less self-conscious with friends. Less concerned with whether I'm well groomed or whether I will say the wrong things. I'll tease and horse around with friends, but I don't tease women I'm interested in.

About half the participants reported not viewing a relationship as having gone beyond friendship until the couple has had sex. As one woman stated:

I can tell by the way I feel the morning after. After I have sex with a woman, I want to be with her. A strong sexual bond develops and I start moving things into her house. After I make love, I feel like, in a way, we claim each other.

Many also indicated that another way to tell that the relationship had entered the romantic realm was if the couple had made a verbal commitment to spend time together, work through conflicts, and be lovers.

The ambiguity of the friendship script as a sexual signal sometimes has an intriguing romanticizing effect, because it increases the tension over whether the relationship will ever be consummated. The uncertainty serves as an obstacle to love, a script device that is a regular component of the romance script described next. By the time the two women finally realize their feelings are mutual, they fall exhausted and grateful into each other's arms.

In summary, the friendship script emphasizes emotional intimacy over sexuality, does not designate a clear role for the initiator, and prescribes a gradual — and often ambiguous — progression toward romantic involvement.

The romance script

The romance script emerged as the second distinct and next most popular courtship pattern in lesbian fiction and practice. Its appeal in fiction was evidenced by the tremendous explosion in romance books available from lesbian presses such as Naiad. The classic plot for the lesbian romance intertwines emotional intimacy and sexual attraction, with one or both women being magnetically drawn to the other. The "love at first sight" formula grounds the script. Initiation in the romance is much more direct than in the friendship script, and the relationship progresses very quickly toward commitment. For example, in the *Edge of Passion*, Micki, a successful buyer in a Boston department store, meets Angela, a younger TV journalist, at a gay bar in Provincetown (Smith, 1991). They are immediately attracted to each other, dance, and make out in a dark corner. Micki implores Angela to "slow down," asserting that what has happened between them "isn't connected to anything else." However, Angela insists, "Yes, it is. It's our beginning" (p. 13). While still at the bar, Angela experiences a moment when she "felt Micki's flesh reach out to her, when she'd felt the lines between the two of them dissolve, so that there was only one being, one beat, one pulse" (p. 16).

Sexuality is much more overtly present in the romance script than the friendship one, but the extent to which it is acted upon varies. More often than not, it is consummated; exciting sex scenes are almost obligatory. Books on display in women's bookstores often fall open to the "hot" scenes. However, sex is most palatable when served with love. If the couple is not already in love before having sex, they are sure to be after unparalleled lovemaking: "Never before had she [Kate Delafield] known such orgasmic rapture throughout a night. Never had she suspected that she could. Or that she would ever want to. Or need to" (Forrest, 1989, p. 190).

However, as Suzanna Rose observes, the true sexual core of the romance is not the sex act itself, but the delightful *anticipation* of fulfillment, the longing for union (Rose, 1985, p. 256). Like the classic Greek romances, the themes of removal to a distant place, captivity, isolation, escape, search, and pursuit characterize the lesbian romance novel. Typically, the smooth progression of the budding romance is jeopardized by some obstacle to love. The subsequent separation or threat of separation stimulates the lovers' (and readers') concerns over whether the longed-for union will be achieved. Once the pair overcome the age, class, or race barriers and is united, they supposedly live happily ever after. It is rare for a romance ever to deal with the issue of how to maintain a long-term relationship.

The "girl meets girl, girl loses (or almost loses) girl, girl gets girl" treatment has some unique twists not contained in the heterosexual "boy meets girl" version. First, the lesbian romance novel frequently contains obstacles that represent real social barriers to establishing a same-sex love relationship that don't arise so often in heterosexual courtship. Parents intervene to separate the young women lovers, angry husbands have the lovers tailed by a private detective or physically abuse the wife, or one of the pair struggles to accept her lesbianism. Second, because there are no polarized gender roles to serve as an obstacle in lesbian relationships, no distance between the sexes to conquer, lesbian romances rely more on age, class, or race differences as plot devices. For example, will 40-year-old Kate Delafield be able to resist the amorous overtures of a "too young" 26-year-old Aimee Grant? Will the wealthy debutante be able to find happiness with a lesbian born on the wrong side of the tracks? Third, more harmonious relationships are depicted in lesbian than heterosexual romances, where the woman often must interpret the man's hostility or indifference as a sign of love and eventually win him over (Snitow, 1979, p. 250). Consequently, lesbian couples achieve intimacy more quickly.

Research by Marie Cini and Teresa Malafi (1991) of lesbian dating suggests that the romance script is followed by some lesbians in practice as well as fiction. Numerous lesbians Cini and Malafi approached were not able to participate in the research because they had gotten involved with a friend and had never dated. However, 23 lesbians between the ages of 18 and 24 were able to describe their thoughts, feelings, and actions on an actual first and fifth date with someone new. Because respondents were asked explicitly to describe their dating experiences, none reported going out with a friend. All the dates were with women they did not know very well, thus setting the stage for the intrigue of the romance script. The anxiety of spending an evening with an unfamiliar person was apparent in their experiences, which played out in a rather traditional date format.

Both sexual attraction and emotional intimacy were important elements of the respondents' first date scripts. In contrast to the lack of emphasis on physical appearance in the friendship script, most of the women's predate thoughts revolved around appearance, signifying a desire to be physically attractive to the other woman. They expressed considerable concern about their looks: "Am I attractive enough for her to like me? I feel fat and ugly." "I usually don't worry about how I look—

but this time I'm really attentive to it." "How do I look? Do I look good? Do I look strong and centered?" "What should I wear? I want to make a good impression." "Should I smoke?" "I wish I had lost that 10 pounds." "What if I wear something she thinks is stupid and she dismisses me right away?"

Respondents also were quite attuned to how the physical rapport was developing. They often mentioned wondering when would be an appropriate time to add a physical component — a touch, a kiss — and how they would respond if the other woman initiated it. Unlike heterosexual women, however, lesbians did not report the need to control sexual activity. Whereas heterosexual women generally make the decision about when to "let" sex happen, lesbians indicated a more mutual decision-making process for initiating physical intimacy.

The respondents' comments also indicated that they used the first date to evaluate their dates' potential as a partner in a committed relationship. As hypothesized above, even at this early juncture, many respondents were interested in discovering if their date was "Ms. Right." Assessing their interest in each other was a significant part of the script. As one woman phrased it: "Could I grow with this woman? Can I see her in my future?"

Accounts of the respondents' fifth date experiences further illustrated the rapid progression or "instant merger" often associated with lesbian relationships (Cini, 1990, p. 7). Respondents usually reported being both sexually and emotionally involved by the fifth date: "OK. If I made it to the fifth time out it means I plan on this being a long-term relationship. . . . Maybe I'll be with her for the rest of my life." "I like the idea that I'm part of a couple and that others know we're a couple." "Yes, I love her." "I don't want to be anywhere else but with her." "Could I spend the rest of my life with this woman?"

The strong attachment that most lesbians reported by the fifth date generally was grounded in highly intimate talks or deep emotional sharing. In fact, it appeared that even if lesbians did not start a relationship by becoming friends, they quickly moved to establish an intimate friendship as part of the coupling process. Some of these talks are described as follows: "Much more open with my feelings, less concerned about protecting my feelings." "I listen to her, putting the pieces of her together." "I hope we look deep into each other's eyes and tell each other deep personal things."

In conclusion, the romance script describes emotional intimacy and physical attraction as being intertwined and obvious from the outset. The attraction fuels the intimacy but may or may not be consummated sexually. Relationship initiation is direct and purposeful, and the couple is expected to enter into a committed relationship very quickly.

The sexually explicit script

The sexually explicit courtship script embraces the philosophy, "Good girls go to heaven, bad girls go everywhere;" it celebrates the active pursuit of sexual pleasure (e.g., Bright, 1989; 1990). The sexual experience itself plays a predominant role in the script; love, affection, and commitment also may be present in a sexual encounter, but are not regarded as necessary to justify it.

Probably the most common fictionalized sexually explicit script is the "lust at first sight" or "casual sex" version. The two women meet, feel a strong physical response to each other, and have a sexual adventure. Initiation is direct and goal-oriented. The bulk of the script is made up of considerable detail about specific sexual behaviors, arousal, and satisfaction. A concern about safe sex practices and AIDS prevention is usually an overt part of the script. The decision to see each other again typically depends on the erotic and emotional qualities of the interaction. If the relationship is continued, emotional intimacy eventually may develop between the couple.

Butch-femme roles sometimes occupy a prominent place in the sexually explicit script. These roles have been defined as representing a lesbian sexual signaling system (Nestle, 1987; Loulan, 1991). The "archetypes" of butch and femme are ways of presenting the self in order to attract another woman. The most frequent combination is butch-femme, but butch-butch and femme-femme pairings also occur occasionally (e.g., Califia, 1988; Nestle, 1987). The erotic appeal of butch-femme archetypes is highlighted in the sexually explicit script. The butch lesbian's lean, muscular body, unruly hair, confident manner, and sexual expertise are celebrated, as are the femme lesbian's beauty, sensuality, and sexual appetite.

Although the sexually explicit script often is downplayed as being inferior to friendship and romance in the courtship script hierarchy, it is nevertheless given its due in contemporary fiction and nonfiction. For example, in *The Lesbian Love Advisor*, Celeste West (1989) acknowledges that "the morning after" the first time in bed could be either the beginning of a continued liaison or the last time the couple will be together. Appropriate manners in the situation depend on whether a repeat performance is desired. If not:

Offer her coffee and a croissant, telling her you have to be out and about. Bustle unromantically, but not rudely. You may mention that you have so much work to do you'll be busy the next six months, but never be churlish. You always owe true politeness to any woman whose affections you have encouraged and won. Naturally you have combined integrity with your romantic glamour, so you have nothing to confess to her, like your special lover of three years is due home imminently. (p. 45)

The sexually explicit script also has had a strong, if unacknowledged, impact on the lesbian romance script. In recent novels, the romance script frequently is pitted against the sexually explicit one (e.g., *Just Say Yes*, McDaniel, 1990). The romance script usually prevails, but not before the author has gotten to describe some juicy casual sex scenes between two women superficially attracted to each other. Of course, those interactions are not as deeply satisfying as ones experienced later between the women once they have fallen in love. Thus, the reader may vicariously enjoy the sexually explicit script without endorsing it. In addition, the romantic scenes must become more explicit in order to compete with the pure eroticism of the sexually explicit script. In effect, the sexually explicit script has sexualized the romance script.

The extent to which lesbians use a sexually explicit script has not been investigated. However, research on lesbian dating indicates that some lesbians consider having, or do have, sex on a first date. Two of Cini and Malafi's (1991) 23 participants reported a willingness to have sex on a first date under the "right" circumstances. In addition, 4 of 20 lesbians, aged 17 to 55, in Dean Klinkenberg and Suzanna Rose's (in press) investigation of dating described making love on their most recent first date with another woman. These sexual contacts all took place within a traditionally romantic setting. For example, in two cases, the couple had arranged to spend the weekend together and went sightseeing, out to dinner, and talked about how they felt about each other. These findings suggest that lesbians quickly tend to establish a context for sexual encounters which includes romance and friendship.

In summary, the sexually explicit script is characterized by an emphasis on sexual attraction over emotional intimacy, direct and purposeful initiation of the encounter by one or both women, and a possible — but not required — continuation of the relationship.

Influences on scripts

To some extent, the distinctions made among the three scripts defined above are conceptual rather than practical. In everyday life, it is likely that different experiences or circumstances favor the use of one script over another or that the scripts may be blended, as in the "sex on the first date" scenario described above. The choice of script appears to be affected by individual differences, community values, and social conditions. One individual characteristic that might affect a lesbian's knowledge of what scripts are available is the amount of lesbian experience she has had. As noted earlier, it is a common pattern for lesbians to become aware of their love for a woman within the context of a friendship. At this stage, many do not identify themselves as lesbians and the friendship often has no sexual component (Vetere, 1982, p. 57). In later relationships where lesbians identify themselves as such, most report that sexual attraction is an element of their love relationships, and that they begin to make a distinction between friendship and romantic relationships. Thus, the singular reliance on a friendship script is probably less likely to occur among lesbians who have been "out" longer and have more developed courtship repertoires.

Another individual characteristic that may influence script preference is the person's attitude about sexuality. A lesbian may regard the sexually explicit script as politically incorrect, for instance, and consider sex acceptable only within the context of a committed loving relationship. Or, if she regards sex as a low priority in a relationship, she might prefer developing a friendship rather than an intimate physical relationship.

In addition, community values often operate to promote one script over another. In the 1970s, nonmonogamy was a widely accepted practice in most urban lesbian communities, and casual sex was not necessarily expected to lead to commitment. Current norms seem to favor the "instant merger" outcome for romantic relationships; there appear to be external pressures on a pair who have become sexual to establish an exclusive relationship. As Sausser (1990) aptly put it:

In our little culture, a lot of women are stand-offish. This is because they marry anyone they date. If you sleep with someone and then move in, date them and then marry them, kiss them and immediately form a permanent relationship . . . you'd better be darn careful whom you talk to! (pp. 20–21)

The expectation that any date should result in commitment might lead a lesbian to reject the romance script in favor of the friendship one, which would at least slow down the merger process.

Social conditions may also affect courtship scripts. For instance, butch-femme roles are adopted more often among working class and ethnic minority lesbians (e.g., Castillo, 1991, p. 37). Ana Castillo (1991) has pointed out that cross-dressing and cross-gender behavior are prevalent among Chicana lesbians, although dominance in the relationship does not accompany the butch or macha role. How these roles are incorporated into courtship scripts for different class and race groups remains to be determined. However, the relative absence of butch-femme roles in the friendship script raises the issue of whether this script is predominantly a white, middle-class lesbian courtship pattern. If so, it would be important for future research to identify alternative scripts that are used by working class, African-American, Chicana, Asian, and Native American lesbians.

Finally, other social conditions such as the advent of AIDS (Acquired Immunodeficiency Syndrome) has affected how lesbians approach relationships. One of the major changes lesbians have made in their response to AIDS has been to reduce the number of casual sexual contacts they have (Rose, 1991). As one 35-year-old lesbian, responding to Suzanna Rose's survey, wrote:

The spontaneous fun of a one-night stand is gone; now it's something to worry about or not engage in. . . . I'm into nice, conservative women now. I run away from women who are outgoing and sexually promiscuous. Even though sex is not as much of an exciting adventure as it used to be, I feel safe and secure with the woman I am with. Sexual variety and variation sure has suffered!

Other responses included: "I'm much less interested in exploring extra-relationship relationships." "I'm just glad I've been celibate." "No more one-night stands." "No more 'free love' philosophy that I embraced in the early '70s when sex was just fun and free of adverse effects." "Fear of AIDS has decreased my sexual desire."

Suzanna Rose (1991) also found that the second major AIDS prevention strategy adopted by the participants in her study was to get to know a partner's sexual history before getting involved. Specific safe sex practices, such as using dental dams when engaging in oral sex, were used by very few lesbians. In sum, the AIDS epidemic appears to have encouraged lesbians to begin with a friendship script rather than a sexually explicit one, in the belief that knowing a potential partner and her sexual history well will reduce the AIDS risk.

Courtship scripts and the Boston marriage

The Boston marriage as described by Esther Rothblum and Kathleen Brehony (1991) can be seen as an amalgam of the friendship and romance scripts. Whether the blend constitutes a romantic friendship or a friendly romance depends on how the relationship is viewed. During the initiation phase of the Boston marriage, the relationship more closely parallels the romance script. There is an emotional intensity and physical attraction between the two women that catalyzes their relationship. Rather than a gradual getting to know one another, the women get close very quickly, either emotionally or sexually or both, move in together, and merge their lives. Thus, as in the romance script, the women are magnetically drawn to each other, initiation is direct in that one or both pursues the other, and the pair moves quickly toward commitment. On the other hand, it is possible to argue that the lack of explicit sexual contact in some Boston marriages makes the friendship script a more exact model. The Boston marriage can be seen as fitting the coming-out version of the friendship script, because it is through a friendship that the women first realize their lesbianism.

The Boston marriage illustrates the difficulty that often occurs in distinguishing between friendship and romance better than any other type of relationship. Friendships exist in which two women are clearly "just friends" and perceive there to be little or no physical attraction between them; in other friendships, the role of sexual attraction may be unclear; and in still others, it may be very obvious. Regardless of whether sexuality is present, the friendship may be very "romantic" nonetheless, with longing and passion for the friend being expressed. Also, there are romances that are physically passionate for a while but rapidly fade into a nonsexual friendship.

The analysis of courtship scripts presented here helps to clarify these distinctions by suggesting that the presence or absence of sexual behavior should not be regarded as the sole criterion for defining whether the relationship is friendship or romance. We identified four characteristics that distinguished each script, including emotional intimacy, sexuality, and relationship initiation and progression. One might hypothesize that the extent to which the pair identifies as a couple is an important criterion in differentiating between long-term romantic relationships and friendships. These considerations are beyond the scope of the present chapter, which only addresses courtship. However, they point to the need to examine what long-term relationship patterns occur among lesbian couples.

Script theory provides another way to view the Boston marriage. Script theory posits that scripts exist at three distinct levels: cultural, interpersonal, and intrapsychic (Simon & Gagnon, 1986, p. 98). Cultural scripts describe social norms regarding the enactment of specific roles. Interpersonal scripts represent the blueprints people develop as they apply the cultural scripts to specific situations. Intrapsychic scripts are those that embody the individual's private wishes and desires.

Examined in light of script theory, the Boston marriage may be viewed as follows: There is no widely available cultural script that describes how two women mate; however, a cultural script for how to enact a friendship does exist. Therefore, in a Boston marriage, each woman's private desires (i.e., intrapsychic scripts) are likely to be enacted within the context of a friendship script (i.e., cultural script), with strong cultural prohibitions against sexual intimacy between two women being incorporated into the couple's interactions (i.e., interpersonal scripts). Exposure to alternate cultural scripts will change the interaction among the three script levels. Awareness of lesbian cultural scripts that define sexuality as part of a love relationship are likely to have an impact on interpersonal and intrapsychic scripts. As in the case described by Rothblum and Brehoney (1991), one woman's intimate involvement with a lesbian jazz group — and her concomitant more personal exposure to lesbian norms — caused her to redefine her 15-year-old relationship as "not a relationship" because it was not sexual. Her interpersonal script changed in response to a new cultural script. Presumably, her intrapsychic script also changed; she then desired to have a sexual relationship.

Lastly, the impact of recent and emerging cultural scripts on the Boston marriage also must be considered. Of the three scripts presented here, the sexually explicit script is the most recent and, as noted above, may have served to sexualize the romance script. The more overt emphasis on sexuality in two of the major lesbian cultural courtship scripts might make it increasingly difficult for couples in Boston marriages who have much contact with the community to sustain a nonsexual relationship. However, operating against the predominance of either a sexually explicit or a sexualized romance script is the emerging "friendship first" script that has developed in response to AIDS. It is also possible that AIDS has resulted in an increase in celibacy among lesbians, even those in couples. If so, Boston marriages may become even more common and widely accepted in the future.

Conclusion

The intent in the present chapter was to identify lesbian courtship patterns as a way of illuminating the processes involved in the Boston marriage. The friendship, romance, and sexually explicit scripts described here represent cultural scripts within the lesbian subculture that differ in terms of emotional intimacy, sexuality, and initiation and progression of the relationship. Differing norms within the community are likely to modify the scripts, as are individual proclivities and experiences. Within this context, the Boston marriage can be regarded as a common variant script that has been affected by lack of exposure to alternative lesbian courtship scripts during its initiation phase. However, because it shares aspects of both the friendship and romance scripts, it definitely must be regarded as a lesbian courtship pattern. This analysis suggests that examining the interplay of cultural, interpersonal, and intrapsychic scripts occurring in the Boston marriage would yield important insights about how lesbians develop and use courtship scripts.

References

Bright, S. (Ed.). (1988). *Herotica.* Burlingame, CA: Down There Press.

Bright, S. (1990). *Susie Sexpert's lesbian sex world.* San Francisco: Cleis.

Califia, P. (1988). *Macho sluts.* Boston: Alyson.

Castillo, A. (1991). La Macha: Toward a beautiful whole self. In C. Trujillo (Ed.). *Chicana lesbians: The girls our mothers warned us about* (pp. 24–48). Berkeley, CA: Third Woman Press.

Cini, M. A. (1990, March). The neglected minority: The place of lesbians in theories of relationship development. Paper presented at the Association for Women in Psychology conference, Tempe, AZ.

Cini, M. A., & Malafi, T. N. (1991, March). Paths to intimacy: Lesbian and heterosexual women's scripts of early relationship development. Paper presented at the Association for Women in Psychology conference, Hartford, CT.

Cotton, W. L. (1975). Social and sexual relationships of lesbians. *Journal of Sex Research, 11*(2), 139–148.

Deaux, K., & Hanna, R. (1984). Courtship in the personals column: The influence of gender and sexual orientation. *Sex Roles, 11*(5/6), 363–375.

Forrest, K. (1989). *The Beverly malibu.* Tallahassee, FL: Naiad.

Gagnon, J. H. (1977). *Human sexualities*. Glenview, IL: Scott, Foresman.

Ginsberg, G. (1988). Rules, scripts and prototypes in personal relationships. In S. W. Duck (Ed.). Handbook of personal relationships (pp. 23–39). New York: John Wiley.

Grammick, J. (1984). Developing a lesbian identity. In T. Darty and S. Potter (Eds.), *Women identified women* (pp. 31–44). Palo Alto, CA: Mayfield.

Harry, J. (1983). Gay male and lesbian relationships. In E. Macklin & R. Rubin (Eds.), *Contemporary families and alternative lifestyles: Handbook on research and theory* (pp. 216–234). Beverly Hills: Sage.

Klinkenberg, D., & Rose, S. (in press). Dating scripts of gay men and lesbians. *Journal of Homosexuality*.

Laws, J. L., & Schwartz, P. (1977). *Sexual scripts: The social construction of female sexuality*. Washington, DC: University Press of America.

Loulan, J. (1990). *The lesbian erotic dance*. San Francisco: Spinsters.

McDaniel, J. (1990). *Just say yes*. Ithaca, NY: Firebrand.

Nestle, J. (1987). *A restricted country*. Ithaca, NY: Firebrand.

Nichols, M. (1987). Lesbian sexuality: Issues and developing theory. In Boston Lesbian Psychologies Collective (Eds.), *Lesbian psychologies* (pp. 97–125). Urbana: University of Illinois Press.

Peplau, A. L. (1982). Research on homosexual couples: An overview. *Journal of Homosexuality, 8*(2), 3–8.

Peplau, A. L., & Amaro, H. (1982). Understanding lesbian relationships. In W. Paul, J. D. Weinrich, J. C. Gonsiorek, & M. E. Hotvedt (Eds.), *Homosexuality: Social, psychological, and biological issues* (pp. 233–248). Beverly Hills: Sage.

Rose, S. (1985). Is romance dysfunctional? *International Journal of Women's Studies, 8*(3), 250–265.

Rose, S. (1991, March). Lesbian sexuality and AIDS. Paper presented at the Association for Women in Psychology conference, Hartford, CT.

Rothblum, E. D., & Brehony, K. A. (1991). The Boston marriage today: Romantic but asexual relationships among lesbians. C. Silverstein (Ed.), in *Gays, lesbians, and their therapists* (pp. 207–222). New York: W. W. Norton.

Sausser, G. (1986). *Lesbian etiquette*. Trumansburg, NY: Crossing.

Sausser, G. (1990). *More lesbian etiquette*. Freedom, CA: Crossing.

Simon, W., & Gagnon, J. H. (1986). Sexual scripts: Permanence and change. *Archives of Sexual Behavior, 15*(2), 97–120.

Smith, S. (1991). *Edge of passion*. Huntington Station, NY: Rising Tide.

Snitow, A. B. (1979). Mass market romance: Pornography for women is different. *Radical History Review, 20*, 141–161.

Tessina, R. (1989). *Gay relationships*. Los Angeles: Jeremy P. Tarcher.

West, C. (1989). *A lesbian love advisor*. San Francisco: Cleis.

Vetere, V. A. (1982). The role of friendship in the development and maintenance of lesbian love relationships. *Journal of Homosexuality, 8*(2), 51–65.

Zand, D. (1991, March). Lesbian courtship rituals. Paper presented at the Association for Women in Psychology conference, Hartford, CT.

The Boston marriage in the therapy office

Laura S. Brown

Introduction

One of the few places where members of Boston marriages have revealed the true nature of their relationships has been in the safety and confidential setting of psychotherapy offices. Such women enter therapy in a number of different ways; one partner may seek individual therapy because of concerns and distress she is feeling about the asexual nature of the relationship. In other cases, a woman may enter treatment because she is feeling pressure to become sexually active and is attempting to find ways to cope or comply with this request. Or, the couple may present themselves for treatment for other problems, and come to disclose in the course of therapy that their relationship is nonsexual. Finally, one or both women may seek therapy for matters unrelated to the primary relationship and find that a therapist wishes to define the relationship as problematic when its asexual nature is revealed.

What is a therapist looking at when she encounters women who have been in a Boston marriage? Are these women lesbians? Could one be, and not the other? Are they partners if they have not been sexual lovers for an extended period? Is there a primary relationship present, or just two good friends in denial? The answers to these questions will have profound impact on how the therapist responds to her clients, and ultimately on the clients themselves. This situation is one in which the values and biases of the therapist regarding what constitutes a "real" relationship can become either a powerful source of support for the clients in determining their own futures, or a powerful catalyst for pain and distress when a relationship and its significance are invalidated.

This is particularly true when the therapist is herself a lesbian, since the average lesbian relationship, with its typically low level of overt genital sexual frequency (Blumstein and Schwartz, 1983) can in many ways resemble a Boston marriage. The therapist's feelings about the presence or absence of sexuality in her own relationship, if she is currently in one, may strongly influence her ability to take a therapeutic stance with such a couple, as the issues raised by Boston marriages can threaten the lesbian therapist by raising questions and concerns about the legitimacy of her own situation.

What constitutes the "real" lesbian relationship?

The most difficult question the therapist must answer for herself, and facilitate the clients' ability to answer, concerns the primacy of genital sexuality as the sine qua non of an adult primary relationship. A related, and almost equally important question, is whether overt genital sexuality between women is the defining characteristic of lesbianism, or whether this is a social construct which reflects certain time-and-place limited values which might be harmful to certain women if applied to them. Celia Kitzinger's (1987) research on the social construction of lesbianism demonstrates that in addition to externally imposed definitions of lesbian identity, lesbians ourselves are likely to describe as many as five different major defining variables in explaining how it is we came to name ourselves lesbian. Leaving aside for the present Kitzinger's critiques of these various explanatory fictions, the important point for the therapist and client alike is that there is no one fixed definition of what constitutes a lesbian identity, much less a lesbian relationship.

The power of these basic questions to impose definition and direction on women's lives in a society where therapists wield enormous influence is illustrated by a case example. A couple have been together in a Boston marriage for more than 20 years. They were sexually active on a few occasions during the first 6 months in which they lived together. They do not define themselves as lesbians, nor are they a part of a lesbian community; however, they do define themselves as a couple in a primary relationship, with shared home, bed, finances, pets, wills, and powers of attorney.

One of these women, experiencing depression and difficulties in her work life, seeks therapy with a competent heterosexual therapist in her community. The therapist, upon taking the client's history, informs her that she is suffering from an arrest of sexual development and encourages her to begin dating men, citing the lack of sexual activity in the relationship as "proof" that the client is not a lesbian but simply a heterosexual person whose sexual development has been delayed. The client, who experiences extreme feelings of internalized homophobia and who is fearful of being perceived as a lesbian by co-workers, finds these suggestions useful. She begins to experiment with dating men, although she finds herself unattracted to them and is not sexual with any of her dates. Under the stress of therapy, the relationship begins to disintegrate, leaving the other woman, bereft and grieving, wondering what happened to their secure partnership.

Whatever ambivalence and concerns the client might have had about her relationship were highly vulnerable to the therapist's view that the relationship was neither "real" nor "lesbian," as well as the assumption that in the absence of evidence of "real lesbianism," the client must be ipso facto heterosexually oriented. Because, as Esther Rothblum and Kathleen Brehony (1991) have pointed out, women in Boston marriages often feel uncertain as to the legitimacy of their relationship in light of popular notions of what makes a relationship "real," they are especially vulnerable to heterosexist assumptions on the part of therapists. This therapist clearly assumed that a "real" relationship is one that includes sexual contact, and that "real" lesbians are sexually active with other women. Rather than supporting the client in her relationship or exploring ways to strengthen and help legitimize it, the therapist treated it as unimportant, thereby widening whatever cracks might have already existed in the foundation.

Thus, the first question that a therapist must clarify for herself and her clients is, what constitutes a legitimate form of adult intimate partnership. Therapists are, like everyone else, a product of the dominant culture, which defines such relationships as having a strong component of sexual attraction and regular sexual activity. The difference between being "just friends" and having a "relationship" is usually defined in terms of sexual activity. Thus, for example, the female protagonists in the French movie *Entre Nous* can be seen as not having a lesbian relationship because they are "merely" intensely loving, nonsexually affectionate, and devoted to one another, while being genitally sexual with men to whom they are tied primarily by law and finances.

However, therapists working with members of a Boston marriage must carefully examine the validity of this assumption and ask whether a certain degree of heterosexism is distorting both her own and her clients' views of what constitutes an adult intimate partnership. Because the legitimacy of heterosexual relationships is typically defined by the institution of marriage, a heterosexual couple with a sexual history similar to that of a Boston marriage are still considered married, whereas the couple in the Boston marriage might not be considered a "real" couple. It is highly unlikely that a therapist would inform either member of such a marriage that he or she was not truly heterosexual, or encourage them to see themselves as being "just friends." The legal imprimatur of marriage made available by heterosexual privilege obscures the reality that such dynamics occur in heterosexual as well as lesbian relationships.

Homophobia also plays a part in responses to these questions regarding "real" relationships. One or both women in the Boston marriage may be avoiding overt sexuality because they perceive this as behavior that would define them as lesbians. Either woman may be fearful that sexual expression, if unleashed within the relationship, will render the couple vulnerable to ostracism in work or social situations. Or, they may fear that it is only the nonsexual nature of the relationship that accounts for its longevity, a response, conscious or otherwise, to the cultural stereotype that lesbian relationships are founded only in sexual attraction, and consequently of short duration. Any early sexual activity between the partners can be, and often is, dismissed as experimentation, less meaningful than their many years of companionship and affection.

Thus, these questions of definition are essential because they frame the direction in which therapy will progress. If a couple in a Boston marriage enters treatment because of problems in their relationship, a therapist must first be prepared to reexamine her own definitions, and then to support the couple in respecting the definitions they have created for themselves as a valid and useful framework in which to make decisions. This may be especially difficult because one or both women in the Boston marriage may be examining the legitimacy of their own definitions. One or both women may be asking whether they have really been a couple, whether their relationship is a genuine one whose boundaries deserve respect, whether their difficulties can be resolved if sexual functioning is not developed or restored. The women may wonder whether it is worth learning to communicate more clearly or negotiate differences if they are not a "real" couple, that is, not sexually active with one another.

At this early stage of therapy, the therapist must be able and willing to set aside preconceptions and facilitate the couple's exploration of the meaning and parameters of an adult intimate relationship. This in turn helps all parties in therapy to make decisions: Is this therapy intended to strengthen a legitimate relationship, with or without a sexual component? Or will it be aimed at securing a separation in recognition of a decision that this is not a primary partnership because the sexual component is absent? Is the development of sexual functioning between the partners an important goal of therapy? Is it more important to preserve the relationship and maintain overt sexuality outside the relationship than to attempt to bring sex into this one?

This exploration may be very threatening to both women in the Boston marriage. If one woman is questioning the relationship on the grounds of its asexuality, this exploration of definitions will require her to analyze her willingness to discount the value of other aspects of the relationship as balanced against overt sexual contact. If one woman is resisting the institution (or reinstitution) of sexual contact, she will be pushed to examine what becoming overtly sexual with her partner may represent for her. Either woman may find herself reexamining the meaning of a faithful commitment; if she is emotionally faithful, but has sexual relations with a third party to whom she has no commitment, has she violated the boundaries of the Boston marriage? In any case, the therapist must be careful to avoid a premature closure, but must create a safe space in which the anxiety evoked by this questioning can be contained and tolerated. The women in the Boston marriage have likely avoided frank discussions of the meaning of sex and its absence in their mutual life; talking about it will probably evoke long-held resentments, fears, and recriminations in which unproductive patterns of relating will be exacerbated and inflamed.

One way to create a safe environment in which to explore this highly volatile issue may be to draw up a contract that binds both women to remain within their relationship as it has been previously defined (e.g., as a monogamous primary commitment) during a fixed period of time as a condition of therapy. This sort of agreement not to "act out" prevents the premature resolution of the conflict via what I have come to call the "non-monogamy two-step" (referring to a Country-Western dance popular in the Seattle lesbian community), in which one woman becomes sexually involved outside the relationship as a strategy for moving the couple more quickly from its current distressed position. Although this invariably does break the log-jam, it also invariably destroys the relationship and allows assumptions about the primacy of genital sexuality to remain unexamined and thus inaccessible to conscious, thoughtful decision and choice.

Also important in creating a safe space for exploration of these important definitional issues is the therapist's willingness to promulgate a social constructivist perspective on lesbianism and lesbian relationships. This perspective suggests that there is no fixed, immutable, or inherent quality of lesbianism or lesbian relationships; rather, it points to the effect of social discourse in creating shared definitions of what constitutes certain phenomena, including lesbianism. Kitzinger (1987) observes that lesbianism as a quality of the person herself is a relatively recent social construction; in past epochs, sexual behavior between women was perceived as a perverse expression by women who were defined basically as heterosexual. Even during the past century in which lesbianism has been ascribed to the person, rather than her actions, the concept has been variously construed as a form of pathology, a sin, and a normative minority of variant of human behavior. More recently within a radical feminist politic, the concept has been construed as a form of resistance to patriarchy. Some of these social constructions require the presence of overt genital sexual contact between women; others do not. By supporting clients in a Boston marriage who challenge their assumptions about the implications of the names they use, or fear using, to describe themselves, and by promoting the therapeutic assumption that there are no givens regarding what constitutes an adult intimate relationship, a therapist can help to create an atmosphere in which each woman can learn how she has come to define herself and her interactions with her partner.

These explorations will also require that the therapist deal regularly with her own fears and feelings about the nature of lesbian relationships. For the lesbian therapist, whether partnered or not, the Boston marriage will frequently elicit feelings of identification with one or both partners, as well as questioning regarding her own history and acceptance of overt expressions of sexuality. Most relationships, regardless of their quality, will have periods when there is a diminution of sexual activity due to illness, stress, overwork, or conflict between the partners. Often a decrease in sexual activity in the therapist's own lesbian relationship, when it occurs during her work with a Boston marriage, can be a source of intense personal distress and concern that she, too, might come with her partner to resemble these clients. Or, the therapist might currently be, or have been, in a Boston marriage, given that this is a phenomenon whose frequency is unknown. The questions raised by the client couple may be the catalyst for the therapist to begin turning over the rocks in her own interpersonal landscape. Whatever the impact of working with such a couple, the therapist treating members of a Boston marriage would be well advised to seek regular consultation, acknowledging in advance that this phenomenon is one that is likely to elicit feelings which, if left unattended, could be acted out in the therapy to the detriment of all concerned.

The Boston marriage: Staying together

One possible outcome of couples therapy for members of a Boston marriage is that the women make the decision to continue to perceive their relationship as a functional primary commitment. It has been my experience clinically that this outcome, although rare given the social context in which such a couple functions, requires a high degree of personal integrity and acceptance of difference from community norms. Both women must be able to embrace, rather than simply tolerate, the value of a relationship defined by factors other than sexuality. They may choose to define themselves as a legitimate lesbian couple. Or they may define themselves as primary partners and decide not to use the term lesbian to describe their relationship. It is important that the therapist not push these women to define themselves as lesbian; rather, the goal is to develop strategies to help the couple validate their choice of one another as life partners within their own system of ethics and values.

The women in a Boston marriage may be faced with deciding whether to "come out" as having an asexual relationship, which they do not see as a deficiency. In this regard, such women are like members of any other sexual minority in that they are resisting society's determination that their partnership is invalid because it fails to fit within culturally imposed notions of proper adult behavior. In one case of which I am aware, and in another example in a collection of interviews of lesbian couples (Mendola, 1980), the partners have decided that the woman who desires to have an active sexual life may have casual sexual encounters with women and/or men outside of the relationship. Each of these situations involves very specific rules governing fidelity and infidelity; a common theme in both of these cases is a commitment that sexual activity not happen with women or men for whom the sexual actor feels strong affection or love. Thus fidelity in these cases becomes defined by faithfulness of emotional intensity rather than by sexual behavior, underscoring that the strength of the partnership is not sexuality, but love, affection, and feelings of deep intimacy and emotional connection. Coming out as a committed asexual couple requires more strenuous communication to friends that the relationship is real and not open to invasion simply because it lacks the element of overt sexuality.

Ending a Boston marriage

A more common outcome when a troubled asexual relationship between two women undergoes the scrutiny of therapy is that the relationship draws to a close. Again, the process of breaking up requires that therapist and clients alike respect the reality of the relationship. Rather than dating the end of the relationship from the end of sexual contact, the closing date should be defined as the time when the two women make a mutual, conscious decision to no longer view the relationship as primary. The therapist must exercise caution not to collude with the notion that the two women have been "just friends," which is a convenient fiction often offered when one of the partners has become interested in having a sexual relationship with someone new and wishes to skip the important process of closure with her former partner. Such labeling minimizes whatever importance these women have had to one another, especially given the dominant culture's devaluation of friendship. Bibliotherapy may be helpful at this juncture; my clients have found it useful to read Lillian Faderman's (1980) *Surpassing the Love of Men* and Janice Raymond's (1986) *A Passion for Friends* as a corrective against cultural invalidation of the importance and passion that exist in nonsexual partnerships between women.

Commonly, as with other breakups, one partner is less willing to leave the relationship than the other and may feel betrayed, abandoned, and angry. When the woman in this position is the one who does not wish to be sexual, she may engage in self-recrimination, shaming herself for her stance and blaming herself for the end of the relationship. A therapist can make very powerful interventions at this point by underscoring the fact that relationships between women who are sexually active with one another also end, and that not being interested in or willing to be sexual does not imply a deficiency or pathology. Such a stance runs counter to dominant cultural definitions of healthy adulthood, which tend to devalue celibacy unless it is chosen outside of a primary relationship. A more radical and feminist re-visioning of healthy sexuality for women includes celibacy when consciously and deliberately chosen as the state which best suits the individual, as equally valid and valuable as all other choices of sexual identity and behavior.

A more difficult resolution is one in which the woman leaving the relationship appears to be acting out her internalized homophobia. As in the example given earlier in this chapter, such a woman may not be interested in beginning a new sexual relationship with anyone, but may be fearful that her current partnership will come to be labeled lesbian. In this case, the woman left behind will also be faced with a struggle regarding her sexual identity and may, after years of putting herself in a category that has no name — in which "Sue and I love and live with one another but are not lesbians," begin an often painful process of coming out as lesbian to herself.

Conclusion

For a therapist working with a Boston marriage, the guiding principle must be one of constant challenge to taken-for-granted notions. Feminist analysis of the nature of intimate relationships can be an important basic assumption. For example, by questioning the patriarchal concept that couple relationships exist to give ownership over the sexuality and sexual behavior of one person (the woman in a heterosexual relationship) to the other (the man in a heterosexual relationship), and by presenting this as the source of the couple's assumptions about the validity of their relationship, feminist critiques and analyses can be powerful tools for deciphering the nature of the couple's problem.

Because the frequency with which Boston marriages occur is unknown, it is likely that many therapists will assess these couples as simply manifesting a sexual dysfunction in the form of mutual disorders of sexual desire. Although the question of sex therapy in Boston marriages will be addressed elsewhere in this volume, it is important to state here that such an assessment may miss the unique nature of such a nonsexual couple by focusing on what appears to be missing rather than on what actually forms the nexus of the relationship. The therapist must be careful not to impose the primacy of overt sexuality upon a lesbian couple seeking treatment. Rather, a more helpful solution may be to present the

Boston marriage as one legitimate form of lesbianism, in order to increase the choices available to each woman, together and separately.

References

Blumstein, P., & Schwartz, P. (1983). *American couples.* New York: William Morrow and Company.

Faderman, L. (1980). *Surpassing the love of men: Romantic friendship and love between women from the Renaissance to the present.* New York: William Morrow and Company.

Kitzinger, C. (1987). *The social construction of lesbianism.* London: Sage Publications.

Mendola, M. (1980). *The Mendola report: A new look at gay couples.* New York: Crown Publishers.

Raymond, J. G. (1986). *A passion for friends: Toward a philosophy of female affection.* Boston: Beacon Press.

Rothblum, E. D., & Brehony, K. (1991). The Boston marriage today: Romantic but asexual relationships among lesbians. In C. Silverstein (Ed.), *Gays, lesbians and their therapists: Studies in psychotherapy* (pp. 207–221). New York: W. W. Norton.

Personal Stories

What's sex got to do with it?

Leslie Raymer

M Y TODDLER just walked in here and pushed the reset button on my computer, crashed the word processor, and lost the last four hours work. This is why I don't have sex anymore.

Actually, I feel like something of a fraud writing an article for a collection about lesbian asexual relationships. I am, after all, in a relationship that is at least in *theory* sexual. I don't like the word "asexual." I associate it with worms. It sounds prudish and tight-assed. "Nonsexual" doesn't work, either, since I see myself and my lover as sexual beings. Nonpracticing, maybe, but sexual. Nor does celibate. None of that thought-out, intellectually motivated or therapeutically healing stuff here. We just seem to be out-of-order.

But I am also a fraud allowing people to assume we have a wonderful sexual component to our wonderful, fulfilling relationship when we don't. We never did, really—not *wonderful* anyway. It was adequate. Now, I am exploring what sex is all about for me and for us. Actualizing this fact and "coming out" about it is strangely embarrassing. Much of our identity as lesbians, after all, is about sexuality (or is it?). The way my friends squirm when I talk about this subject leads me to believe this is one of the many things we need to discuss with each other at great length. The squirm also leads me to wonder how common this situation really is for lesbian women. It is not exactly big news that the level of sexual activity in lesbian relationships drops more significantly than it does in heterosexual *or* in gay male relationships once the initial infatuation passes. Some researchers suggest that because women are the "emotional glue" that holds heterosexual relationships together, when we love each other, there is enough emotional bonding at every level that the ritual of sexual intimacy is less essential to maintaining the relationship. Personally I like this concept more than the idea that we simply have a lower libido than men. I've had some pretty horny times. This isn't one of them.

Maybe it's the 30s. I would never have guessed at 18 or 22 or 26 I would find myself in this place. I feel so settled, safe and well loved. Ten years ago, had I listed my top 10 needs for a relationship, good sex would have been number 2 or 3 . . . maybe even number 1. I think it's still in the top 10, but floating down there with those other theoretical considerations like "maintaining our independence" and all that happy garbage that is impossible to measure and, while possible to maintain, probably impossible to create from scratch.

I have always liked women best. Being lesbian is being home. Though I dated a couple of young men (now gays) in high school, I didn't really love them like I have women. It makes sense to me to have sex with the people one likes best. Except for a couple of meaningful one-night stands — with dear friends — I have lived the "have sex, get married" lifestyle. I am pretty entrenched in monogamy at this point also, having experienced that it is damn near impossible to pull it off another way in this culture at this time without creating a lot of avoidable pain and stress. Besides, I don't have enough time to spend with my partner, and I can't imagine trying to squeeze in another relationship.

I grew up in a single-parent household with three brothers. Even though my mother and I are both strong personalities, we were still outnumbered. My first woman-gathering was Girls' State. Girls' State is an ultraconservative gathering sponsored by the American Legion Auxiliary where young women learn about U.S. government. I attended between my junior and senior year in high school, and the Auxiliary would no doubt be pleased to know that Girls' State was a life-changing experience for me. The energy was incredible. I met my first female lover, Ruth, there. We did not consummate our relationship at Girls' State, but we did talk about what it might be like to kiss other girls. And a few of us were involved in (gay-bashing) gay-play. I cried for two days after being at Girls' State for six. I loved those young women. And I vowed not to lose track of Ruthie.

After a couple of visits back and forth during high school and early college, Ruthie came to my hometown "to look for a job." Within a few weeks we were lovers. We had wonderful, exploring, creative sex. We challenged everything we knew about sexuality and gender roles. We tried dildos and vibrators, screwed each other with popsicles and giant candy canes, took turns being on top, and did it in every position we could think of, and sometimes I had so many orgasms I passed out. Ahhh, nineteen.

Ruthie had some childhood issues to resolve. Maybe sexual abuse, definitely other physical abuse, and lots of baggage to figure out with her family of origin. I was just beginning to actualize my own childhood sexual abuse.

I believe most women are sexually abused/exploited during our childhood or young adulthood. Most of us. Statistically, then, it seems obvious that most relationships between two women would include at least one survivor. JoAnn Loulan and others have documented the impact this has on our relationships. We feel safe enough with each other to identify our toxic histories, and the grief and pain of it is often destructive.

After having been together a couple of years, Ruthie decided maybe she wasn't lesbian after all. I have seen a lot of women do this — the old "I just happened to fall in love with a woman" denial. I felt it too, at some point, but was long past it when Ruthie verbalized it to me. I had begun taking women's studies and framing my world in feminism. I was receiving validation for my sexual identity and finding community. She decided maybe she wanted to do men or whomever and was done being "married." Objectively, I know Ruthie's position was reasonable. We had, after all, just stumbled into a relationship, and it was great fun, but not for life. I, however, could not imagine being without my first true love.

When Ruthie shared her decision with me I was devastated and did not hesitate to show my feelings. The following day my brother and soul mate died in a tragic accident. This left me totally devastated and feeling very alone. Ruthie assured me she would not leave me in my grief, and that she loved me very much. I know she did care about me very deeply.

Death and dying expert Elizabeth Kuhbler-Ross would be impressed that I generalized my denial to include the conversation with Ruthie the day before my brother's death. We bought a house together and lived as partners for quite some time after her decision we weren't "right for each other." (I have since taken heed of the advice: "Celebrate romance, but keep the real estate in your own name.")

Although Ruthie and I had been friends for a couple of years before being sexual and had managed to maintain a good friendship throughout our relationship, I came to a place where I defined the relationship as finished because we were no longer sexual. I had withdrawn from everyone, including Ruthie, so even if I had been able to clarify these issues for myself, they were not expressed or discussed between us. I initiated a new sexual relationship which in effect ended my relationship with Ruthie.

My relationship with Di was as erotically charged in the beginning as I could imagine. She is nearly 30 years older than I and appreciated my sexual appetite. I appreciated how appreciative she was. We had a great deal to teach each other. We made love to the sounds of Bob Seger, Ralph Vaughan Williams, Christopher Cross, Richard Wagner, and, of course, our lesbian contemporaries, Holly, Cris, and Meg. Di was just coming out as a lesbian, and both of us were clarifying our feminist consciousness and our individual therapy experiences. She was also into the then-new Hospice movement — a perfect ally for me and my new unfinished business. After my brother's death my family of origin withdrew from one another in a way I had never seen before, and I planted myself firmly in this new relationship. Di was everything to me — best friend, lover, sister, mother. And our sex was good. She turned me on and fed my ego in a way Ruthie never had. We were comrades at a special time on our individual journeys. Di was starved for sex that was not male identified, I was seeking "home" and challenging every rule — ageism, sexism, heterosexism — I could. We were social-service executive women on our way to somewhere big.

Di has children my age. When we met, they did not live with her, and I carefully explored whether she thought they would again, wondering how this would affect our love/life. I moved into her home, and shortly thereafter her youngest daughter (a few years younger than I) moved back home, too. I had great difficulty with their dynamics and worked at staying out of their relationship. Her presence in our lives made a big difference for me. She didn't like or respect me, and had no qualms about letting it be known. I didn't like the way she treated Di and clammed up to avoid conflict with someone who reminded me so very much of my asshole father. Di also had frequent duty with the Hospice beeper. While I still commend her and others involved in this work, the constant reminder that beeper imposed was too much for me. Often losing Di during dinner, from a party, or from a quiet romantic evening to rush off to the bedside of someone breathing his or her last was quite a downer.

My interest in moving to a larger market with my employer and Di's interest in obtaining more education dovetailed, and we tailspun into a move out of the town where I grew up and she had lived for 30 years. While the move was probably right for me professionally, it was not a good personal fit. Nothing felt right between me and Di — I was working so hard to compromise and she was working so hard to give me every-thing. Within a few months of our move I was commuting back home to maintain old ties and develop a relationship with a sexy and needy woman named Gail, who was in my consciousness raising group. My family was coming back around, too, and I wanted to be close to them. My little brother was married and ready to start his own family. I wanted to know his children — and I did not want to lose track of my deceased brother's son, either.

I specifically remember discussing Di with Gail, explaining that we had come to the point that we just kept each other's back warm at night. Again, the quality and quantity of orgasm-oriented sex was the barome-ter by which I measured the life of our relationship. My breakup with Di was painful. I had been honest from the start that I did not see our re-lationship as a "forever thing" and that I was not in a place to commit to monogamy. She heard this, but we did not deal with it until I bla-tantly challenged the boundaries of our relationship by seeing — actually, sleeping with — Gail.

Gail was probably bad news for me from the start, but she was an attractive package deal because I also got her son Toby. Gail wasn't the world's best mom and had a lot of bad breaks, so I rode in on my white horse to fix everything for her and Tob. Gail and I had great sex at first, and we made love until the sun came up sometimes. After a short time of free (actually she was very controlling — I once contemplated whether she was the devil incarnate) sex and love, Gail began feeling secure enough to share some of her horror stories about previous sexual experi-ences. She had been abused and raped as a child by at least one male relative, she had lived a lonely, promiscuous straight bar-scene life for years and been used by lots of men. Her only other sexual relationship with a woman was with her therapist (the/rapist) and that woman's hus-band in three-way sexual encounters (he wins, he wins). And Gail would sometimes cry after a really intense orgasm.

Still dealing with my own childhood issues and pushing Gail to deal with hers, I to this date could not tell you who was withdrawing or who was withholding. Sometimes control was very subtle, sometimes more overt. I have only recently been able to name the relationship what it was — abusive. I know that when sex became a power issue, I wanted out.

After prolonged soul-searching and a couple of years of working harder for her than I ever will for anyone again, I literally moved her out of my house over her ranting and raving body. I stayed in that relationship for Toby, not wanting to leave him with that crazy woman, and got out of it because it became clear he would soon be living with two crazy women if I didn't.

Then, for the first time in my life, I spent some time learning to be alone — finding and defining friendships and trying to sort out my shit — doing therapy seriously this time.

Of course I learned a great deal from each of these women (and even from my one-night . . . okay, two-night . . . stands). I probably learned the most from Gail. Had I not known her, I probably would still be carrying a lot of pain about my jerk father. I learned that for me, sex is really better when it's part of love. I learned how to work on a relationship. I learned that loving someone (even intensely) is not enough. Gail's abuse and self-abuse frightened me, and I learned that I cannot allow myself to be as vulnerable as I feel during sexual intimacy when I am not safe. I learned to spot an abuser a mile away. And I learned I really like kids in my daily life.

From there, I came to here. The story is not quite as clear from here and a lot harder to articulate.

Maureen was on my list of "Interesting Women I Would Like to Know Better" when she asked me to meet her for lunch. She wanted to explain that she would not be attending a gathering I was hosting, not because she didn't like me but because she was bulimic and the gatherings had really come to have a binge focus. I was very cautious, hoping to have left my white horse to pasture. Maureen is a gentle soul, and I needed gentle badly.

Our relationship had a slower emotional start than my earlier relationships. We were both rather fearful; I coming out of a truly dysfunctional relationship, she unsure she was finished with her previous relationship, out of which she had just klutzed her way via an unfulfilling affair.

Sex has never been our strongest suit.

I have never been here before. I want my primary relationship to be sexual and it is not. I've also never been in a relationship this long. I feel like I practiced everything in the first 3 years several times and did all that pretty well this time — I just don't know what to do now, 5 years into this partnership. I want to be an old woman with Maureen . . . a sexy old woman, at that. I am in a safe and solid relationship, and have every intention of staying here, sex or no sex. This time, it doesn't mean it's over, and that is very different for me.

I do not mean to imply that somehow our lack of sex is Maureen's responsibility or choosing. It does belong to both of us — I am not particularly interested right now either. In fact, I more frequently initiate sex in our relationship (if not the act, the mood), and Maureen is quite OK with or without it. I *want* it to bother her that we aren't making love, but I don't want it to bother her so much that if we can't get it together she finds it elsewhere. I *want* her to have a greater sexual appetite, but I love just who she is, too.

My sexual appetite seems to grow or decrease in geometric proportions. If I am having lots of sex, I want lots more sex. When I have less, I want less, and I think I'm hanging around here in zero-land examining every facet of this before I plant my feet and try to find the balance point. (Being consumed with lots of great sex is not really an option in my life right now, and would take a great deal of coaxing to enlist Maureen's cooperation.) Maureen and I never clicked sexually like I have with others, but our similar world view has always more than compensated for this shortcoming between us. I really have fun living with her, and I think we are good for each other.

Sex is not completely gone, of course, in the broad sense. We have the best cuddling ever. We touch and hug a lot. We respect each other and demonstrate that in our interactions. We are tender and affectionate. We kiss often, but not "seriously," and we have not had orgasms together for quite some time. We have discussed doing sex/therapy together, but are not motivated enough by our circumstance to do it. Right now, I am fairly confident this isn't pathological in our relationship and fairly confident that my thinking so is not denial. (But who knows?)

I can think of lots of reasons why we don't have sex. Perhaps, more appropriately, why I don't have sex, since Maureen doesn't really care that much.

I'm a little chubby again. As much as I try to overcome it, I still feel sexier when I'm thinner. I don't generally find skinny women attractive, and in fact prefer soft round types. I would probably prefer me, if I wasn't me. Moving the extra weight around is cumbersome and tiring. I prefer the way I feel about 40 pounds lighter. Coincidentally, I've usually left relationships chubby and have lost weight in the process of moving into a new relationship. The implication of this pattern is somehow a factor in my current situation. I had great eating habits when I met Maureen. In fact, my diet was one of the things she found attractive. She managed to get her bulimia under control with a little help from me (and others, of course). I love to cook and feel that sharing a meal is one of the pleasures of any relationship. Despite putting my white horse to pasture, I have also become quite aware of Maureen's food and body issues, and I feel especially unattractive knowing she really doesn't like chubs.

I really started gaining weight in this relationship when we began trying to conceive our cute kid. The process itself was really fairly simple once we identified a willing and appropriate donor. He did his thing in a jelly jar, and we did the rest. It took 5 months to get pregnant. While this is not a great deal of time, the stress was incredible. Becoming pregnant is an emotional roller-coaster ride. Always affirming a pregnancy, I spent half of each month eating as though I was pregnant, and half of each month grieving and psyching up for the next insemination.

Since I was confident I could lose weight and not so confident I could carry a child to term, when I did get pregnant, I blew off any concern for weight gain and concentrated on eating lots of quality foods. There was no satisfying my appetite. Our child is 18 months old and I still am carrying the weight. Chub is a definite factor.

While trying to get pregnant, I was afraid to have sex. I was really concerned that we'd jar our little zygote loose if we had sex. When we accomplished the first step, I was paranoid for the first trimester, and pretty much out of the sex habit after that, and soon got bigger by the day.

Having a baby around and physically birthing a baby are also factors. Being a mom really does change your life. In the beginning, I was so damn sore, there was no way I could even think about sex. Delivering Ali was long and difficult, and I am just now no longer sore. Immediately after her birth, there came a period of complete exhaustion for about 3 months. A child at every age keeps parents hoppin' . . . but I actually feel sorry for women who are expected to perform sexually after working and/or keeping up with a small child for 14 or 16 hours. Both the discomfort and fatigue are major factors in my lack of interest in sex.

There are some other factors associated with having our Ali that have affected my sexual appetite. For one, I am trying on this new identity of mother. My own childhood experience was that we came first to my mother. My biggest concern when considering parenthood was that I had only this model for parenting. I believe that a healthy family is about adults relating to adults first, and then to children as well. But the needs of a small child are so *in your face*, that it is impossible to clip your own toenails, much less make your partner feel special. This has become more manageable over the past few months, and I want to learn to be a sexy mom. I did not perceive my own mother as sexy — she dated a few men, but not many, or any for very long. Most moms I knew weren't particularly sexy. I don't know how to change my image of "mom" in this regard.

The childhood sexual stuff is perhaps a factor, again, too. Healing from childhood sexual abuse is, as Anne Morrow Lindbergh says about life, like an onion. I peel off a layer or two, cry for a while and go on. I think I had pretty well processed my experience to death until I had Ali. The pain in my crotch was not just physical — I experienced some psychic pain, also. My vulva and vagina felt so bruised for so long, there was some association with being manipulated with fingers, as I was as a child. While I thought I had dealt with all of the onion, recovering from childbirth must be at the very core of the thing. I am still allowing myself this plateau, if that is the case. I have a hunch that leaving relationships in the past had something to do with where I was with the onion. There may be more hidden here, too. A whole new onion, maybe? This is a terribly frightening possibility to me. I have learned, though, that these things don't come up until I am capable of dealing with them. For this I thank Maureen for her patience and concern.

Maureen has conceded that there may be some childhood issues for her, too, but she cannot find any specifics. At the very least we are all socialized in a culture that eroticizes the imbalance of power and all must work very hard to unlearn these images. I sometimes wonder if in this process we make our world pretty nonerotic. There must be a middle ground.

The reality is, too, that Ali gets a lot of our affection and sensual energy. This is wonderful but frustrating. I believe the roots of that pop-psych co-dependence stuff are right here, and I want us all to be healthy. I believe Ali needs to see that Maureen and I share a commitment to each other, and to learn that our love for her was born from this.

So. There are lots of reasons for not being sexual. But there have been reasons, for me, with this woman, since I have known her. I have other life-long commitments that aren't about sex — a few fine friends, family. I work hard to create my own reality in a culture that is not designed to meet my needs. I now refuse to allow myself to measure the value of any of my relationships by such male values as how often I "get some."

Maureen and I might be able to address the chub factor, the fatigue factor, the body-image factor, and the abuse factor, but it still might not make a difference for me or us.

Then what?

One friend suggested that this sexual appetite stuff comes in cycles. Maybe so. Maybe I've just changed relationships on the downside of the cycle every other time. I have a sense that this time, while waiting for the upside, I lost track of most of my sexual self . . . I'm not even interested in masturbating. I hope this part of me will come back around. I do know that if it doesn't, I still want to be in this relationship that gives me so many of the other things I need and never had before. If everything else stays healthy, I think I could be happy snuggling and keeping each other warm . . . and happy.

That's what.

When we were whatever we were: Whatever it was that we had

Laura Moxie

I T WAS ME and Violet. I've been a lesbian for about four years now and I haven't had a lot of lovers. My first relationship was with an emotionally abusive lover. It took me ages to get over it; it was awful. I had only been lovers with that woman when I moved into this house, where I met Violet. I'm 28 and Violet is 34.

She was not here when I moved in. I moved in because of a lesbian friend who lived here. Violet was away for three months. It seemed that Violet was this *dread* presence: "Oh, Violet wouldn't like that." So I lived in terror of the day that she would come back. It's funny, because I had a connection with her before she came back. There was a morning when I got up and I thought: I shouldn't leave this towel sitting out here because Violet might be back today. We didn't know when she was coming back exactly. Sure enough, she did come back that day.

At first she was slow to warm up. I was trying to be very, very friendly, because I wanted to stay in the house and I knew that her approval was important. I'm not sure when it changed or how this ended up happening. I moved in here in August three years ago and we weren't great friends by Christmas. But some time after that we started becoming friends.

Violet had been on a six-month trip to Asia, and so she was really mellow and feeling good. Usually she gets very depressed in the winter and had been through a hospitalization for that in the past and medication every few years for her depression. But I didn't experience any of that the first winter with her. She had broken her cycle.

By the summer we were really good friends. She was straight but interested in women and had lesbian leanings which of course I encouraged. We were both looking for lovers. I was looking for a woman lover and she was looking for a lover of undetermined sex. During the time that I lived with her she did have a couple of male dates, one-night stands. The house is situated so that both our bedrooms are upstairs and they're all that's upstairs. It was the "Laura and Violet area." By that summer two different friends of ours — a friend of hers and a friend of mine — said to us, "Well, you're both looking for lovers, why don't you become lovers with each other?" I don't remember what Violet said to that, but I instantly said no, forget it, we're roommates, we cannot be lovers, it's not allowed.

That summer was Violet's 15th high school reunion. She asked me to go as her date and I ended up going. She thought this was a lark. She had been straight in high school and basically her whole life. She had been thinking about whether she was a lesbian for 11 years or so but had never done anything about it, although she flirted with the idea. She was also part of a lesbian game playing group where she let the other women think she was a lesbian.

Anyway, we went to her high school reunion together. It was not far from here. She could have brought me as a friend. And really that's what she did. At the time I wouldn't have said that we were lovers. It was a weird experience for me because she introduced me to everyone as her girlfriend. People didn't pay much attention to that. It wasn't that big a deal. They accepted me as a friend and didn't really "catch" it, the game she was trying to play. I was annoyed because I thought it was clear that it was a sham. It was clear to me that we did not relate the way lovers do. Even forgetting the physical side, there was a way that we related that wasn't as lovers did. We didn't slow dance, and we could have. If she really wanted to be provocative, that would have done it. There was a little awkwardness there. To me, masquerading as lesbian lovers seemed like a strange thing to do.

That event sort of set the tone for our whole relationship. We had a very nice time together in San José. At that time I was selling jewelry and scarves, and Violet would go places with me and sell with me. She was really helpful to me because my job was very stressful. She even became part of the business, making scarves and helping with jewelry.

Neither of us had a lot of social functions to which one brought a date, but we would often go together to things. I went to see her music concerts (she was a singer).

We got to be very close. We had some problems that second winter because of one of her depressions. We fought about that once, but the result of the fight was talking about it and admitting that we were really important to each other.

There was one point in the winter when Violet was playing games on one of our roommate's computers. We were going to watch a movie that I had rented. She had said she would finish the computer game and then come up. And I waited and waited and she didn't come. Finally I went down and asked where she was and she said she thought I was going to start without her. I blew up at her and said this wasn't about the movie, this was about her spending all her time playing computer games. It was really an addiction. I had a very hard time with that. She cried, and I felt awful. The next day, we talked about it. She said she just needed to retreat in the winter. It made me feel much closer to her. She gets very depressed in the winter and, even though she had told me, I didn't really understand. I thought I could make everything better in her life. It was a rough time for us until baseball season started. She's a baseball fan — I started to go to baseball games sometimes and now I'm still going to them even though I'm not going with her.

I had one brief affair with a friend of mine during this time, but it did not work out. I didn't have a lover and wasn't really that much in the market for one. There was a point at which I started to feel interested in having a girlfriend. I'm not sure when I started to realize that I was committed to Violet in some way. We had never talked about it but we did a lot of things together. All my friends knew her, and I knew all her friends. We were family. For all her moods, we got along really well always. We talked about everything. Finally I realized that I *couldn't* have another lover until I resolved things with Violet. Violet was in the way for me. The other component of this was that some people thought that we were lovers because of the way I talked about her. I never said, "she's my lover," but we did everything together, and I talked about her all the time. Our lives were wrapped up together the way lovers' lives are.

Violet knew about people mistaking us for lovers and at some point I said we should really say we're not lovers. But she said, "Oh no, just let them think we're lovers." She liked other people having that impression. I didn't mind them having that impression, and it certainly made it easier when we broke up, because those people immediately grasped the situation.

Anyway, she had a birthday, and I orchestrated a surprise party for her. I took her little black book, called all her friends, called her brothers. It was really a great moment for me. We took her out to dinner, brought her back, and there were about 15 or 20 people in the living room with presents, decorations, and video cameras! She was totally in shock. To me this was a great act of love. I thought she should understand how I felt about her from my having done this. She was very excited and thrilled and it made me feel wonderful.

I had been attracted to her for a long time. She would take long, long hot baths, and I would spend time with her when she was in the bathtub. We'd chat, and she would sit around in a towel or naked afterwards, cooling off. And so I started feeling very, very attracted to her. I would tell myself, this has to pass, she's straight, she's my roommate. At this time also she was seeming more and more woman oriented. She was bringing fewer male friends home. I was able to convince myself that she was turning lesbian.

That spring, I was selling at Women's Weekend, which takes place at Russian River, a lesbian mini-music festival. Violet and I went for the weekend and camped out. That was the weekend that things came to a head for me. I realized that we had to move one way or the other. I thought I really had to tell Violet or do something, but I didn't quite have the courage. We got fake tattoos that were little hearts with each other's initials. She said, "Oh, let's go back and tell everyone that we're married." And we went back and we told them, but I was very half-hearted about it. It felt strange to me. Because I was a lesbian, there was something missing for me, but I don't think there was for Violet. I think she was playing in a way. I think she liked the idea of it. I don't doubt for a minute that she loved me and was, in her own way, very close to me. I don't think that part was a put-on. But something about the "trappings" of it was what she was into.

Anyway, it took me about a week, with encouragement from my roommates, to finally say, "I don't want us to play at being lovers any-more. I think we really *should* be lovers." Her reaction was, "Great. Wow!" I was sure she would say no. We spent about three weeks kind of trying to be lovers. But it was hard. It was a weird thing. I think part of it was that she was an incest survivor and I was just starting to deal with my own childhood abuse. So I was feeling weird about my sexuality. Later I realized that it was commitment I needed from her, not sex. But that was the only way I knew to change things — if you're going to have a relation-ship, you have to have sex. We didn't; we spent a couple of nights to-gether and kissed, that's as far as it went. It just always felt kind of weird. We were very, very close but it wasn't quite working. We were both too scared.

When we first got involved, I had been talking with some friends of mine who had been encouraging me to get a lover. I said I got involved and their first guess was that it was with Violet. They knew how I felt about her and that she was the person in my life.

Anyway, she finally said she didn't know if she could do this, she didn't know if it was right for her, and she'd let me know at the end of the weekend. I thought, "Oh God, my world is coming to an end!" And it was then that I fully realized how important she was to me. And the mag-nitude of the situation. We spent about another month having horren-dous fights and not speaking to each other much. Things were stormy and awful.

Then we went into therapy for about five weeks. We both acknowl-edged that our friendship was important, and this was a way to salvage it. That was a helpful experience, even though it seems to me now that our friendship may not have been salvaged. The therapist was really good. I told the therapist that Violet had internalized homophobia and that she was afraid her friends wouldn't like it. Violet denied this. By the end of therapy, she was admitting it. This didn't make me feel better, it made me angry. She did love me and she said that she did; there was just something in her that couldn't make it happen.

The therapist did one thing that was very validating. We told her what our situation was and she said, "Oh, you were in a sexless marriage." And Violet agreed. It validated for me what had happened, because it hadn't felt like the breakup of a friendship, although that can feel very devastat-ing too. It just felt like my whole world was shattering. And it still feels like that a year later.

In therapy, we were trying to decide whether Violet was going to stay in the house or move out. I did not behave well in all of this either. I was just miserable and let everyone know it. After our last session when she talked about her friends' not accepting us, I wrote her a long letter. I said, "This is part of you, whether we're together or not." I don't know why she's even friends with some of these guys — they're real jerks. I think it's her insecurity. Her friends seemed to accept me, and they knew that I was a lesbian. So they would probably have accepted Violet just fine. There were gay men in her circle. But still, it would have been an adjustment, and she's not good with that.

I was willing always to work it out and recognize it was a difficult process, but to stay together. To be a couple. I was very much in love with her. If she had not felt the same about me, I think it would have been easier. But the fact that she did love me and somehow something within her wasn't allowing her to go any further was devastating. She also had other reasons — being afraid to be in a relationship, being afraid of getting hurt. One of her big fears was that the events that precipitated her hospitalization would repeat themselves. One of the major events was her breakup with a male lover. She left him because he was making dates with other women while she was present; it was a bad situation. She was afraid that if something happened between us it would be the same thing. She didn't trust me to stick with her through her depression. I think part of it was that we were much closer than she's probably ever been to her male lovers. That kind of closeness was scary. She said that she felt comfortable with all her friends, a lot of whom were ex-boyfriends, but if she came out to them about us it would destabilize her whole friendship network. That is what coming out does; I couldn't argue with her about that. But it also made me angry, because she had wanted all *my* friends to think that we were lovers. Lesbians would ask if we were lovers when they saw us together. Especially later in the relationship, when I'd talk about her or when they would see pictures of us, lesbians would assume that we were a couple.

Violet had a straight best friend who was married. I remember her repeating during the winter and spring that "Ellen is my best friend." It really hurt my feelings. I thought, What am I, chopped liver? I think she said it as part of her denial.

There were a lot of other things too. She has a lot of phobias and I do things that drive her crazy. She's a neat freak; I'm not. She can't stand the smell of cantaloupes or broccoli. She can't stand spiders to be mentioned. When we split, I thought there would be that period when I would think, oh thank goodness I can talk about spiders, I can eat broccoli, and I then I thought, I don't care, I want Violet back. I didn't have that sense of relief. I have a feeling that maybe we would never have been lovers, and that was okay with me. But I felt we had unfinished business. We had to take our relationship somewhere and see it through, see what could happen. We never got that chance. Maybe that's why I'm still plagued by this relationship. If it had come to its logical conclusion and we really had been together too long and gotten on each other's nerves, that would have been one thing. But that wasn't it. It was because I am a lesbian and she is not.

I would say we were together for a year and a half and it's been a year now since she moved out. I still feel incredible loss and grief. The house has not been the same. We've been through all sorts of roommates. My boss has talked to me about my work performance because I've been really grumpy. It's been a difficult year.

I've seen Violet once or twice very briefly since she moved out, when she came to get things from the house. I have been tormented that she never responded to my letter, in which I mentioned her internalized homophobia. It may have been a harsh letter. We had less and less contact, but even when she moved out we still cared about each other. We had been doing almost everything together. So we still talked life details for several months. At some point I asked whether she was going to respond to my letter. She said yes, but that moving into her new place was making her too busy, which was just an excuse. She said she thought about it every day. Violet is like that. She's not good at dealing with things and being up front. She still hasn't responded to that letter.

I was feeling a lot of nostalgia this spring. So I wrote her a letter for some closure for myself, saying that I missed her. She wrote back right away, and her letter was very disturbing to me. I meant to reply but I had to go to Women's Weekend and there was a whole cycle of anniversaries of our relationship. Her reply made me realize that if we became friends again I would have to deal with the reality of Violet, not just the good parts. Not just the closeness we had, and maybe not closeness at all. I don't know if I can be close to her again, because she said that she missed me too, but basically she thinks she is straight but not "straight-straight." So what does that mean? I feel like saying it means that she's straight, that's all. One thing she did that really makes me angry is that she masqueraded as a lesbian. And I knew her history, and I knew her history was men, so a lot of this was my own self-deception. A friend of mine who's a therapist said I have delusions of grandeur if I think I can convert straight women to lesbianism! Violet went to lesbian events and put herself out as a woman-centered woman. I do think she's woman centered. But that's not honest or accurate if she's basically straight, if she knows she doesn't want to be in a lesbian relationship. I think she may not really know that. I'm not sure what it will take for her to know that.

What I realized in couples therapy was that the sex part was not really important nor was what we said to other people about our relationship, but it was the commitment we had to each other that was important. I could live with Violet and not have a lover, but I couldn't live with the idea that she might go off and start having sex with some man. And I could not deal with the thought of her really liking a man. That's one of the things that's keeping me from being friends with her now. She's had very bad experiences with men, so I can't imagine that she would end up married. I would feel a lot better if she became involved with women. Then I would feel happy for her and I could deal with her as just a friend.

Straight women are very unsafe for me. I've had a few bad experiences with straight women friends. I had another straight woman friend a few years ago, a schoolmate who really pursued my friendship. There was sexual energy between us and I brought it up. I wasn't sure I wanted to be lovers with her but I wanted to talk about it. She said a lot of homophobic things. We did continue to be friends but I finally broke off the friendship because she still flirted with me. I told her it bothered me and she got really upset. I said it was disrespectful to me because I'm really a lesbian. She was flirting with something that I live. Violet was very flirty with her best friend Ellen. Violet's trip to China was to see Ellen. She never talked about it. I don't know how Violet felt about Ellen getting married. She said she liked Ellen's husband.

I'd like to see Violet make up her mind. I'd rather be friends with her as a woman who is definitely straight than as someone who's wishy-washy about her identity. What I know I can't deal with is her indecisiveness because I find that hurtful. She wants lesbian love and energy but she doesn't want the social stigma of being a lesbian. She's very straight-looking. She has long blond hair and she's small and cute, and the way she dresses is little-girlish. I think she doesn't want to lose that heterosexual approval. She's had a hard life so I can understand this, but I wish she would be honest about who she is. I think being sexual with women is very scary for Violet. She has been socialized to be straight and has taboos against lesbian sex. If you've been straight for a very long time, you have to really want to come out, or to be totally in love and lust to forget all the socialization. I don't think that was true for Violet, although it was for me — I was in love and in lust. But some of that was missing for her.

The hardest thing about our breakup was the reaction of my lesbian community. One roommate was very supportive, although she moved away shortly after. For a while we were a close-knit household; everyone liked everyone. Home was very important to me. I didn't tell a lot of people that Violet and I were involved. Then when things went awry I couldn't tell them. They had never known that we were together. I didn't get the kind of recognition that people normally get during a breakup. Although, if we had been an acknowledged couple and had broken up, I don't know how much I would have wanted to talk about it anyway. I probably would have done just what I did, which was to wait awhile and then start talking to people about it. My friends were supportive when I told them, because they knew how close I was to Violet. I had some way of explaining to them what was going on, but it was really traumatic. My boss was supportive because he thought we'd been lovers. He gave me a day off when we first split up.

I don't know how much support Violet has. She has one good friend who is a lesbian, but she moved back to the East Coast. I don't know how much she told her about this. I know this friend was always encouraging her to be a lesbian also. Violet has had mentors along the way, many of us encouraging her, but it clearly hasn't done any good. The therapist said we should each have our own support network. Our roommate Hana would have talked to Violet if Violet had wanted to talk. Never in all this process did I say that Violet was a terrible person or that I hated her.

There is part of me even now that wants her back. I'm beginning to finally say that I don't want her back, that I want a lesbian to be lovers with, someone who doesn't have all the problems that she has. We have been able to avoid each other because we have different friends. If she were a lesbian, we would have friends who saw each other, we would see each other, but as it is, we don't. Just the other day my sister ran into a friend of Violet's and heard that she is moving. Apparently Violet doesn't like living alone and is looking to move in with somebody now. And I thought, Oh, she could move in here. But then I thought, it's now a lesbian house, and men aren't allowed after a certain time at night. We've changed, and I've changed. I don't think my new housemates would even like Violet, quite frankly. But I still miss her and the thought ran through my head that maybe Violet and I could get an apartment together, just the two of us. That's not practical, but it was in my head.

I've had another lover since Violet. It was another disaster. I've gone through a lot of stuff that I haven't acknowledged, and in a way that was why the relationship with Violet was so perfect. Being sexual is very problematic for me. It's not easy and it's not necessarily something I want to do. What I came to realize is what I really crave is closeness and affection and commitment, someone who is my best buddy. My relationship with Violet filled a need for both of us. It was much nicer and safer and more comfortable than a sexual relationship would have been, with all of the charge that has to it. I think that at that time in our lives being sexual wasn't appropriate for either of us. But I had no other ideas, no way to think, much less talk, about what I really wanted until we'd been through the whole process and it was too late. Maybe it would have been better if I had gone to her and said, "You're really important to me and I want some commitment here." I don't even know if she would have understood if I had said that. Neither of us had a frame of reference for having a committed, monogamous, nonsexual relationship. That was the important element. She could have other friends, but I didn't want her to sleep with other people. With men. I don't know if she would have been willing to do that.

It's hard to know how she would have felt if I had had lovers. When she was upset she closed herself off in her room. I think if I had had lovers she would have closed herself off. I think she might have been jealous, it depends. If I just had a one-night stand, I don't think she would have cared, although it's hard to say. I think she would have totally devalued her reaction and decided she had no right to feel hurt or upset by it. But it would have been hard for her to be supportive and encouraging the way friends often are. I think I would have reacted the same way if she had had a lover. This is almost a moot question because I couldn't have had a lover, because the situation between Violet and me totally precluded other lovers.

I've never lived with a lover before. I've had male lovers and I've had female lovers, but I've never had someone with whom I was as close as I was to Violet. Whatever it was that we had. Partner was the word I used a lot. It was a good term because she was working with me, and only I knew how ambiguously I was using that term. It didn't just mean business partner in my mind.

When I talk about it now, I don't use the word "lovers." I usually say, "when we were whatever we were." Most of my friends know enough about it to understand. I don't explain it to people who are new in my life. I don't go into the short explanation, I only talk about it if I can really tell the whole story. In my mind there is no quick way to explain it without sounding like I'm making excuses. To say, "Well, we were, but we weren't really, lovers" sounds almost defensive. Still, it was important, even though we weren't really lovers.

When I explain it to friends, they often remember high school girl-friends they were totally bonded with. I think often those relationships go unacknowledged from beginning to end. At the same time, they are monogamous and they do have breakups. I've had a lot of understanding from friends. Maybe the circumstances were a little bit different, but it's not that unusual. It's just unusual to acknowledge it.

Violet and I have a lot of interests in common. I'm still debating whether to be friends with her, because I'm friends with other ex-lovers. With one it took us 2 years. We had been friends for a year, and then had a very brief, unhappy affair. Then we tried to be friends again a year later. It didn't work then but it's working now, 2 years later. It took us time to get over the trauma. Another friend and I have managed to be friends the whole time. But that was only a low-key affair.

I don't even know what I want in a relationship. Part of me thinks Violet really tricked me into falling in love with her. On the other hand I view the infatuation I developed for her as organic and natural. That was part of why I had such a strong feeling. With other women, I have met them and felt I *should* be attracted to them. She was totally the wrong person and I knew that, but my logic had no influence over me. I felt it was fate, it was meant to be. That's part of my frustration that it ended so abruptly.

I had been very politically active and radical, and I have a fear of being involved with someone else who is political and radical. Not that I would want to be involved with a Republican or even someone who is apolitical, but politics puts pressure on me. I feel stress from the pressure to perform and to live up to standards. I like the idea of having a lover who is less political, and who says, "Oh, don't go to that demonstration, stay home, you need to rest," someone who takes care of me. Violet was somewhat political, but she never put pressure on me. She's a real feminist but her life wasn't centered around that. I really liked that. I thought that type of person would be my ideal lover: someone who was more conservative, less political, and more nurturing. At the same time I have a crush on a woman now who is very political and very much a lesbian. A friend of mine said that lesbians are very scared by lesbians. That was true for me, although it's less true now, but I think it was part of my feelings about Violet. She was safer for me because she's a straight woman. I can't figure out what that's about. Maybe if I were with another lesbian I would be measuring my identity against hers. Since I'm newly out maybe I would fall short. With Violet, I was the dyke, I was the one who was more lesbian.

There's a pro and con to the familiarity I felt with Violet. There weren't any surprises. I trusted her emotionally and knew her foibles. She had a lot of them but I knew what they were. Even the risk that she might go on meds or be hospitalized. I worried a lot about her this winter, living alone, and being depressed. But I guess she made it through.

Violet is very nurturing, and very sweet, and affectionate, and loving. She just didn't have good boundaries around her sexual identity. I think the problem is that straight women just don't understand how lesbians can take relationships with women so seriously. If I were a man she would totally understand.

I think a nonsexual relationship is functional. I think there are a lot of relationships in our lives that we don't give the importance we should because they're not sexual. One of the experiences I have had in San Francisco is that a lot of women I have become friends with have moved away. It's a very transitional city, and I feel very settled here. I feel if a friend is thinking of leaving town, she should come to me and say she's thinking of moving, what do I think. But they don't. One of my good friends, an ex-lover, did come to talk to me. She wanted my opinion and validation. She didn't ask permission or ask me to move with her, but she included me in the process. I wish we gave each other more importance. I have some friends who are deliberately asexual, they want to be single. I'd like to see us have a broader definition of couples, or lovers, or even three friends together. I have one friend who is committed to her friends and even jealous of them, and I respect that in her. She takes her friends very, very seriously. I'm that way too, although I've had to let go of it because my friends won't cooperate. When I was a child, that's how my friendships were. I've had best friends who were really, really close. I have very close lesbian friends, and I would like to see us have more options. We need words to say we're committed to each other, and that we will talk about life decisions together, but that we're not lovers. Too much of what gets recognized in our community is not who we care about but who we are attracted to and who we end up in bed with, which may be based on very dysfunctional urges.

I'd like to think that, as lesbians, we're part of a community, not just individuals moving around. I would like to say, "I'm moving to this city. Who would like to move with me?" My sister, who also lives here, has said that she would think twice about moving away from me. It seems more socially acceptable, because we're sisters. If she did move, I would seriously consider moving to be with her. I wish friends would do the same.

I have a real dilemma about the friends and lovers issue, because the heterosexual model is that you meet someone you don't know very well and you instantly become lovers. And every male in your life is a potential lover. It's not quite the same with lesbians. There are women who I don't feel are potential lovers, and I'm very close to them. There are other women who are potential lovers. It's very confusing. Do I want to follow the heterosexual model and meet someone and become lovers when I don't really know her? Or would I rather get to know someone? But once you get to be friends, are you allowed to be lovers? Can you become lovers with someone with whom you are good friends? I don't want someone who will be disjointed, in and out of my life. The model is that sex has to come first and then you get to know each other — I think that's kind of backwards.

I couldn't possibly say when Violet and I stopped being friends and started being more than that, whatever that means. Sometime during the winter I guess. During our second year together. Or maybe it started when I went as her date to her high school reunion. I don't know. It took me a long time before I allowed myself to feel attracted to her. Then it took a long time before I admitted I had to do something about it. When the whole thing blew up, I really kicked myself. I thought, as long as we didn't acknowledge it, she probably would have been willing to go on and be committed to me. But I couldn't deal with the lack of acknowledgment. Our growing together happened so gradually and naturally, but the breakup was so stormy. It's interesting that I accepted the breakup immediately. Everything this spring reminded me of something we did together. I still have the fantasy that she'll come to me and say she's a lesbian and let's try it again. It's fading, I'm getting over it, and I wouldn't get involved with her now. I do think about the time we were together, and I think she does too. Living here, in the predominantly gay and lesbian Castro district, was her way of dipping into the lesbian life. I wonder what she would say now, a year later, about what happened between us. When I've run into friends of hers they've gone out of their way to be nice to me.

What cuts me to the quick is being rejected because I'm a woman; I consider it sex discrimination. That is the anger from which I will not recover. I don't trust Violet because of that. I think I've read too many lesbian novels in which these two straight women meet each other and get together. I just don't understand why falling in love isn't enough.

It's very hard to come out when you're living with people who are lesbian and pressuring you to come out. So I had this fantasy that maybe she just needed to be on her own and get away from this pressure, and come out. But I guess she is still straight.

Violet had more power in the relationship. She was the one who decided what image we portrayed to the straight world. She went into it as a game, seeing if we could shock people, but it was my life. At her high school reunion, she wanted to show people that she was different. She wanted to say, "I have changed." But it wasn't what I would have chosen. It's different saying, "This is my girlfriend," from saying, "I am a lesbian." There's a T-shirt that says, "My girlfriend is a lesbian but I'm not" and it made me think of me and Violet. It's sold as a joke, but who knows how often it's true?

Postscript

One year after this interview, Violet and I have become friends again. I am happy to say that the sweetness there once was between us has not been lost; though our relationship has changed, we still care about each other. At the time we became close again, we were both involved with other people, she with a man and I with a woman. She helped me through a difficult breakup and then I helped her through one. A lot of issues came up and we were able to process things we had never dealt with from the time when we were together. We have been able to talk about how her wishy-washy sexual identity was hard for me and about some of the other factors that influenced our relationship and breakup. This has been a gift for me. I have given up trying to find friends to make commitments with, though I still wish for this. I think our culture just isn't set up for it at this time. I see straight women, especially the ones that like to flirt with lesbians, as dangerous and don't get too close to them. I try to be very clear about relationships and expectations with the women I am close to and honest with myself about what I really want. I'm glad I still have Violet in my life; she will always hold a special place. And I am glad for the clarity I have gained since the time we were together.

She will never have the access to the total person that I have

Elizabeth

I FOUND from the beginning that Marianne was a very interesting, challenging, stimulating person in spite of the fact that she was rather young. I liked her thinking and I particularly liked that she was not intimidated by me or my age. Because I'm older, I frequently find that young women can feel intimidated in my presence. They may see me as this accomplished, middle-aged person. Marianne was not intimidated by me and that made me very comfortable with her. She's very bright, very intelligent. You know, there are people who are very intelligent, but somehow they cannot take leaps of imagination, they cannot go to another level of understanding that seems new and creative. Marianne has the capacity to do this and that impressed me very much.

So I found myself looking forward to hearing her voice and enjoying going out to eat with her once in a while, and I also found it a little ridiculous that I was attracted to someone so young, who could be my daughter. We met at a time when I was feeling depressed because I had just come out of a long-term relationship, and I was very sad and lonely. I started confiding in her that I was feeling this way, and her response was wonderful. It got to a point when I knew that if I were feeling bad, all I had to do was give Marianne a call and she would be there or she would ask me to come to her place and stay there. She was coming out of a relationship that had been short-term but significant. At that point it had been her only lesbian relationship. So there was a lot of pain there for both of us, and we served as each other's supports at that transition time in a very deep and meaningful way.

But all along we were involved and we were not involved. At some level we were each other's primary person. We would travel together for weeks at a time, we would spend weekends together. But at the same time I was saying that I was looking for a woman my age, and she was saying that she was looking for a man. Because after the pain of that first relationship, Marianne was saying that she wanted to stay out of the lesbian world. She would talk about people she was meeting and I would talk about people I was meeting, but at some level we knew that none of these people was really "it." For instance, I went out with a woman one day and I got home around 11:00 at night, and Marianne gave me a call to see how I was doing after my meeting with that person. What ended up happening was that Marianne came over and stayed the night. So in a way her call was a way of making sure that nothing had happened on my date. If in fact I had connected with this woman in a way that she was coming home to be with me, obviously a call from somebody else was going to be an interference. But I guess that Marianne knew that it wasn't going to be an interference and that I would welcome her coming to stay with me that night. When I say that Marianne stayed the night, I would like to clarify that. Although in reality we were sexual a few times, when we traveled together or even slept together in the same bed, nothing would happen. It would just be very nice, some embraces, some kisses, but not really sexual.

There was a short period when we were actively sexual, but then Marianne decided that she did not want that. That the age difference was too big, and that to leap over those twenty-some years and to leap over the fact that I was a woman when she was not sure she wanted to be with women was too much for her at that time.

I would say that this has been one of the most significant relationships of my life. I haven't been able to let go of this relationship yet. Marianne is now in a relationship with a woman, Eve. Eve is a person I don't like, partly because of my jealousy and partly because I don't think she is the right person for Marianne. I think both components are there.

Marianne and I met almost four years ago. We got very involved about three years ago. We've been living in different cities for one year now. But for this past year we've been seeing each other at least for a weekend every six weeks or so, very consistently. The longest period of time we haven't seen each other has been two months. We have also continued to talk on the phone pretty regularly.

There have been some hard times, like when she started this new relationship. I was hurt and furious, mostly because I was terrified to lose her. She got into this relationship after I had moved away. And I think that had I not moved, Marianne would not have become involved with Eve.

Part of my feeling is that there is a way in which our connection is so very important that I feel that I compare everybody with Marianne, and every woman that I meet falls short. I think that is true for her too. She might call and say, "You know me better than anybody else, and I don't really feel that Eve and I have that much in common." Yet it's almost as if Marianne's relationship protects her from me and me from her. We are very clear that ours will not be a sexual relationship, so we can go about relating to each other in the way we always wanted to relate.

Marianne described me to Eve as a former lover, and explained to her that we were not involved anymore. At the time Marianne met Eve, we had not been sexually involved for over three years. I met Eve before she and Marianne got involved and I disliked her instantly. I thought she was being intrusive in our friendship. Marianne said that Eve was a new person she wanted me to meet and I had to say, "I don't like her. I don't like her style, and I think she's being very intrusive. She's just met you and she's acting as if she owns you." I said this not knowing that they were going to get involved. Then they got sexually involved, and when I heard, I felt very hurt and I told Marianne how I felt. During the past three years, I did not constantly say, "I'm in love with you." But when I heard about Eve, I told Marianne, "I have been in love with you all this time, and I still am, and this is very hurtful." Marianne's immediate reaction to my confessions was one of anger, and I think that was because she was feeling guilty. In reality I had no reason to be hurt, because we had spent years telling each other that we were free to get involved with other people. On the other hand, when it happened, of course it hurt!

Eve made noises about being friends with me. She's the type of person who is friends with her ex-lovers and the new lovers of her ex-lovers. I have never gotten into that with any relationship, I have never been friends with lovers of ex-lovers. I am not going to get into that now, particularly when I'm still fairly raw about the whole thing, and when she is a person I don't like. If Marianne were with a person I liked a lot, then perhaps it would be possible, but I don't like Eve so I don't have any desire to be her friend.

So when I've been back to visit, there have been some attempts at including me in activities with Marianne's whole group of friends and I mostly refused all such activities. I've said that I'm not interested in being with those friends; I'm not interested in being with a pack. I said, "If I'm going to see you, I want to see you alone. I don't want to see you with a bunch of people and I don't want to see you with her. I'm here very few times and I don't want to spend those times with her." I used to stay with Marianne every time I came back to visit. After she got involved with Eve, I found other friends to stay with. Eve was assuming that I was going to stay with them, as if nothing had happened. And I said, "I'm not going to sleep on the sofa in the living room while you're in the same bed together. No way." In a way, what Eve was doing was trying to get me to be her friend so that I was less of a threat. That's one of the reasons I think why so many lesbians have these entanglements with lovers of former lovers, because being friends means less danger. (But I think that increases the danger!) It seems that for Eve, trying to get me to be her friend meant that if Marianne and I were meeting in front of her then Eve would know what was going on. And also, if I'm Eve's friend, then I have to be loyal to her, too. However, the reality is that Marianne and I had three years in which we could have been sexually involved with each other if we wanted, but we never did, so Eve should have nothing to fear. Yet on another level, the reality is that Eve will never have, I don't think, the same access to the total person of Marianne that I have. Marianne says to me, "You know me better than anybody else."

Being with them together would be very difficult. On the other hand, Marianne once said that she would make a point of not being physical with Eve in my presence. I said, "I don't have the right to tell you how to be with your lover just because I am there. However, I don't want to expose myself to that and that's why I don't want to be with the two of you together." Marianne has said that Eve is anxious and angry when she hears that I'm coming to spend time with Marianne. When I last visited, they had a battle about it. I said, "Why is she so worried about this? She has you and I don't." Marianne said, "Well, she has me, but she doesn't. There is a way that you know me like nobody else and when I really need to talk about something that matters to me, I need to talk about it with you. So Eve knows that and knows that in reality she doesn't know me."

I don't want most friends to know how I feel about Marianne. I think

they would be judgmental about this. With so many people I've pretended that Marianne is only a friend because I feel ridiculous about
being in love with someone who could be my daughter. However, this is
the truth. And if I cannot talk about the most important thing that has
happened to me in the last three or four years, I really cannot talk to
them at all. I cannot fully be their friend, it's sort of like not being out.
When you're not out, you can still have conversation, but you're keeping
a part of yourself out of the picture and that doesn't let you fully communicate. I make it out that Marianne is not the most important person in
my life. But the first part of my schedule when I visit is to see Marianne,
and everyone else comes after that.

Marianne and I both agree that we have been the most important
people in each other's lives in the last few years. And were it not for the
difference in age, we would be in a different type of relationship. We
would be in a "real" relationship. The age difference is coming from
Marianne's perception; I think I would have given it more of a chance.
When we were sexually involved and Marianne didn't want any more of
that, I said that there are very few times in a lifetime, precisely because
I'm now middle-aged, when a person who is so perfect for you comes
along. A person who likes the same things and encourages you to do the
best, who is so protective and challenging, and does both at the same
time. Who is encouraging, and sexually exciting, and attractive, and
stimulating intellectually, the perfect person. Not that Marianne doesn't
have quirks that I don't like. But even though the age difference creates
some things for me that I don't like, I was willing to put up with them
precisely because, being older, I knew that this was the chance of a
lifetime. Because Marianne is younger, I think she still is in a place of
thinking that a person like me will come along but be 20 years younger.
She has the luxury of waiting for the perfect person to come along. I
don't have that luxury.

However, there are times, particularly when we've been with people
who are in their 20s, when I get bored. I don't get bored with Marianne, I
get bored with those people. Marianne has a circle of friends of all ages,
so her friends would not be an annoyance for me. But there are other
things, like Marianne wanting to go dancing every Saturday night, or
getting on a windsurfer, or going skiing. When we do some of those
things, Marianne is always teaching me, which makes me feel very cared
for, but it does curtail some of her freedom. This whole thing has also

been difficult for Marianne because I've pretended that this was not a relationship in front of a lot of other people my age. She has felt badly treated by those people, like she's this "little person," an attachment to me. To many of my friends, Marianne is still a girl. So Marianne feels treated like a girl, and humiliated. Also, her family knows me and is very nice to me, but would consider me undesirable and would believe that I had seduced her if they knew there was anything more there. I would not have been welcomed into her family if I had been seen as the seducer of the innocent girl.

In terms of my professional world, the age difference is a problem. But Marianne made the decision to end the relationship before I was ready to make the decision to let go. It's perfectly possible that if we had stayed together for another 6 months, I would have decided that I didn't want the relationship. Part of the reason why I may have stayed "hooked" is that I had discovered this wonderful person and she said no, so I have spent the last few years living on the joy of those three months in which we were sexual. That's an exaggeration, because there are things we have built in these 3 years that have solidified this relationship. But I know there is still a lot of fantasy on my part even though I know very well that we will never be more than we are now.

On the other hand, what we are now is wonderful, meaningful, and unique. Just the other day we started talking at 9 in the morning and separated at half past nine at night. We did not stop talking. At other times, we would go to a restaurant for dinner at 7:00, and then somebody would come and say, "Do you want anything else, because we're closing." That meant that it was 1 o'clock in the morning! We were just sitting and talking. And the times we've been sexual, it's been very intensely passionate and wonderful. The problem for me was that I did not have time to let this relationship run its course. I always have been wanting to get more than what I've been able to get. And at the same time I was getting so much that there was no way I was going to let go of it.

Part of the reason why I moved is that I wanted to be away from Marianne. I wanted to keep the connection and I kept it; as I said, I've been traveling regularly and she's been traveling too. But I wanted to be in a different geographical space so that my first move would not be to call Marianne to ask her if she wanted to go to the movies. Here, I need to think of somebody else to go to the movies with. I needed to get out of that, and that was one of my big motivators for getting away from my old town. And I think the year apart has worked that way. Marianne started this relationship with Eve that she would not have started if I had been there. Or if she had started it while I was there it would have been ten times more painful to have it start right under my nose. So now it's at a distance, when I can come once every two months and we can say that we haven't seen each other for so long and so we can spend a day together, and that's good and that's enough. And I don't need anything else and I'm not interfering in any way in her relationship and in other things.

Now that I've moved, I feel more comfortable talking more about our relationship. I say to the people here, "There's this person, and she's younger." I want her to meet a number of people who I have met here. I'm assuming that Marianne's relationship is not going to last. And even if she starts a stable relationship with another woman in the future, I know that I'll always be in her life in some way and she'll always be in mine. I'm hoping that someone else will come along in my life so that my attention will be directed toward this new person and not always toward Marianne. At the same time, I know that the reason I cannot find someone is because my attention is focused on Marianne.

Even if Marianne and I again live together in the same geographical area, I don't think it will make a difference. We had all the chance in the world to get involved during those past three years and it didn't happen. And I would be very afraid to pretend that we are going back into our relationship, because I might get hurt again. The fact is that my physical attractiveness is fading as I age, while her physical attractiveness is increasing. Relationships are hard even when people are sharing life stages. I don't want to find myself at age 70 with a 40-year-old woman who is having a mid-life crisis and trying to find somebody younger! I think that could be ten times more hurtful than what is happening right now. At this point in time I still feel reasonably attractive and energetic. I have a pool of people around me, and I can still try to find a companion for myself in that group.

I think Marianne has the same ambivalence that I have: thinking that moving to my area is not a good idea, but at the same time wanting to be around me all the time. If our relationship won't change, why keep warming it up? It's better to let the fire die and let things be. But I know that neither one of us wants to let the fire die.

Her being in this new relationship, although painful, has been very reassuring, very comforting. It preserves the importance of our relationship in a way that nothing else could have done. If Marianne were still without a sexual relationship, I would think she was just holding on to me until she got into a sexual relationship. I used to tell myself that during the last three years. This has made it obvious that, regardless of who is in her life, I will always be important. It has made our relationship deeper. When I was with her this summer, we were more able to tell each other how much we loved each other and how important we were to each other, than we had been in the last few years. Because in the past, we had been afraid that any declaration of love meant that we were going to go back to being sexual, and neither of us really wanted that. I was afraid that Marianne would think that I was inviting her to do that, and I think she was afraid that if she heard an invitation from me she would have to separate from me and keep her distance and make it clear that she didn't want that. She is sexual with Eve, and faithful to her, so there is no question that we'd be sexual. I guess she feels protected from her own temptations or my possible invitations, and maybe she wants to keep sex and emotions separate.

We've had a lot of history under our belts

PART I: ANGIE

WE JUST CELEBRATED our eighth anniversary. I met Cedar at the Michigan Women's Music Festival. It was quite romantic, as you can imagine. We had a wonderful flirtation in getting to know each other.

The first six months of our relationship were very romantic and very sexual. Then it started to taper off. I didn't want to be committed. At that point I considered myself to be dating her and not really in a relationship with her. And so I was dating other people occasionally. Then after about a year we broke up — I broke up with her.

It was a situation where I wanted nonmonogamy and she wanted monogamy. We were separated for about 6 weeks. At the end of the six weeks we both had made major changes in our thinking. Before we broke up, Cedar was rather dependent and sort of like a puppy dog, is the way I've teased her about it. I was rather aloof and distant and independent. But when we were separated for those 6 weeks, she felt she *could* live without me and she felt much more independent, and I felt that it would be *hard* to live without her and felt that I was more or less willing to make a commitment.

We had a dinner date set after 6 weeks, our trial separation. At dinner, we both felt we wanted to commit to the relationship, but from different angles. She wanted to commit to it not from a position of desperation but from a position of being peers and equals. I wanted to commit to it because I realized that she really did have everything that I wanted in a partner. So that was the most romantic part of our relationship.

We went through the next year just thoroughly enjoying each other's company and being very romantic and very sexual. I think the prime ingredient in our relationship has always been laughter. We make each other laugh a lot and we both thoroughly enjoy a good laugh. And enjoy each other's company because of that. We can tease each other and enjoy — not really laughing at each other — but teasing, the kind of teasing that makes you really giggle. Cedar's got a really good sense of humor, she's extremely witty. I've always enjoyed that, and I can get her to laugh in a similar way, although I think she's the funniest.

During the first year we lived in separate residences in Las Cruces, New Mexico. We spent a lot of time at each other's houses, but not 100% of the time. Then, during the second year, when we decided to make this commitment, Cedar was actually at my apartment almost 100% of the time. So, I would say that we sort of started living together during the second year.

At the end of the second year we actually moved into a house together. We've been in that house now for the past 6 years. I can remember that when we moved into the house, during the first week, we made love. And that was the last time. And that was 6 years ago.

The first year we lived together, it was so nice to be living in a house together. She had her possessions and I had my possessions. It wasn't like one or the other of us was at the other person's house and our things were someplace else. We enjoyed setting up house and becoming more comfortable with each other. It wasn't like dating or entertaining a guest, as it had been in the past. It was like being at home together.

And we would occasionally talk about why we weren't making love. What's wrong? But neither of us had a very strong motivation to do anything about it. It was nebulous. I think it bothered me more than her, or maybe I was more verbal about it. She would say, "I don't know. If you want to, I can." And I would say, "No, no, I don't always want to be the assertive one. I want you to be the initiator at times." She would say, "Okay, I will be the initiator sometime soon," and then I'd wait and it would never happen. And then, internally, I would say to myself, "Well, you don't have to wait for her to initiate. If you want to make love, then you can initiate." And, I don't know, I would feel too tired, or not in the mood, I don't know what it was but it seemed that there was no motivation there anymore. And we went through about a year that way. We were sleeping together, in the same bed, even though we each had our own bedroom.

In the meantime, we both started to gain weight. I used to joke with Cedar and say that we had supplanted sexual passion with eating, that eating was our passion now. Because we would both come home from work and make big, elaborate dinners. On some level I kind of believed this, and it didn't feel real comfortable. I had a whole lot of messages in my head, and I didn't know which ones were right. I told myself that we had both gained weight and so neither one of us was feeling good about our looks. I felt a little embarrassed — it seemed so curious, I'd done a lot of reading about fat oppression and there are fat women in the community who I think are really attractive, and I'd ask myself why I couldn't have the same attitudes toward my *own* body? I tend to think that a woman is either attractive or unattractive and it doesn't seem to be based on her weight. It seems to be based on how she carries herself, what her personality is like. Cedar would tell me that she was embarrassed about how she looked.

In the first year when we slept together, we wouldn't wear any clothes. And then, in the third year of being together, which was the first year in the house and the first year of not being sexual, we started to wear T-shirts to bed. And when I asked Cedar about that, she said she didn't want me to see her body, she didn't feel good about her body. And then we started to fight about it. I would say, "We're never going to be romantic if you never snuggle with me naked like we used to." Then we'd fight about it, and then we didn't want to do it because we were mad at each other!

One day Cedar came home and said she'd been talking to a friend of hers, and that that person slept apart from her lover one night a week, just for them to have a sense of their own independence, and so they could do whatever they wanted to in their own bed, even if it meant staying up half the night and reading. They didn't have to worry about keeping their partner awake, and they could get a better night's sleep apart. So Cedar said, "Why don't we try that," she would like to try that. I didn't really like the idea, because it always seemed to me (as a TV addict, and a movie addict, and a novel addict), that once you had a partner you always slept together. That was *part* of the point to me, to have somebody to sleep with, because sleeping together is so intimate. But she seemed to want to try it, so I did. We went through a couple of months when every Sunday night we slept in our own rooms.

Then something started happening, for example, one night she might have a backache, so on Monday night she would want to sleep apart. A couple of months went by, and then she would say she hadn't slept well and she wanted another night alone. And another night. It was a very gradual phenomenon, but it got to the point where we were sleeping apart almost 50% of the time. I was starting to get more and more annoyed by it, but when we started to talk about it, we'd fight.

At some point, I started to snore. Still to this day I don't know why I started to snore, whether it was weight, or stress, or whatever. Then she would say she couldn't get any sleep because I snored and woke her up all night. We started to sleep apart permanently. But I didn't like that, because it went against everything that I thought of in terms of a partnership. And I felt so helpless because I didn't want to keep her awake so it was *my* fault we didn't sleep together.

We were still enjoying each other's company, making each other laugh, enjoying doing the same activities. I mean, we were and are really super-good friends. When I am upset, she's a really good person to talk to, and when she's upset, it seems like I'm a really good person for her to talk to, so in many ways we are best friends.

I finally put up a fuss, and Cedar agreed to sleeping together one night a week. We decided to sleep together on Saturday nights, so that neither one of us would have to get up early on Sunday. So, over the course of 2 years, we had gone from sleeping together completely, to sleeping apart 1 night a week, to sleeping apart completely, to sleeping together 1 night a week.

And then, somebody else came along. I don't feel good or proud of this, but I ended up having an affair. It lasted for about 3 months, and I told Cedar right away. Of course, she was devastated. It was so confusing to be sexually attracted to another woman and feel guilty about it, even though Cedar and I hadn't been sexual for 3 years. I didn't feel that I deserved to be asexual — that's an awkward way to say it — I didn't ever "choose" to be asexual. If someone had come along and said to me, "We love each other, we have a great time together, how would you like to make a commitment to me and we'll never make love together again" I would have said, "No. Thank you, but no." And yet that was the situation I was in. When I told Cedar about the affair, it was very dramatic and emotional, and we fought a lot. Even though we had not been sexual Cedar felt that we definitely still had a "monogamous" relationship.

Cedar and I presented ourselves to the community as a couple. We presented ourselves to Linda, my new lover, as a couple. This is what Linda said to me. She said she had a crush on me and she felt guilty about it because she didn't want to interfere with an established relationship. I thought she was really attractive and as soon as she said the words, "I have a crush on you," I knew I was going to get involved with her. And I told her that Cedar and I have been together for 5 years, and that we're a couple, and that we live together, but we haven't been sexual for 3 years. Linda let go of some of her guilt when she heard that. It seems like if you're sexual you're a "couple"; if you're not sexual, you're not a "couple." For the length of our affair, the impression that Linda gave me was that she thought that I would leave Cedar for her, because Linda was offering me a sexual relationship. When I said I was going back to Cedar, Linda really questioned it. She wanted to know why I was going back to a nonsexual relationship. I told her that I had hopes that that was going to change — Cedar and I had started therapy and I was optimistic. But it didn't change.

At some level, though, I knew I wasn't ready to give Cedar up. The therapist had said that the deal was that I stay with Linda totally guilt-free for one month. At the end of the month, it was really clear to me that I wanted to be with Cedar, not with Linda. So I moved back into the house and Cedar and I said that we wanted to work it out, so I broke off the affair with Linda. Cedar and I started to really pursue counseling on a weekly basis. The counselor was a good therapist and a lesbian. My biggest complaint was that we weren't sexual, and so the therapist would give us all of this wonderful homework. We were supposed to go home and rub each other's backs, just one night. We would go home and would rub each other's backs, and that was it. No pressure. The whole idea was that she would help us to become sexual again gradually. For the first month or two, we did all the homework assignments.

And then there came a time when one of the homework assignments was to actually be sexual. Well, we didn't do that. We went back to the therapist a week later, and on the way into the door, we kind of colluded. I said, "Let's just tell her that we didn't feel like it, okay?" And Cedar said, "Okay, we'll tell her that." We went to therapy for maybe another month, and we weren't doing the sexual homework. At the end of the month, we looked at each other, and said, "We're wasting our money." So we agreed to stop going to the therapist. The therapist had theories about why we were not sexual, but who knows why. I certainly don't.

That was 3 years ago. In the past 3 years, what we've done is slept in the same bed together once a week on Saturday nights and I snore and

Cedar wears earplugs. What I've noticed, though, is that since we're not used to sleeping with each other, we inevitably both wake up with backaches. We're not having sex.

We've just celebrated our eighth anniversary. We have a monogamous relationship — that's a curious term when there's no sex involved — but we're monogamous unless we negotiate a different relationship. That's kind of where it is. I don't know what will happen next. Now I'm 40 and I think that when I was 20 I could bop from one relationship to the next and look for the "perfect" relationship. But I'm not 20 anymore. Maybe I need to be satisfied with a relationship that's good in every other respect. We're comfortable, we amuse each other, we enjoy each other's company, we're good counselors for each other.

I came out when I was 28 and I've had quite a few relationships with men and, after I came out, with women. Cedar came out to herself when she was 15 and she's never had a relationship with a man. She's had 5 or 6 fairly long-term relationships with other women. She believes in monogamy and I believe in nonmonogamy, even though I'm willing to make this commitment. I had one relationship with a woman that lasted 2 years, but all my other relationships were fairly short term and frequently were nonmonogamous. It was sort of like I went through one adolescence being interested in men, and when I came out I went through another adolescence, being interested in women.

I was out to my mother, who died recently. She adopted Cedar as her second daughter — it was a really nice relationship. I felt she included Cedar in the family as though Cedar had been a "spouse." She's the only one I came out to. I'm not out to my father, even though for the past 8 years whenever I've talked to him on the phone, I've said something about Cedar. I think in an unspoken way I'm probably out to him, but we've never talked about it.

When we broke up after the first year, Cedar went to talk to my mom. And my mom said she didn't understand "why Angie is doing this." That Cedar was the best thing that had ever happened to me. She encouraged Cedar to hang in there. My mother was very supportive and wanted me to be happy.

Sometimes I think we've never broken up permanently because we really do like each other and enjoy living together. Sometimes I think we haven't broken up because I'm 40 and I'm scared that I'll be alone for the rest of my life if I break up with her.

Cedar and I can snuggle, and hug, and kiss, but if I don't get that funny feeling in the pit of my stomach, then I don't call it a sexual encounter. But I know that's different for everybody. Somebody else might get that funny feeling in the pit of her stomach but not have a climax and not consider it a "sexual encounter." Somebody else might consider hugging and kissing sexual. We snuggle around our friends and in private too, and I like that part.

We've had a lot of history under our belts. We're very physically affectionate. There's a lot of snuggling and hand-holding and hugging. But it doesn't go beyond affection. We call each other "my partner" in public. I can't speak for Cedar, but I know that I'm embarrassed for people to know that we haven't been sexual for 6 years. I do not tell people that. I guess I have some stigma attached to it in my mind. I think that if I'm in a partnership with someone and we're not sexual, that I have a sexual dysfunction. I don't want people to know that. Another reason is that it seems to me that lesbian couples who have been together a long time and (I assume) are still sexual, that they're the ones that are envied. I want people to think that we're still sexual. When we're with friends and we're snuggling on the couch, I think that when they see us being affectionate they will think we're also sexual. And that's the way I want it to seem.

PART II: CEDAR

I'M A 35-year-old woman. I've been "out" since I was about 16. By "out," I don't mean to the world, but to myself. I've had maybe 12 women lovers — none of them one-night stands, and I have never had a male lover. For the most part, the relationships followed a predictable pattern. I would feel very passionate, very sexual. Almost obsessively in love. I would chase and charm them, sweep them away with romance, gifts, flowers. Sooner or later I would win them over. I didn't consider these to be just conquests. I seriously believed I was in love. If the relationship lasted six months, a few of them did, it continued to be romantic and sexual. I wanted to live with my lovers right away. I wanted to spend all my free time with them. I wanted to become them, in fact. If the relationship lasted longer than six months, especially if it included living together, I began to feel less sexual, less romantic, and rather impatient with anything remotely resembling a demand for sex. Even though I may have still considered myself in love, I simply did not feel as sexual or as attracted to my partner. This, by the way, had nothing to do with their competency as lovers. For the most part they did not see it that way and *many* arguments would follow as I was accused of not caring anymore, of wanting to end the relationship. In some cases the complaints led to outright demands that I either be sexual or the relationship would end.

My feelings about my lack of sexual desire toward my partner varied. I felt guilty, certainly. I didn't want to stop hugging, kissing, and being affectionate — I simply didn't feel sexual. I alternately thought something was wrong with me, that I wasn't "normal," or that something was wrong with my partner, like she was "over-sexed." Some arguments ended with me promising to change, others ended with both of us angry, stubborn, each saying that the other was at fault.

Some interesting points in all this are that I never stopped being sexual with myself, I always insisted on monogamous relationships, and should my partner suggest, consider, or take another lover, I would be furious and usually jealous. However, more often than not, I would be the one who had an affair and ended the relationship. I did not necessarily *want* the relationship to end but I wanted the passion and the "in love" feelings of an affair while insisting that my partner stay monogamous. I managed to not see the glaring double-standard involved.

I convinced myself that the excitement was all in the chase and that no matter who I ended up with, the passion would not last and the length of the relationship would be determined by how much we cared for each other and liked and loved each other apart from the sex. I didn't find a relationship like that until I met Angie.

Angie and I met 8 years ago. It was not love at first sight. In fact, she practically had to hit me over the head to make me realize she was attracted to me. At the time I was recovering from the breakup of a 3-year relationship and I was not actively looking for another. Angie was determined, however, and once I got over my surprise we became lovers. It was not a smooth beginning. I remember the first year as being rather rocky. We broke up once, but both made changes and got back together. With Angie's help I let go of some bad relationship patterns. I stopped trying to be the other person. I learned how to use constructive criticism instead of yelling and screaming. I regained a lot of lost self-esteem. I realized I had finally met someone whom I could deeply and permanently love. However, one pattern did not change. In time the passion faded. I became pretty much asexual and I still am. I honestly cannot remember how long it's been since we've made love, although I'm sure Angie can. I love her very much, I think of her as my life partner. I want to touch her, hold, kiss her, and be playful with her, but I do not feel sexual. I *want* to be lovers with her but I don't know how to find the passion again.

We have done couple counseling about it more than once. We tried some of the suggestions, but they never seemed to lead us anywhere. At one point Angie had an affair. She told me about it only after it had been going on for a few weeks. I had been out of town a lot, distracted by family problems, and I never realized what was going on. I was shocked, infuriated, jealous, and very hurt. Angie told me that she didn't want to leave me but wanted to be *sexual* with the woman for as long as it lasted. Because of the fact that I felt guilty over driving her into another woman's arms, I tried to accept the situation. It drove me crazy — the thought of her sleeping with, making love to, someone else. I finally issued the "it's her or me" ultimatum and, though furious with me for forcing her to choose, Angie chose to stay with me. We still did not become sexual.

Time passed, we love each other dearly, but we are not technically lovers. Every once in a while, I convince myself that if I only liked my body better, I would feel more sexual. You see, when we stopped being sexual, we both put on a lot of weight. We've wondered if we've substituted a passion for eating for our sexual passion. I'm sure we've both come up with rational excuses for our behavior. Of course, we don't talk about it to each other. I speak of it only to a close friend. We don't tell other couples for fear they wouldn't understand. Perhaps they would understand better than we think. I know that I thought there weren't a lot of other couples like us. My certainty was shaken when, upon attending the National Lesbian Conference in Atlanta, we found women conducting *workshops* on the subject. I was amazed to hear other couples, both older and younger than we, asking the same questions we've asked ourselves and each other. Is it "normal"? Why is it happening? Is it a "bad" thing? Should we call ourselves just best friends, or can we still be "lovers" without being sexual? Does anyone out there understand? Do we understand it ourselves?

I find that, regarding myself and the nature of my relationship with Angie, there are many questions . . . but where are the answers?

Cast of characters

———

Pat

Pat: Teller of this tale Little Cathy: Cathy's niece
Cathy: Pat's ex-lover Barbara: Little Cathy's roommate

CATHY AND I met at work. We were both teachers; she's still teaching. I'm 60 and she's 48. She was a new teacher in our county and I
had been teaching for several years when we met. I can't remember how
we met. We had worked together for a couple of summers and had been
friends for a long time before I even realized that she was gay. She knew
I was gay even before I knew she was gay. I know when that happened.
I asked her if our principal was gay, and Cathy changed color, and I
thought, "Oh, my God, she must be too!" I was right. This was in the
1960s.

I first came out when I was in college, during my last year, about ready
to graduate. I was attracted to a younger woman who was friendly with
me. We spent nights together, and I can remember wanting to kiss her
and finally doing it. We did nothing more than kiss. But it was very
exciting to me and I knew then what my orientation was. I really hadn't
faced it before that time.

Prior to Cathy, I had been in an 18-year relationship with a woman. A
good part of that was without sexual activity. Cathy had a gay relationship when she first started to work in the school system, before I knew
her very well. That was a very short relationship. By the time I knew her
she had a roommate that she had brought out who was a couple of years
younger than she was. They were together for 6 or 7 years. That ended
up being a nonsexual relationship, a Boston marriage, also. She went
into another relationship that was very abusive and didn't last very long,
and we got together at that point.

Cathy is vivacious and fun to be around. She loves her work and is very good at it. She was exciting to me because she was young and full of life. It's hard to say now whether I'm seeing what I want to see or what was really there. I try to be objective, but I don't know how objective I am. Now I have a feeling that she was not very open with me from the very beginning. She was not a very sharing person. She talked about me not being able to communicate and that's very true, because I was never allowed as a child to communicate. I was the youngest child by 9 years, and we had my grandfather and my great-aunt to care for until I entered school. I don't think they said I couldn't talk, it was just that they didn't have time to listen to me. I think they loved me, but everyone was so busy and I was so much younger that they didn't have time for me. There wasn't enough talking space. I still find myself in conversations not being aggressive about getting my points across.

I don't think Cathy was a good communicator either. Often conversations would go on around Cathy and we would think she was involved in them. Then a few minutes later she would say something pertinent as if she hadn't heard what was going on before. It wasn't unusual, but it always surprised me when it happened. So I'm not sure how successfully either of us was able to communicate.

I'm sure that that was a factor in our relationship. If things didn't work out the way they should I didn't push for them. When I finally took a stand, which I did occasionally, that was such a jarring thing that it made her very unhappy.

We lived together for 16 years. She had broken up with her lover and I had just broken up with my lover. She had no place to live and I needed someone to help with expenses. So I asked her to move in. She was happy to do that, because she needed a safe haven from someone who was abusing her. And then after a week or two she said, "Let's share the bed because I do not want to sleep by myself." I said, "Okay." I had some reservations about that but I didn't feel anything wrong with it. I had become very sexually attracted to her when she was in my bed. I acted on that and she seemed happy to do that so that's how it started.

We were sexually active for about 4 or 5 years. Then it was once every month or so and then even less than that as time went on. I can't tell when we stopped having sex, but we were celibate for at least 5 years before we broke up.

We didn't talk about not having sex at all until the last year. Then

Cathy brought it up. She said, "This is not good. We should do something about this." I agreed. But neither one of us did. Somehow I got the feeling that she was handing this problem to me, and I didn't know how to do anything about it. She wasn't placing blame, but it was just my responsibility. In all the time that we were together, she initiated sex less than 10 times. When we did it, I initiated it.

We had a lot of gay friends and I saw us as a gay couple. I think she did too. We gave gifts together and we were always invited as a couple. We entertained together, we vacationed together, we visited family together. Both families accepted us together as a couple. I am out to my family; she is not out to hers.

"Lover" was never a comfortable term for me to use because in my generation that term was what you called an illegitimate love, like an affair. So I did not use that term, but I began to use it during the end of our relationship because that was what other gay people were using. I was always a little uncomfortable with it. I would use "roommate," "buddy," or sometimes, "lover." Or I would use her name.

Cathy has a niece we called Little Cathy. When Cathy and I first became lovers, Little Cathy was with her family in Germany. Her whole family came by and visited us in the United States and I met them. They were fun to be around and they were young. Little Cathy was probably still in junior high at that time. So I had known her for a long time. Later on, Little Cathy lived with a roommate, Barbara, in Baltimore. Cathy's big sister invited us up one Christmas to visit Washington, D.C. Then we saw Little Cathy and met Barbara, her roommate. They were both about 25 then. Cathy and I began to wonder whether Little Cathy and Barbara were gay. They did everything together. Barbara, when she went out without Little Cathy, went out with a group of men, as one of the boys. Not as a date, she would go to bars and play with them. Little Cathy did not date, except maybe very occasionally. Most of her social life was with Barbara.

We kept in touch with them through Cathy's sister. Then they started visiting us, they would stop in Jacksonville on the way to Disney World. Cathy and I have property in north Georgia, a little mountain cabin, and they would visit us there. Cathy's parents live there, so Little Cathy was able to visit her grandparents and Barbara would come along. Once Barbara got sick and asked if she could spend the rest of the time with us, and we said yes. These visits happened over a period of two years.

Then Little Cathy and Barbara invited us up to spend time with them and visit Washington. That's when I think things got really serious between Cathy and Barbara. Barbara was courting Cathy at that time, right in front of me. I saw it and didn't want to see it. It was not a happy time for me. Looking back, I found that Cathy and Barbara had found lots of time to be away from me and away from Little Cathy when we were all together. There was a long period during the Washington holiday when this happened. Once Little Cathy and I were stranded in a shopping center while they were gone for a long time. That was very disconcerting.

Later Cathy told me that she had talked to Barbara and Barbara had told her that she might be gay, but that Barbara had never had any kind of homosexual activity. Barbara said that Little Cathy definitely was not gay. During that time, Barbara was planning to move to Texas for a job there and Little Cathy wanted to go also. They were having some discussions about that because Barbara did not want Little Cathy to go with her. And Little Cathy did not know how to make up her mind. Innocently, I asked Little Cathy, "Is this going to help your job? Are you going to be able to advance because of this?" She said, "Yes." I said, "That's how to make up your mind about whether to go or not."

Barbara and Cathy talked a lot, but did not include me in their conversations. Barbara had one conversation with me about going to Texas. I asked, "What are your long-range plans?" She seemed upset and wide-eyed and said, "Well, I plan to get married and have babies." I said that if she planned to do that, she had better get started on it. Even though I didn't know what was happening, I knew that that didn't ring true! I think she said that to throw me off. She was very uptight about anything leaking back to her job and the possibility of losing her job because of this. She was very, very closeted.

Cathy and I usually went to the mountains to spend Thanksgiving with her parents. Last year, Cathy told me that she did not want me to go. She wanted time alone. She was going to spend the Thanksgiving Day with her parents and then she was going to go off somewhere where she could think. Well, that didn't make sense to me. Before this, she had talked to me again about not being sexual and not seeing our friends. She felt that was wrong and that should change and, again, she implied that it was my responsibility to make those changes. We had stopped being social with our friends. I don't know why that happened. I loved being with our friends. We had a group we would camp with, we had a group we had dinner with often, and that stopped for some reason. Before Thanksgiving we went on a weekend camping trip with some friends and on the way back Cathy started talking about her unhappiness. She couldn't stay on track and I kept trying to direct her back to talking about her unhappiness. Finally I said that we needed to get help with this. I said, "Let me make an appointment with a therapist and let's go together and get some help." She became furious with me. She flipped her head and made an exasperated sigh and refused to even talk about that. That surprised me and left me not knowing where to turn and very frightened. That was about two weeks before Thanksgiving, so when she told me about Thanksgiving, I knew that she was going to meet someone. And that she was breaking up with me.

I hot-footed my way to a therapist. Before she even left I had already had one meeting with the therapist and told her what I thought was happening. The therapist is gay and very helpful. She gave me coping skills which I desperately needed to get through that time.

When Cathy came back from that four-day holiday, she told me that she had a new interest, a new relationship that she wanted to pursue. Of course I was distraught and unhappy. I moved out of the bedroom that night and went to work that next morning before she got up and went downstairs. When she came home that night she was furious with me "for leaving a hole in her life!" I was so shocked at her reaction, I couldn't answer her. There were no words. So I stayed at home until she went to work. She was then unhappy because I was crying in the morning. When we had talked the night before, she said that there was something we were leaving out of the conversation — the person she was with. I said I didn't want to know about the person, it was none of my business, and if it was someone I knew, I wasn't going to like that person and I would be angry with her. Cathy got angry with me because I wasn't sleeping in my bed — I was sleeping on the couch. I cried at night and that interrupted her sleep. It didn't progress very well, as you might say!

That went on until Christmas. I tried to control myself and I wasn't very successful. I am a chomper of teeth and a displayer of feelings. My friends asked to help. I said we're breaking up and didn't talk about why, because I didn't really know. Once Cathy's lover called in the evening while I was there and they talked in front of me. They talked on the phone every evening. And finally I said, "You know, Cathy, it's very painful for me, and it would be so simple since I have a hearing problem for you to do this once I've gone to bed and removed my hearing aid. I wouldn't even hear the phone ring." I was so resentful that it was necessary to explain this. And so she did that.

Then she let it slip that her lover was Barbara. It seemed like she just had to tell me that. After she said that name, she said, "Oh" and put her hand in front of her mouth. It was kind of phony. Barbara called and said, "How are you doing, Pat?" And I thought, "You bitch. How do you think I'm doing?" That was very hurtful.

I put Cathy on the plane to meet Barbara in Texas, and she gave me a big hug. When she came back, she put her hands on my shoulders so I couldn't get too near. I spent time in my room and made sure I didn't see her anymore. I wrote her notes, she wrote me notes. I said that I'm not doing this to be nasty or mean. I need distance, and you've made your distance! I think she wanted to continue living here but spend all her play time in Texas with her new lover. That was not acceptable.

My therapist helped me work out a plan of action for Cathy moving out. I wrote Cathy a note, telling her to move out by February 1. That gave her 2 weeks. Cathy told me that she could not move out by then, but she moved out 2 weeks later. She talked to our mutual friends and talked to me some about being friends. But any contact since she's moved out has been my doing; she has not initiated any contact. She did sent me a birthday card this summer.

She's in Jacksonville, teaching still. She has a few more years before retirement. I'm retired, so I don't run into her. As far as I know, she is still involved with Barbara. My friends tell me that Cathy is enjoying the relationship but that it's on hold. That's more than I need to know, so I don't question further.

Little Cathy and I were in contact for a long time. I was glad to be supportive of her. Cathy talked with her and told her that she was involved with Barbara. Little Cathy was upset and felt rejected by Barbara. Little Cathy moved to Texas with Barbara and she did not want to move out. She is still living with Barbara, even though her aunt Cathy still spends long weekends with them in Texas. Little Cathy asked me if I had ever thought of hurting myself, as she put it. I got very frightened for her, and talked with my therapist about that. Through my therapist and another friend I gave Little Cathy hotline numbers for Dallas and Fort Worth and several referrals. I think Little Cathy is into denial and cannot accept that she might need help, which is sad because her mother has a degree in social work and might be of help. Little Cathy was very dependent on Barbara for social life, financial affairs. Barbara was her caretaker in lots of respects. I think Barbara fostered that. Little Cathy is in her late 20s but she isn't having sex with men either, she says.

I want Cathy to be happy. I don't want her walking out of one relationship into the same kind of relationship, with a woman who is over 20 years younger than she is. Cathy can't leave her job, with five more years of teaching, and lose her retirement. Barbara is doing wonderful things in her job, so she can't move. There are many people in Jacksonville who would be happy to have a relationship with Cathy. Why did she pick Barbara, who is inaccessible to her?

It hadn't occurred to me to talk to my friends about our relationship. We have a male friend who is homosexual who likes to talk about his sexual escapades. I think he talks a lot but doesn't really do anything. Cathy used to think that because I wasn't telling him that we weren't having sex, I was in essence lying to him. That bothered her a lot. I think now that Cathy was always a little bit embarrassed by my presence in her life. I don't know why.

I have not talked with my therapist about our relationship being asexual. It had not even occurred to me to bring that up with her. We've been talking mostly about how I can get through my mourning period! I am anxious to move on past mourning now. It's time.

I'm seeing someone now with whom I'm sexual. I'm not living with her, and we've decided that we want to go very slowly with that. We have the same values and we have fun together. We want to be sure that we'll have a good relationship before we make any long-term commitments. She too had stopped having a sexual relationship with her ex-lover. We've talked about why that happened and that we don't want that to happen with us. I've been reading as much as I can get my hands on about that topic. I've been reading JoAnn Loulan and Betty Berzon and some things about heterosexual relationships and how to keep them going. I hope I can learn the skills needed to keep this new relationship working for our mutual benefit.

"I think it has to do with the fact that I love her"

Janet and Marty

MARTY: This is our third summer here in Vermont. We're in our mid to late 40s. We started our relationship in 1980. Well, we met in 1979 and we moved to Boston in 1980. We met in Provincetown, through a friend. Janet was involved with someone else at the time. It was about a year later that we finally got together. Initially it was a sexual relationship. For 10 months maybe.

I was drinking and doing drugs. That was the way most relationships had been. I feel very fortunate in meeting Janet, because I don't have to be sexual. It's hard; I don't drink now, so I can't have sex. In fact, I'm going to do some counseling for sexual abuse starting next month. So I've been blessed with Janet, because I just can't have sex and so we haven't been sexual for a while, for about 11 years. But Janet is not as fortunate as I am, because she would prefer to be sexual.

JANET: The community perceives us as lovers, but they know we're not sexual. We talk about that—I tell everybody! There are two types of reactions. There are people who say it's my problem and not Marty's. For a long time Marty said that too. She felt very content with the way things were. And there are other friends who say, "Gee, that's awful, how do you do that? What are you going to do about that?" We considered being nonmonogamous, but we haven't done that.

MARTY: This is how we met. I had just gotten back from working in Alaska, and I was with a friend in Provincetown. I was living there, working at a restaurant. Janet came in, it was her birthday, and I bought a bottle of champagne for her and her friends. That's the first time I saw her. And I was in love immediately. Everything about her — her hair, her voice, so quiet — I just had to know more about her. She was the person I had been looking for. I did get to know her after the summer season was over. I had injured my hand which precluded my working on my previous job in Alaska on a crab boat. I was kind of in a bind, and a friend let me stay with her. This friend was in love with me and I was not with her and I was stuck there. Janet came to town a couple of times. I was drinking and drugged out most of the time. But we managed somehow to meet. It was almost summer again when we began sleeping together.

JANET: Somewhere between Easter and Memorial Day Weekend we began sleeping together.

MARTY: I've always been a lesbian, since day one. Of course I tried not to be, I slept with guys for a while. That didn't work. But I've always been gay. I joined the service and I was thrown out for being a lesbian. I was sexually active with other women when I was a teenager, even before that, at 11. I had one "particular friend," you see. We spent a lot of time together. I started working when I was 13, so I started getting involved with older folks, doing drugs and drinking, carrying on. In Alaska, I was on a crab boat, way out on the Aleutian chain. I was closer to Russia than anywhere else.

JANET: I was horribly straight. I was horrible at it, and I didn't know I had any options. I thought I had to do this, but I never could do it right. When I was 19, I had a baby girl. Because I wasn't married, I had to surrender her for adoption. I didn't have any work skills, couldn't support her, and had no support at all from my family to keep her. This was a terrible price to pay for a brief and unloving sexual relationship. And I was 32 before I got involved with a woman, Harriet. That was the woman I was with when I met Marty. And that relationship was sexual but it was nonmonogamous on her part which was very painful for me. Harriet often abandoned me in a bar to leave with someone else. It was a constant series of women, there was no end to it. She was out of control in a lot of ways, including sexually. I had left that relationship emotionally probably a year before I met Marty, but couldn't leave it financially. I was trying to get my money together to separate from Harriet and was able to do that the summer Marty moved to Boston. I was finally able to cut the ties to Harriet. When I met Marty, I had been a lesbian for about four or five years.

What attracted me to Harriet was watching her have such a good time! Harriet thought she was straight, too. A mutual friend said I should hang out with her, because she knew how to have fun. I was at that time dating a married man, and I was always at home waiting for the phone to ring, feeling depressed. I had been seeing him for 6 or 7 years. And this friend said that I was just wasting my time. Harriet used to drive to the Cape almost every weekend. One weekend, I went with her. And that first weekend, we fell in love. At that point I was open to anything because I was just so miserable. Even my father said it was great I was gay, because I was happy. He knew how unhappy I had been as a straight woman. Being straight was like wearing the wrong pair of shoes. It didn't fit and it was very painful.

When I met Marty, I liked her eyes and her cheekbones. And I thought it was interesting that she had come from Alaska and worked on a crab boat. She was pretty.

MARTY: I had a safety pin in my cheek.

JANET: And the way she looked at me, I knew that she liked me a lot. That was obvious.

I was living in Boston and coming to the Cape on weekends. I had a lot of friends there and I loved Provincetown. To dance and be around gay people.

We began living in Boston; after 6 months or so, we stopped drinking. We used to drink a lot. And then Marty announced that we would not have sex. She just couldn't do it anymore.

MARTY: I couldn't do any of it, none of it, which surprised me since I had been so sexually active. With alcohol, I could do things that ordinarily I wouldn't do. It's not that I don't get aroused, but following through with it is scary and distasteful. Probably because of the problems I had with my father, and it's all related to that sexual abuse. It made me physically ill.

JANET: My reaction was "bullshit." I was really upset. I said, "Do you really think I'm going to go for the rest of my life without sex?" I thought it was me, that there was something wrong with me. That was a stage I had to get through. That I was ugly, or smelled bad, or something.

And then I began to notice that I had a lot of energy for other stuff. I was more creative. I had more time to spend on my writing. I began to think about what sex had meant to me and why I was sexual, which didn't come out of a good place most of the time, and about the sexual experiences I had had. What percentage of them was good and what percentage of them was bad, and how many were downright dangerous or unpleasant.

I understood at last that it was not me, that it was something about Marty. I finally came to that conclusion. She just kept telling me it had nothing to do with me.

MARTY: I think it has to with the fact that I love her. If I don't love somebody, I can do just about anything. I don't know how that works psychologically, but when I first meet somebody, I don't really love them. Not like I do after 2, or especially after 11 years. So I can be sexual when I've just met someone, and being sexual is part of meeting someone. It's all chemistry. It has nothing to do with a relationship or caring. All you know is you're turned on and they're turned on and it draws you together so that you get to know each other as more than sexual objects.

JANET: It took me a few years to realize this. We had other problems, we were coming off alcohol, we got sober on our own. We had other things to keep us busy, besides the sexual stuff. I was working at a feminist magazine at that time and that gave me a spiritual support system that was helpful. We started planning to build our house in Vermont. That directed our energy.

My friends don't pressure me to have sex, but they say, "You have a big problem. What are you going to do about it?" Because every once in a while I'll say, "Oh my god, what am I going to do?" But no one pressures me to have an affair. That's a big thing, you don't do that without some forethought and consideration. So my friends would never advise me to have an affair, no matter what. And people like both of us. They also understand the incest issue because there's a lot of it in our community. Most of them know that for some survivors of sexual abuse, sex can trigger memories of the abuse. I'm a psychiatric nurse and I work with sexual abuse survivors. Seventy-five percent of my patients are sexual abuse survivors.

Some friends have said it's my problem and have been supportive of Marty. I suspect that the two women who support Marty are also not having sexual relationships, and for similar reasons. They're both heterosexual. There seem to be two groups of women: the women who do have sex and the women who don't have sex. The women who don't have sex feel that they don't have to and they shouldn't have to. Before this relationship, I thought that lovers stopped having sex because they were bored with each other. It never occurred to me that one partner might not want to be sexual while the other still did.

People see us as a couple, because we very much are. We own a house together. We have joint checking and savings accounts. We plan to stay together for the rest of our lives, which is also rare. People don't make that kind of commitment a lot of the time. That's a strong commitment no matter what happens.

MARTY: I use the term "friend," or "partner," or "roommate," or "housemate," when referring to Janet. I like "friend" because that seems to fit most situations. When speaking to other lesbians, I use the term "lover."

JANET: I'm out everywhere in my life, and I like to tell people that Marty is my "lover," not my "roommate"!

MARTY: I wish that sex could be taken out of the relationship context completely. It really can have nothing to do with a relationship. It would be a lot simpler if it were that way. We use heterosexual standards. I don't know what married women do. Does their sex drive with their mate calm down after a period of time? Do they have sex once a week or every five minutes, or never? Men's testosterone makes them more horny. It's all about creating babies in the first place.

There are times when I feel more sexual than others. Somebody looks really good. But as a general rule I don't think it's as prominent in our lives as the rest of society would have us believe. We don't walk around thinking about sex all the time.

Marty and I celebrate the anniversary of when we began to live together, not when we began to have sex together. We made a commitment that week. We've remade that commitment a couple of times. I don't remember when we first had sex together, as a matter of fact. We made a commitment sitting down together on the living room rug. We did a ritual.

JANET: We have regrouped since, about not having a sexual relationship and still continuing our relationship. And the answer is yes, we do want to continue.

I think about having sex outside the relationship. But it's a serious thing to do. I don't know whether I want to do that or not. Marty can say it's something I should think about doing. At one point she even said to me, "Do that!" That was a couple of years ago. She said, "*Please* do that. Go away, have an affair, leave me alone." But I don't know what the reality of that would be for me emotionally, to be involved with two women. I'm not a person who acts without giving it serious thought.

MARTY: It kind of makes you examine what sex is all about in the first place. Do you just want to have sex and feel good for 15 minutes and then go your separate ways? Or do you do it once a week or once a month? You figure all that out. How would it be between us if one of us or both of us were sleeping with somebody else?

JANET: At this point, it just hasn't felt right. One fantasy is that I would meet someone I had never seen before and would never see again, and have sex, and that would be the end of it. But I don't know if that would ever happen or where that happens. And I would worry about AIDS.

MARTY: Occasionally I have an urge, but I certainly don't act on it. I have never had good sex, out of love. To me, loving someone, you don't *do* that to them. Think about it, the term "fuck you," what does that say about sex and love?

There's no way we can have sex, thinking about it as I do. Maybe if we both thought about sex the way I do, we could.

JANET: Pretend we don't know each other, meet somewhere, at truck stops?

INTERVIEWER: Are you out to your family?

MARTY: Yes. My stepfather used to call me names, which made it difficult for my mother. But she said as long as I was happy, it was okay.

JANET: My family knows I'm gay. My parents are in their 70s, and don't talk about it. But they know that I've lived with either Marty or Harriet for the last 15 years. My father once said to my sister, "I don't know what her relationship is, but she sure is happy." My sister knows I'm a lesbian and that our relationship is asexual. My sister is supportive of Marty. My sister's first husband cheated on her in a very cruel way, and so she can't abide me cheating on Marty. That would get her very upset. And she says, "And for what? For sex? What the hell is that for? Where are your priorities?" She thinks Marty has been good to me and for me. Which is true, very true. At the beginning of our relationship I was physically sick. And Marty helped me to get better physically and sort of grounded me emotionally. I was in therapy and she stuck with me through that. I eventually felt stable enough to search for the daughter I'd surrendered for adoption in 1963. Soon after I found her, I told her I was a lesbian because if I was going to lose her again, I wanted to know right away and not somewhere down the road. But she accepted me and Marty too, and she also knows that we are celibate.

MARTY: Our relationship is based on love and caring, and I promised to help Janet to be all that she can be. To help her in every way that I can, to love her. Even to clean the bathroom.

JANET: Marty taught me how to love someone. Before I met her, I thought that relationships were all about sex. A relationship meant you had sex together. Other than that, you both took care of yourselves first. You had to be careful not to give away too much and be sure that you weren't being taken advantage of or used. And I didn't expect much in return. That's what I'd learned about relationships so far. When I talked about my sister's relationship with her husband, which was very abusive, I'd say, "But he loves her!" And Marty would say, "Oh, really? That's love?" She would say, "Life is very hard, and the purpose of love is to have someone who can help you to get through it, because it's a lot easier if there's two of you instead of one." That's very true. If anything goes wrong, we both know that the other person is going to be there. With Marty, I know that I won't even have to call her. She just shows up. She'll always find me if I'm lost. She's a rock.

MARTY: And so is she.

JANET: So, when I look around me and see all that we have, what we've built over the years, sex doesn't seem all that important. And it's not just the material things, because I don't think we would have the material things if the love wasn't there. It's also the security, the growth, we have fun together. We've both grown, and we keep changing.

MARTY: I think sex was necessary to get the thing going. Don't you?

JANET: Well, yes, I think so, but now that I've been through this relationship I don't know anymore. But at the time it seemed like a good idea! I think it was necessary. To let each other know how we felt, to identify each other as lovers. Because if you're lovers, you kind of have to make love, at least, at first.

I think the sex that we had was some of the best sex that I've ever had. And I thought, I want to spend a lot of time with this woman, because she can teach me a lot about sex. Little did I know. . . . And I'm still sexually attracted to her, I might add.

MARTY: If I were going to have sex with anyone, it would be Janet.

JANET: I really don't have a lot of casual lesbian friends. I have a couple of good ones. And I talk with them, they're my support system.

MARTY: I should add that I am not going into therapy to become a sexual person. I'm going because of other matters in my life. And that's important for both of us to keep in mind, because otherwise that can be a real trap.

JANET: When Marty says, "Why don't you do it yourself, masturbate and get it over with?" I respond that it's not the same thing as a sexual relationship with somebody else. Not very long ago, I was masturbating and I suddenly felt Marty's hands on my hips though I was alone in my room. It felt very real. It wasn't at all alarming, it was wonderful. I thought, wow, that's what it feels like to have somebody else with you while you're making love, another presence, the warmth of another human being in the room. It was an intense experience. Maybe it was a flashback. It reminded me of the loss that I feel not being sexual with somebody else. I was startled and then felt very sad.

One time, Marty said, "All right, I'll make love to you." This was about 5 or 6 years after we were together. She said, "Lie down." She tried to make love to me, but I said, "we can't do this. This is not the way to do it."

MARTY: I would like to make her completely happy. I would like to be the total lover. It's not easy to know that I'm not making that possible.

JANET: And I often say, "If we were sleeping together, we might be celibate by now anyway. To judge by other relationships."

But I also think lesbians have sex less than other people because they reject the heterosexual way of life. Lesbians don't have to prove anything, which men do. And straight women have to prove that they're sexually attractive, and straight men have to prove that they're macho. And lesbians don't have testosterone floating around in our bloodstreams! I think it's too bad we have to have heterosexual relationships as an example.

We have bliss

———

Ruth and Iris

IRIS: We have "bliss." We just had bliss this morning, so we just came from that place, and we're still a lot in that place. I picked Ruth up at a car place and we went to her house. We took off our clothes and got into bed. When we touch each other, it's like going to the goddess. It's not like anything — I don't know how to talk about it. I feel myself open on every level. I feel my skin become permeable, feel my atoms move aside so that her atoms can come and fit in between them. It's ecstasy and it's a spiritual place too.

RUTH: It's spirituality on a level that neither of us has ever experienced before.

IRIS: I've never been in love with anybody so deeply. I never knew it could exist. When we go there, nothing else is there but us and something like heaven and the goddess with spirits in attendance.

RUTH: It's as if we go to a place that's like heaven.

IRIS: And part of it is memories. Memories of times that I've been there before, with Ruth or with other women. Memories of Ruth as my mother, as my sister, as my daughter, as my lover, everything. It's as if I remember everything. I know her. I know her in a way that I've never known anyone. Part of why I know her, part of why we can do this, is because this is not sex. I've got sex in some kind of category in my mind, in my body. I've learned something about sex. That it is a certain thing. And this is not sex.

RUTH: We do feel sexual feelings come up when we do this. There is a point at which I consciously move that feeling up from my vagina up into my heart. It just flows into her heart and it's a connection like nothing I've ever experienced. I have not been a particularly spiritual person and I find myself spouting all kinds of what I would have previously called spiritual claptrap! It is coming to the goddess.

IRIS: I have always responded to sexual feelings by having sex. Ruth and I are both very sexual creatures. This is the first time I've made the choice to do something different with these feelings. Bliss is a sort of emanation. I find myself using medieval and Renaissance Christian concepts to describe some of what happens. It's a spiritual experience. It's also an emotional experience. It's an entire experience.

RUTH: There is a physical experience too. Our skin changes when we are with each other. You can feel a difference in our skin, everything changes. It is an experience on all levels and all planes.

IRIS: I experience all those sensations, all those openings and surroundings and closings, enfoldings, all those women words, all that water. I also experience a happiness that I've never felt. A true bliss. A happiness of incredible knowledge. I know something. I know something about Ruth, and something about myself, and something about everything. I know everything. It's this one-ness.

RUTH: There's a poem that I sent Iris. It talks about that place in us where the universe resides.

RUTH and IRIS: "I honor that place in you where the universe resides."

RUTH: It talks about your peace, your uniqueness, your love. If you are in that place in me, there is only one of us.

IRIS: That is what our bliss is like. We have an experience being one, becoming each other. While still maintaining autonomy. That is very important to me. As a lesbian, I've lost my autonomy sometimes, I've lost myself. I've never lost myself with Ruth. I don't fear losing myself. Because if I lose myself, I lose bliss. I have to be in myself to have this. The deeper I'm in myself, the deeper I'm in Ruth. That's how it works. I'm learning things that I thought were probably out there. I never thought that I would learn these things at my age with this bisexual woman who is married to a man!

RUTH: She hates it too!

IRIS: It doesn't make any sense. It wasn't part of the plan! There is no map, we're doing without a map. This feels really dangerous. It's emotionally terrifying to be this open to someone who is committed to someone else. And to be this open to someone who I'm not having sex with flies in the face of everything I've been taught about how to protect myself. And how to be smart in relationships.

RUTH: It's not easy. We both get really afraid. Afraid of all kinds of things. I do get afraid sometimes of losing myself, but that's a common fear for me in relationships. I get afraid because we have trouble figuring out how to integrate this relationship into the rest of our lives. When we go away together, we're great, we're perfect. When we're here, the transitions are hard, the other parts of our lives intrude, coming between us. So there's a fear of not being able to do this within the context of our lives. And in that there's a fear of losing Iris. There's a fear that since we're not being sexual, if she is sexual with someone else, she will be giving her something that I can't give her and so she's going to leave me.

IRIS: Since I'm in a nonmonogamous relationship with my partner Joann, that means I can also be sexual with other women besides Ruth.

Ruth and I try to talk about our relationship to other people. We also are careful, because this is a tiny community and everybody talks. We worry. People are incredibly respectful, I've noticed, but they also love to gossip. There's a lot of speculation, a lot of assumptions, and people feel threatened.

It's important to me that people get used to this relationship. That's why it's important to not be secret. It's important as a political statement, which is an important part of my life. It's not just a social statement, or a personal one, but a political one too. To raise people's consciousness that there are more than two kinds of relationships in the world; there's more than friends and lovers.

This relationship, as far as the impact of passion on my soul, is the most important relationship I've ever had in my life. That's how I feel about it. People need to take it seriously. We've had trouble with people taking it seriously — lesbians, straight people, therapists. We both happen to see the same therapist.

RUTH: There was a time in the summer when we were both having a lot of difficulty. I was in therapy but I didn't like the therapist I had, so I switched. Iris was having a hard time, and she ended up seeing the therapist (a heterosexual woman) before I did. Then Iris had to talk her into letting me see her. Since then, we see her together.

IRIS: Separately and together.

RUTH: But together only when things are particularly hard.

IRIS: Bless her heart, she's trying. She's doing better than anyone else, but even she is having a hard time. This relationship is real slippery. You can't put it into a category; it's challenging for our friends, our therapist, our lovers.

RUTH: But the therapist gets how important this relationship is to us.

IRIS: You need to ask about sex, sex is important. But then, fine, then you talk about what's really going on. This level of passion, you've got to change your vocabulary. We have categorized relationships in this culture based on sex. That to me is a patriarchal model. Based not only on sex, but on orgasmic sex. Part of the women's movement which I would like to take a look at is how important orgasms have become to women's sexuality. I'm sick of that, but oh, I'm a terrible feminist if I say that! It's real politically incorrect for me to say that there are things I would much rather do than have an orgasm.

RUTH: One of the things that we have discovered, and we discovered this because we don't have orgasms together, is that there are two places: sex and no sex. Orgasm and no orgasm. And they draw a straight line from one to the other. That's how they see it, there's no other place. That's the road and they put walls up so they can't go anywhere else. Well, Iris and I blocked off the part about sex and orgasms. We can't go there. So we have discovered all these side roads all over the place. Iris got a lot of these ideas from the lesbian writer Sonia Johnson. What we have discovered are those side roads and where they take us, and that's where we go. The concept that there are other places to go besides orgasms is just revolutionary.

IRIS: It's so exciting that sometimes I don't want to go the orgasm route anymore. Sometimes I do want to go there, and sometimes I want to go there with Ruth. But for the most part I don't want to go there with Ruth.

We struggle to find a language to describe our experience, and also to expand the consciousness of others.

RUTH: And to give our relationship some validity. But inventing new vocabulary to describe these concepts wouldn't mean that, say, "Jane and Sally's" experience would be the same as ours. It would be used to describe that they are having this experience that is other than orgasms.

IRIS: But for Jane and Sally, that might be great. I can remember when I was 18 and I came out as a lesbian and I got involved with other women, I didn't know what the word lesbian was. I'd never heard the word. I grew up in the South, in the mountains, I had no vocabulary. No context. I didn't know what "dyke" meant. And when someone called me a lesbian and when someone said there are others like you, my heart almost burst from joy, from knowing I was not the only one. It was beautiful. Also a terrible loss, because this thing that I thought no one else knew, other people knew.

Ruth and I met because we were introduced by friends. We quickly became aware that we were very attracted to each other. We work together in the same field. We also found out when we met that we were both in deeply committed, long-term relationships. Me with a woman and Ruth with a man. Ruth had promised to be married to Michael. She already had a date and everything. We've both been with our partners for about seven years.

RUTH: Our partners are very much alike, in a lot of ways. They like to do the same kinds of things. They are both very different from us in the same ways. Michael is very different from me in the same way Joann is very different from Iris.

IRIS: It's important to say that we're very much in love with our partners. In the beginning of our relationship, our not being sexual was a lot about keeping our commitments to our partners. But now our not being sexual is about being on a journey together that's incredibly important.

RUTH: It is a journey, it's a spiritual journey. And what's important to say is that we see ourselves as committed to each other for some kind of a life-long relationship. We live seven miles apart.

IRIS: At least once a week, we have time for each other that is focused time. We even spend the night together.

RUTH: There are other times when we do things with other people, we work together, our lives intertwine in a lot of different ways.

IRIS: We're very open about our relationship too. It's not behind closed doors. How we introduce ourselves to other people depends on who they are.

RUTH: We don't even have words to describe it to each other. We use the term "bliss-mate."

IRIS: It's fun to come up with new words.

RUTH: My mother does not know about this relationship. I just spoke with my brother and sister-in-law about it. My mother doesn't know I'm bisexual. She's not a very supportive person.

IRIS: Michael's family doesn't know. Joann's family doesn't know. My family knows. They are supportive, they always have been of me. I come from a very unusual family. They're really progressive people in this pocket of progressiveness in the totally intolerant South. Mountain people are different — more liberal.

I have a commitment to Ruth to be her partner. I also have a commitment to her to give our relationship credence in its full way in our life. It's been very hard to do that without hurting Joann, without hurting Michael. It's been so hard and we don't say a lot about our other love relationships to each other. Every time one of us talks about them, we get more information and that can be painful. It's not as if we pretend they don't exist, it's just that we're both so delicate. So we try to be sensitive. Discreet. Birthdays, Christmas, New Year's . . . I spent New Year's with Ruth because Michael was out of town. I'm sure I wouldn't have spent New Year's with Ruth if Michael had been in town. It's been harder for Ruth than for me, and I think that has to do with me being a lesbian.

RUTH: It also has to do with the kind of relationship you have with Joann. My experience of seeing a lot of lesbian relationships from the outside is that even a lot of lesbian relationships are very monogamous, very coupled. It's not only heterosexuals who choose this. You and Joann are not, you lead very separate lives anyway, before I ever came on the scene.

IRIS: That's true, but it's also easier for us. It's easier for our lesbian culture to accept and support something that looks quite different from a traditional heterosexual relationship. Ruth and I have taken one giant step away from the norm. That's why people are always saying to us, "Just be lovers!"

RUTH: Either stay with your partners or be lovers. There's too much tension here!

IRIS: People talk about how hard they feel it is for us, but it's hard for them too. Yes, it's difficult, but here it is. A lot of people assume that we're friends. Just friends.

RUTH: Imagine saying, "just lovers," like some people say, "just friends." What if people said: "We're not friends, we're just lovers."

A Boston engagement

Sarah

I'M INVOLVED with a woman, Hannah. I had a regular lesbian relationship for about a year with Joann. It was a pretty good relationship,
but it did end. What got me to end it was I realized I was in love with
Hannah. I met her during the Gulf War. There was all this organizing in
California by Jews about the war. She actually had known Joann, my
lover, a little bit. Hannah was also in another group, which is women
protesting the occupation.

Hannah has been around, she's older than me, in her early 30s. I'm in
my mid-20s. I looked up to her and saw her as this ideal. I was finally
trying to get more in touch with my Jewishness; partly because of the
war, it was freaking me out. So Hannah came into my life when I was
trying to get to know people like her.

I couldn't tell whether she considered herself straight or bisexual. It
was hard to tell. It became pretty clear that she considered herself bisexual. But she had been in a long relationship with a man, Sam, and was just
ending it when I met her.

I started to come up with reasons why I had to hang out with her all
the time. It just developed in this way, and it wasn't sexual, partly because
at the time it seemed I couldn't be sexual with anyone except Joann, she
was my relationship. Especially not with someone like Hannah, where it
was obvious she would be an option and not just a little fling. I was in
love with her.

When I first met Hannah, I was fascinated. I started coming over to
her house; she started having meetings at her house. It was pretty soon
after I met her that I started feeling in love — kind of obsessed with her. It
was weird, because I felt she was returning it. She was talking a lot about

me to her friends, I found out later. She would refer to me, saying, "Oh, Sarah and I had a conversation." Her boyfriend was very hung up on her (he still is) and was getting very jealous. And Hannah would say to him, "Look, she's just a friend, there's nothing going on." Hannah had another close friend who was staying with her, and Sam was never jealous of her. Hannah would say I was just a friend, but it was the way she was talking about me that made other people think about it. Hannah had an affair with a guy who was in our group. He was a friend of mine and I was really upset. I wasn't acknowledging my feelings. So I thought this jealousy meant I was in love with her and should pursue her.

I ended up breaking up with Joann and just pursuing Hannah. It felt like I was the lesbian and she was the straight woman. It was all very standard, somehow. I called her a lot and was always coming up with reasons why we had to hang out. It was stupid, because she wanted to hang out with me anyway. But somehow I felt that I had to provide explanations. Finally, I started to get weird. I would be over here and it would get later and later. Then I would say, "Okay, I have to leave," and just get up and go home. I say "here" because I'm now in her apartment while she's in Israel. I've basically moved in with her.

I finally told her I was attracted to her. She got really mad at me. She didn't believe me. She said I'd been treating her like shit. We were both thinking along the same lines but acting really strange. Not showing up. She would not show up for dates and then be very apologetic later. And then one night we went out and got kind of drunk together in this very methodical way and then she went back to my house and we sort of started making love and it was really *bad*. She was talking in the middle, she was saying, "This is really interesting." She's an incredible intellectualizer. She's about to get her Ph.D. and she's very smart.

It turns out she had a relationship with a woman, Christine, that was suspiciously like our relationship. The difference was that Christine was completely in love with Hannah and very attracted to her. Christine would have sex with Hannah and Hannah would just sit there. They lived together for two years. They weren't really lovers and they weren't not lovers, and they were both involved with men. That ended about a year and a half ago and then Hannah got involved with Sam. So Hannah was single, she sort of was with Christine and sort of not with Christine, and then she got together with Sam.

Hannah has also been with women, she's had women lovers in the past. Never for very long. She had a relationship with a woman where they had a lot of sex but that was about all they had. They weren't really close friends. There seem to be two characters that she has, both with women and with men: one is lots of sex and not friends and the other is close friends but no sex.

The latter characterizes our relationship. Now we're both sure what it is. Our relationship has leveled off and it makes sense now. I feel like we're having a primary relationship, but we're not having sex. And we are seeing other people, at least I am. She's gone a lot, in Israel. When she is around, we're totally domestic, we just live together and are not interested in seeing anyone else.

And Hannah is telling everyone, and I guess I am too, that I'm her girlfriend. She's angry now, because in Israel people aren't taking that seriously. And she's not even telling them that we're not having sex. Especially her lesbian friends consider her straight, partly because she is still attracted to men.

We're both kind of neurotic about sex, but in different ways. This arrangement seems to be working for both of us. I guess we're having a Boston marriage, or at least a Boston engagement, because we've only been together for 7 or 8 months.

Since she's been gone, I've had a few flings with men. I feel guilty when I have sex with a woman; when I have sex with a man, it doesn't count. I don't think Hannah has ever acted jealous, and I have to discern what's going to bother her and what's not. I think it bothers her less with a man. At least that's the way it was with Christine.

Since I've been with Hannah, my whole identity as a lesbian has been kind of shaken. The person I'm involved with and having a relationship with, I'm not having sex with. The people I've been having sex with have been men. And so now I'm associating sex with men. That wasn't true for a really long time, I had an intense relationship with a woman, with Joann. But the sex just blows me away, it's impossible after a while. It wasn't working. Part of the problem was that it was so sexual that it wasn't working as a friendship. My current life just feels so comfortable, but I feel my identity is in question. It's comfortable for me to have this not-very-sexual, loving thing. And to have sex with men.

I tell different things to different friends. A very select few of my friends completely accept this as my relationship and the fact that I'm not having sex is sort of irrelevant. My sister is in that category. She just sees me as being in a relationship with Hannah, and my not having sex is not even relevant, it's my relationship. It doesn't affect my sister's view of my identity. She knows me pretty well.

And then a lot of people we know in the lesbian community think that we're lovers. It's been strange, because a lot of people were really disappointed that I broke up with Joann and so, out of loyalty to Joann, I was not going to acknowledge that I was having sex with Hannah. It was easy to not acknowledge it because Hannah and I weren't having sex! I'd say, "She's my friend. What do you mean?" Those people who always knew me in relation to Joann are beginning to see that maybe Hannah is my lover now. They're not sure if we're sleeping together, and I'm not saying. They're assuming that we are, basically. A lot of people that we know assume that we're sleeping together. It's kind of a recent phenomenon, because we decided to test out being lovers by telling everyone that we were and seeing how it felt. Because we feel very ambivalent, we're both in this mode of not wanting to be in a couple. We feel like we're allies. When you're in a relationship, on some level you're allies but on another level you're adversaries. And so we feel like we're allies and we can tell each other everything. That's why I feel that jealousy hasn't been a big issue yet. We can talk to each other about stuff that we're going through with other people. But it's getting more difficult. We've had this 3-month period in which we tried to value our relationship and say it's different from other people's view of a relationship but it's ours. That we are together and everybody will just have to accept us this way. Once we started saying that, it started looking more like a relationship. Then it was harder for me to tell Hannah that I was seeing other people.

She's pretty good about jealousy, and so am I. However, now that she's in Israel, she mentioned that she's working for a man and I asked, "Are you sleeping with him?" and I realized I was asking it in a jealous way. So I think I am slightly jealous. It's getting more difficult. If Hannah were to get involved with a woman, I would be totally flipped out. She keeps saying she's going to do this.

Hannah feels she can't have sex with me, it's just beyond that point. She admits that she used to play the role of the "straight woman" being pursued by a woman and so even when she was having sex with women she was just there and didn't acknowledge her own desires. And now she's beginning to acknowledge her own desires, as a woman who loves women. She has that very intense coming-out feeling, that all women are beautiful. So I really think she's going to sleep with a woman, she could be doing so in Israel, she hasn't mentioned it. Which would be good if she would just have the relationship over there, because she goes there pretty often. That would be okay with me. But over here, forget it, I couldn't just share her with someone else. Not as tenuous and difficult as things are. And I would just be relegated to friendship status. That's been the big fear on both of our sides. Rather than being jealous of affairs, which is what people do in relationships, we wonder when is one of us going to get involved with someone, and fall in love, and do it the normal way, and which of us will it be? And with Hannah, I'm sure it would be with a woman, she's not interested in men right now, and it's obvious that she's pursuing this. I can't imagine myself getting involved with someone now. Even less than when I was with Joann. But I've gotten involved with people at really inappropriate times, so it could happen.

The dynamics in our social scene are really bizarre! We'll go out together and we'll seem like such a couple. And then other times both of us or one of us (especially her) is flirting, and I'm the "friend." That could happen if we were sexual too. On some level, the fact that we're not having sex isn't even relevant. But what makes it relevant is that we can't completely define our relationship and use the old rules. If one of us sleeps with somebody, it's not like we're having an affair, exactly. The actual act of having sex is not the issue. It's the undefined relationship that is the issue, where it's not clear what the rules are. If we started having sex it wouldn't change that much. We might think that it would change a lot, but it wouldn't.

But then, I also feel that one of the reasons we're not having sex is because we're afraid of getting too involved. Sex would make us even too intense, given our closeness. Yet the one time we did have sex it was far from intense! But then again, I've known Hannah a lot longer now. I feel that sex itself wouldn't be that intense, it might be sort of bad.

Our relationship brings up all the hidden things about lesbian relationships. Hidden things like, What are the rules? How do lesbians get together? Do we just follow the heterosexual model or do we do it differently? And usually lesbians try to be different or alternative, but they end up following the same rules as heterosexual relationships.

I'm sad that it's never worked for me to have long-term, passionate, monogamous relationships. I came out when I was 19, 5 years ago. I didn't really deal with it, I came out in stages. I went through a stage where I was a lesbian and didn't sleep with men. It wasn't a very long stage. A lesbian who occasionally fucked men, was my working definition. Occasionally I've had relationships with men, but they haven't been very long. My last relationship with a woman had a ragged ending, but went on for about a year. It was really standard for people my age. We fell madly in love, jumped into bed within 2 seconds, and didn't get out for 6 months! We were such a couple. We didn't completely merge, we tried to maintain our lives to some extent. But we definitely had some merging. She's very attractive, she's younger than I am and she had never been with a woman. It was a great turn-on for me, corrupting the youth. Now she's completely out, a dyke. And it was very romantic. But I felt that I wasn't getting that much out of it, I was giving a lot. I was running the relationship. It was intense and romantic, but the ultimate contrast was that I never had interesting conversations with Joann. And all Hannah and I do is sit around and have interesting conversations. I feel very supported by Hannah intellectually, but I never felt supported in that way by Joann. Joann's development was extremely central to the relationship because she was the one who was developing! So I never got to be a kid and I never got to be in development.

Hannah is my mentor. I really look up to her and she is empowering and intellectual. She comes from a really interesting background in that her parents are Holocaust survivors. She was brought up Orthodox and grew up in Brooklyn where everyone was a survivor. We talk about that a lot, and she has educated me about Jewish issues that I didn't think about or realize before. So my entire intellectual approach these days is profoundly affected by Hannah.

I had a good role in the lesbian community when I was involved with Joann; I was really solid in the community. It was my big chance to be a real lesbian. And now I've fallen from grace! It's hard to reconstruct how Joann reacted to Hannah. We went through this drama about our breakup, and eventually it came out that Hannah had something to do with it. But we never talked about it directly. To think that I was leaving Joann for Hannah would have been an incredible blow for Joann. Hannah represents so many things that Joann feels she lacks. Joann, for example, is very conflicted about being Jewish because she was raised Catholic. Her whole family is Jewish but her mom converted, and they were banished from the family because of that. Joann is conflicted about being Jewish and I was really getting into it and in that way Hannah is a very threatening figure for Joann. And I worry that things are dribbling back to Joann, since Hannah and I are sending out a lie to the world that we're lovers.

Even though we have no good word to describe our relationship I know that part of calling ourselves lovers is not really true, we're not lovers. I wish we were lovers, that I could be more physical with her. But on the other hand I'm terrified of being physical with her. She has the attitude that there would be something incestuous about us sleeping together.

It's very rare that we meet new people and say, "This is my lover." That's never happened. But when I'm talking about her, sometimes I say, "my lover." Or I say, "my friend" but the word "friend" has this accent on it. When people ask where I'm staying, I say, "I'm subletting my friend's apartment." If I were just subletting an apartment of someone I knew I would say, "I'm subletting an apartment of someone I know," or "I'm subletting someone's apartment." When I say, "my friend," I'm trying to make it clear that she's my Friend friend. It's very complicated!

And when I have affairs with people, I describe Hannah as my primary relationship so that they know that I won't get involved with them. I describe it briefly as, "I'm very close to a woman and it's like we're lovers," or I say we are lovers. The few times I've been in that situation I've basically been very honest about it. I'll say, "we're not lovers, we're not physically close, but our relationship is primary." It explains for a lot of people why I refer to her constantly. She becomes the standard person that gets referred to.

I think Hannah refers to me as her girlfriend. In Israel, she was saying that she wanted to tell everyone that she has a girlfriend. And we have this mutual friend in her department, Joshua, he's a gay man. He and I went to a show. And Hannah had told me that she had talked in depth about me to him. I described this book project to him and he asked why our relationship was part of the book. I thought Hannah had described that part of our relationship, but he was completely shocked. Obviously, she talks about us as if we're lovers. He finally said, "How do you get off? Are you seeing other people?" He is playing a weird role in our relationship; he's the gay man that Hannah and I flirt with together. He has this thing about lesbians. He never has sex with women but he loves to flirt with lesbians. Whenever we're all together, the energy is just bouncing off the walls, between me and Hannah too. It's not as though Hannah and I are just these buddies who never think about having sex. We have these intensely sexual discussions and we just flirt with each other all the time. We're always hugging, especially in public. It's really safe and it identifies what we are. Hannah loves that, and she told me a long time ago that what she really wants in a woman is someone in her life to hold hands with as she walks across campus. And that's exactly what we do. And my image of our relationship before we even got together is that I wanted this calm, friendly, domestic relationship in which we hung out in our apartment all the time. And that's exactly what's happened. It's like a movie in which there's a fade-out, a movie about our relationship.

We do all the things that people in relationships do. We have breakfast together and we go to bed together and we sleep together pretty much every night, all wrapped around together just like people who have just had sex. And we have all these rituals. We get into bed and turn on the TV and watch "Star Trek." Then we turn it off and talk for a little while and go to sleep. And then we get up and go to this particular coffee shop, and we do this every morning. And then we figure out our day. About two weeks before Hannah went to Israel, I was letting myself in and out of her apartment and not going back to my house. Just like we were living together. It was incredibly domestic, like being married. I guess people in long-term relationships stop having sex anyway. And I guess they're distressed about it, and Hannah and I are not distressed about it. There is something very beautiful about our relationship. She's this anchor holding me together, and keeping me in school, and keeping me going. That's why I feel that I would be devastated if she were to have a real relationship with someone else. Hannah was talking about taking a job in Wisconsin and I thought about living there. I see her in a long-term way and feel linked to her. On some level it is very frustrating also. I'm a very sexual person, and the one relationship I'm having is not at all sexual. Very confusing.

The last time she talked to me on the phone, she said she might be teaching in Israel, but I'm not ready to live in Israel. But before that I told her I was thinking about moving with her to Wisconsin, and she thought that was great. She said, "Oh good, I won't be all alone there!" And as soon as she said that, I thought I shouldn't do that, it would screw me up. I mean, Wisconsin!

There have been points in my life when I felt I was closer to my sister than anyone else in my life, and that I would end up spending the rest of my life with her. I think Hannah has kind of replaced my sister. I'm still close to my sister, but Hannah has taken on that role. And even with Hannah saying it would be incestuous if we had sex, that our relationship would be too intense if we had sex, it's as though she's my sister. People have asked me if I want to have sex with my sister, which I find really offensive. With all this talk about such painful incest stuff, they shouldn't joke about that. But I answer that I'm so intense with my sister already, that if I were to have sex with her I would just drown. It would just be absurd to cross that line for me, just unimaginable. Not just because of the incest taboo, but because we are just too entangled. My sister and I moved out to this area together and we are the only people in our family that we can count on. Our whole family is in disarray, but she and I have stuck together. It really is similar to Hannah. I look up to Hannah in the same way. Hannah comes from a big family, and all her sisters are still Orthodox and have big families.

I think it has to do with the sense of familiarity about relationships. When I have sexual relationships, there is something very unfamiliar going on and I'm never sure what it is. Like with Joann, I felt like she didn't really exist at all. Now that I'm starting to be just a friend of hers, I can see she is interesting and I can see her characteristics. But when I was in a relationship with her, those things just kind of collapsed. I didn't recognize her, I would look at her and not know her at all. There was something alien about her or so much part of me that I couldn't see her.

Hannah and I are allies, there is something organic about our relationship as we are getting to know one another. There's something nice about that — if you never go to bed with someone, somehow you have this ability to be allies. With a lover, all this shit immediately comes up, my ego gets completely wrapped up in having sex with someone. When we're not having sex, I can distinguish between her and me. I never see Hannah as being so close to me that I can't recognize her. I definitely see her as this distinct individual and I'm in this data-gathering mode with her all the time. It's so refreshing after Joann. There are so few things you can talk about in a sexual relationship, you feel like you're treading on some very shaky ground.

Hannah is older and has a completely different life, although I'm kind of molding my life to hers. I admire her and want to be like her, and every once in a while I get weirded out about that. I'm in graduate school, thanks to her influence. She got it out of me from some place that was very far removed.

Our relationship is working, which is not true of other relationships I've had. I guess all relationships have strong points and weak points, and usually sex has been my strong point and everything has been off the scale. And now I'm having a relationship in which sex is not the strong point and everything else is good. It's a good trade-off. It's too bad that it has to be a trade-off. I'm not a frustrated person who is trying to get Hannah to have sex with me. I'm ambivalent.

And things shift back and forth. First I wanted sex and she didn't. Then there was a long, horrible period where it was the other way around. I felt very guilty. I would rack my brains and think about why I didn't want to have sex. But I felt that Hannah was acting like she wanted to have sex but she really didn't. Otherwise, I felt that I would have wanted sex with her more. I so much operate on other people's needs that I knew that she didn't want sex! She does believe that I'm in love with her, but she doesn't believe that I want sex with her. And I don't believe that she wants sex with me. One reason that sex is even an issue is because it's expected that people in our situation would want to have sex with one another. If we were in a value-free society, it would just never come up.

Sex is a part of our relationship. There are sexual elements, there is a sexuality between us. It doesn't culminate in a physical act, but it's definitely there. Like when we're in public. She'll take me to her office and the secretary will be there, and it's obvious that she enjoys doing this. She really wants me to be there, she's demonstrating to her peers and her professors that there's this dyky-looking person standing there, connected to her. When Hannah had a motorcycle, my favorite thing to do was to get on the back of her motorcycle and ride with her. It was such a turn-on. I didn't have orgasms, but I loved holding on to her and going very fast. That was the way we had sex. And when the motorcycle broke down, there went our sex life! Maybe without the motorcycle, we'll end up having sex!

Television and books and just people talking make it seem that there is more sex going on than there really is!

Maria Briani and Kathleen O'Reilly

MARIA

I AM 42 YEARS OLD and I'm about 5'6½" and I weigh about 230 pounds. I have olive-colored skin. I have blue eyes which are accented by the turquoise contacts that I wear. I have short brown hair that is crew cut from the middle of my head on down and a perm on the top of my head. I am the third oldest child of a family of 6, 5 girls and 1 boy. My parents were divorced the same year that I was divorced, which was in 1974. I have an associate degree in nursing.

Well, to get on with Kathleen's and my relationship. Previous relationships for me: I was married when I was 24 years old. I had lived together with a man who was about 7 or 8 years older than I was for 4 years, from the time I graduated from nursing school. My husband and I lived together for 4 years, got married and the marriage lasted about 6 to 8 months and we then divorced. And shortly after I was divorced, I was at an Al-Anon meeting (my ex-husband is an alcoholic) and I met the first woman that I had a lesbian relationship with. She was almost 20 years older than I was and our relationship lasted about one and a half years, but during the time that we were having a relationship, she was still carrying on a relationship with her former roommate. When I decided I couldn't live with her having that going on in the household, I decided it was time to call it quits.

I was the nursing director in a 50-bed residential facility for chronically mentally ill folks and it was there that I met Kathleen. Actually I hired her to work for me. She was a licensed practical nurse at the time and I fell in love with her, just the minute I met her. And I found myself spending a lot of time at work just to be around her. Because I was Kathleen's first relationship with a woman, the courting period was rather extensive and it was fun, it was great fun. I didn't really have a courting period in my first lesbian relationship and I did with Kathleen. I remember staying at work 16 hours a day because she worked the evening shift and I worked the day shift. I would stay at work into the evening hours to be around her, and then she'd start coming over to my apartment on her days off, and then I'd start going to her apartment and we just spent a lot of time together.

We didn't really talk about the relationship and what it was all about, we just talked about our likes and our dislikes and shared our philosophies about nursing, about people, about living. We just spent a lot of time talking and sharing and getting to know one another and it was a great time. We gave each other lots of cards with lots of positive affirmations in them.

Probably the neatest thing about the relationship between Kathleen and me is that we have grown together and grown individually, and by growing I mean we have outgrown some not-so-healthy behavior patterns and we have developed and grown into some new and healthy ones. And I remember, I don't know exactly when in our relationship it was but sometime within the first 5 to 6 years, Kathleen was having a problem with drugs and alcohol and I decided that having been married to an alcoholic and having been raised by an alcoholic father, I was just not going to have that happening in a relationship of mine, and so I asked her to stop and she did. And that was really neat, I was really impressed with that. Along the same lines, one time, there was a period when I didn't know what to do with my anger, and when I'd get angry, I'd beat up on Kathleen. Finally one day she told me that that behavior had to stop, and so I went to therapy and I stopped. I learned how to control my anger and how to deal with it in other ways.

Our first sexual encounter was kind of an exciting and a pleasant one for me. We were at Kathleen's apartment. We hadn't yet moved in together, well, we had but we hadn't. We were actually spending a lot of time at her apartment, but I was still maintaining mine. Kathleen had a mirror above her bed and I remember her being real cautious because she didn't know what to do. This was her first lesbian relationship and she didn't know what kinds of things I would like or what kinds of things to do, and I just sort of guided her along and it was a wonderful evening and a wonderful night.

We continued to work at the same place for a few more months and we eventually moved on to another place of employment. Both of us worked together for maybe three or four years of our relationship, and then she went to work at the state mental hospital and I kind of drifted from job to job.

Somewhere I had developed some problems, some major depression problems and I was seeing a psychiatrist almost weekly. Kathleen was married to a manic-depressive man for quite a number of years and so she had had her fill of living with people with mental illness. She had learned to detach herself from those kinds of things, which I think was really healthy for her because my behavior kind of spiraled downhill for a couple of years. It finally culminated in a suicide attempt in 1981 and for a short time I was at the state mental hospital where she was working. She was able to easily detach herself from my behavior and we made it through that particular struggle. And that is kind of what our lives have been like. For each of us personally, we have grown and given each other the space that we needed to grow.

I remember when I had decided sometime, hmm, I don't remember when in our relationship it was, but there was a time when I decided that I didn't want to sleep with her anymore and so I asked her if we could have separate bedrooms. Well, she agreed, I don't know if it was okay with her, but she agreed and . . . I'm the one with the poor memory in this relationship, so Kathleen's going to have to fill in a lot of the details. I don't know what was going on with me at the time, but I just needed some space, and she gave it to me and, again, that is what our whole relationship has been about — giving each other the space and the room to grow and to be who we are.

We went through couple's counselling together for a short time and we learned what kinds of behaviors we did to sort of keep things stirred up in the household. I learned that it was difficult for me to deal with her or to be around her when she was sick because my mother was sick quite a bit when I was younger and I hated that. It was difficult and hard on me. Kathleen, on the other hand, doesn't like being sick and doesn't like being taken care of. She has always had to be the strong and healthy one in her family, and so having her sick in the household was always a difficult thing. Me, on the other hand, I'm a real candy-ass, but she loves to wait on me. I personally think she is extremely co-dependent, but we have never talked about that.

I can't remember exactly when we stopped having sex. I do remember why. I also remember that in the early years of our relationship some of the sexual behaviors that we had were, in my opinion, extremely dysfunctional and I think the kinds of things that we did to and with each other were really bizarre. But eventually I think our sexual relationship kind of normalized a little bit. I have always found it extremely difficult to make love to Kathleen and I think that that probably has more to do with the fact that I don't really know how and I'm not really comfortable talking about it with her and so . . .

I do remember maybe 2 or 3 or 4 years ago we were at a weekend retreat with a group of our friends and she had just finished making love to me, and I made love to her, and she told me that she really enjoyed that and she liked it a lot and she wished I would do it a lot more. Well, that was kind of something that I probably did not want to hear because I think from that point on I decided that I didn't really need sex and I didn't really want it. That it was enough for me just to be close to her, to be held and to be cared for and cared about and to be hugged and kissed and caressed. But sex, the actual act of making love, was not something that I needed or wanted and I had the right to say no.

There have been times in the past few years when we have been asexual that I have felt some kind of passion and some kind of desire to have sex. Again, it is not something that I am comfortable talking about, and it is not something that I have ever been able to ask for when I have wanted it, so I have just lived without it, which has been fine with me.

Well, for the past year, I have been in a corrective parenting therapy group. I am in the process of learning who it is that I am. Eventually as I go through my stages of development in my therapy process I will reach the stage of integration which is sexual independence and I will be able to take a look at those issues. I will be able to deal with and resolve them for myself and, I know Kathleen and I will then be able to resume our sexual activity. Until then, I am really comfortable not having sex, and although I know that Kathleen is not and she would like to have it, and it is something that is somewhat important to her, again, all of our relationship has been based on giving each other the time and the space and the right to be who we are and to grow. It's just been a real neat relationship. It has become very important to talk openly about things that are difficult for me to discuss. I know as I begin to do that, Kathleen also will do the same because we have grown together, and where one learns a new skill or a new way of behaving in a relationship, the other one picks it up, learns it, tries it on. What fits for her or for me we keep, and what doesn't fit we throw away and that's, again, what our relationship has been about.

Some more thoughts that have come to my mind are that it is probably important to note that in my first lesbian relationship, the entire year and a half we were together, she made love to me, I never made love to her. She would never allow that, and during my married life, my ex-husband also made love to me and I never made love to him. So again, it sort of reinforces in my head that it's a behavior or something I just never learned or explored or attempted or even wanted to learn to do myself. I am not sure that now is particularly the time that I want to learn. But I do know that because it is important to Kathleen that I will begin to explore it in my therapy process. Her needs, her wants, her desires are important to me. She is important to me and our relationship is important to me. Sex just is not at the top of our priority list, at least it is not at the top of mine and she doesn't bring it up that often.

We have many friends in our local lesbian organization and we always meet everybody first and sort of bring people into the organization. Consequently we have a wonderful network of friends. Kathleen was telling me that she was uncomfortable with the fact that when we're together with our friends, sometimes I intimate in a joking way that we are sexually active. She is uncomfortable with that because she believes it's dishonest, and since that time, I have shared with one of our friends that our relationship is asexual, but I have not shared that with anybody else. I'm not sure that that is something I would be comfortable sharing with people, partially because our relationship is 14 years in duration and so we are the couple who has been together the longest in the community that I know of. We are looked up to as role models in terms of the longevity of our relationship. My guess is that our friends are friends enough that whether we are sexual or asexual wouldn't be important to them, but it is not something that I would willingly want to discuss with them. It would depend on how close the friends were. I mean, we have some really close friends, some wonderfully close friends, and some people who are just acquaintances. I'm not sure who I would be comfortable talking with about the fact that our relationship is asexual right now, other than the one person that I have discussed it with. I did that simply because it came up at a conference we attended.

Kathleen and I are not closeted, although we do not discuss the fact that we are lesbians around my mother. My father is now dead. With my second oldest sister and my two younger sisters and my brother, Kathleen and I are open and talk about our relationship, but we do not talk about our sexual activity. In terms of Kathleen's family, she has two brothers, her mother and father are both dead, and she is kind of having some difficulties with her younger brother right now.

I've always considered myself never to be out, especially at work, although at my last two jobs my co-workers knew about Kathleen and they knew about our relationship. I considered that something that I was not comfortable talking about at work. In terms of being out with my family, I think ever since I met Kathleen and moved in with her they have known about our relationship, and because I was in a relationship before that, I think they knew that it was a lesbian relationship. In terms of coming out myself, I remember shortly after I divorced my husband, I attended a few of the local lesbian support groups, a coming-out support group and, a first relationship support group, and I learned a little bit about what it meant to be a lesbian and a lot about discrimination. It was really an important time in my life and very helpful to me in confirming my lesbianism.

KATHLEEN

MY NAME is Kathleen. A description of myself: I am 47 years old, I weight 203 pounds and I am 5'4". I have blonde hair which is blonde because I spray it to keep it up; it is kind of in a crew cut. I have been a nurse for 26 years. For the last 3 years, I have been going to college to earn my B.A. Eventually, I want to continue my work with the chronically mentally ill.

My interests: I love to cook, I like to garden. I love to read all kinds of things, which is probably a good thing since I'm going to school, and I love being with my friends. I love getting together with friends: having potlucks and parties and this sort of thing. I'm from Washington. And that's me.

Let's see, how we got involved. I had been married for 9 years to a man and then I got divorced. For 2 years I had worked at the local mental hospital and I decided I didn't want to work in psychiatric nursing anymore because at that time I thought I was burned out. Actually it was the bureaucracy that burned me out, not psych. I went to work for a nursing pool, and they called me and wanted me to go to work there, and I said no at first, because I didn't want to work in psych. But they talked me into it, and so I went out there and I met Maria. Maria was the director of nurses at a psychiatric nursing home. She showed me around the place and I fell in love with her at first, you know the first time I met her. I just thought she was wonderful.

I had never had a lesbian relationship or a lesbian love that I knew of. I mean I have had various attractions to women in my life, but I never knew what it was. I never understood. But when I met her, I knew. I knew that I was interested in her sexually and relationship-wise. It took us about a month, I think it was, of kind of hemming and hawing around each other, writing each other letters and notes and this sort of thing and getting together, not saying anything for long periods of time and then finally talking. I found that she had been in a lesbian relationship and was just getting out of it, had just gotten out of that. And we went to bed one night and here I was in this lesbian relationship and I had no idea what to do and I just know that we lay there and we kissed and I didn't know what to do from there and she placed my hand at strategic places and I went from there and I enjoyed myself thoroughly. I really enjoyed the sexual part of our relationship.

We had a sexual relationship for some time after that, in fact, we began living together not long after that and about a month after we had lived together, I remember Maria said that she felt that we were having too much sex and we ought to cut it down. Now sex was defined back then as manipulation of genitals, kissing, hugging, but also reaching a climax, sexual climax. We had been having sex every night and we cut down then to, I don't know, probably once a week. It is hard to remember since we have been together for 14 years, and there were various stages of our sexual and nonsexual relationship. For a few years, we had a sexual relationship. In fact, Maria had a sexual relationship with someone outside the partnership at one time. Since then, we have both been monogamous. And we both felt, I thought anyway, that it was important to be monogamous.

About 8 years ago, maybe 9 or something like that, Maria wanted to sleep in separate beds, so we did that. So for 2 years we hardly had any contact at all. She had some real psychological problems at the time and we were more roommates than anything else and then finally she said, "Well, let's; I'd like it if we could sleep together again, you know, be together in the same bedroom." So, we did and we have been ever since. We've had kind of a sexual relationship since then, but what it was, was that every once in a while I would initiate some sexual relations. I don't think she ever initiated it. And I would enjoy myself to a point. At times it was very sexually frustrating because Maria didn't manipulate me and it was more of a one-way thing. I would manipulate her and that would be that. Even when I would place her hands or ask her to do certain things, she didn't want to. And then later in the relationship, I realized that she really wasn't being sexually fulfilled and I felt I was kind of forcing myself on her, that she was just pretending to enjoy herself and wasn't really. So, I quit doing it until she would ask for it or it would be mutually agreed upon and that would be okay. But she never did ask. So if I ever wanted any kind of sexual relationship, I had to ask. It got like once every 2 months, once every 4 months, once every 6 months and then pretty soon a whole year went by and we didn't have any kind of sexual contact. Now, like I said, I am talking about arousal to a climax, that kind of a sexual relationship. We did still at this time have a second kind of a sexual relationship where we would cuddle a lot, hold each other and kiss, kind of a sexual relationship if you will. We quit having the climax type of sexual relationship about a year ago even though I wanted it.

We don't talk about it. She doesn't like to talk about sex for some reason. I understand that because I have some reservations myself from our Catholic upbringing where we were brought up to believe that sex is dirty. I mean, I like sex, it feels good and I would like to have some, but Maria doesn't, so I am respecting that at this point. I have been hoping that she will come around and want to have a sexual relationship again. At this point it is particularly difficult because for a long time we at least had the part of a sexual relationship where we would hold each other and touch each other a lot and kiss. We don't do that anymore. She started a therapy group about 8 months ago and they do a lot of touching and holding and nurturing in that group and she has told me that my wanting a sexual relationship, or my even wanting more of this kind of relationship, is my problem. I don't happen to agree with that and I get real angry about that because I think it's our problem. I think it is a relationship thing and I have told her often that I feel jealous of her that she gets these needs met in her group and I don't get my needs met at all. So I feel left out. I feel bad, I feel something like that. I do wish we had more of at least a cuddling, loving, stroking kind of relationship, even if we can't have a sexual relationship. I am hoping that some time in the future we can have a sexual relationship. I really miss a sexual relationship. I have considered going outside our relationship to get my sexual needs met, but decided that's not "right" while I am in a relationship with Maria, and I don't intend to end my relationship. There are other parts of our relationship that are very important to me and for those reasons I want to stay with her.

Do our friends know that it is an asexual relationship? No they don't. In fact, I have told Maria, she knows that I get upset sometimes because she'll make jokes every once in a while that sound like we are having a sexual relationship when we are not. About society changing to be more accepting of nonsexual relationships, yes, I think it should be. I don't like shoulds, but anyway I really do believe that society should be more accepting of nonsexual relationships. I think that there are a lot of nonsexual, or at least relationships where not much sex goes on, that are happening in society and I think that television makes it seem, television and books and just people talking make it seem that there is more sex going on than there really is. I don't think there actually is that much. We're kind of forced into thinking that sex is the be-all, end-all of a relationship. Our relationship is not totally about sex. It is also about being with each other, allowing each other to grow, doing things for each other, being there for each other. I don't know how else to say it.

What would it mean to end our relationship? Well, I don't know. Our relationship has gone through various stages over the past 14 years and some people would have thought that it would have ended at various times, like when we slept in different rooms and this sort of thing. I guess I could say our relationship has ended several times and gone on into a different kind of relationship. Our relationship today is not the same one that we had when we began, nor is it the same one that it was 4 years ago or 4 years before that. It has changed, I think for the better, for the better of both of us each time. And I think it will continue to change because both of us are growing. I think a lot of it is luck in a way. We've both grown and luckily we have both grown in the same direction.

I've already told you the history of my relationships. Well, let's see, I was in the convent for a little over a year right after high school and then I dated men for a while and was married for 9 years. I have had several sexual relationships with men, about 8 or 9 something like that, not long-term though. My long-term relationship was with my husband. How long have I been out as a lesbian? Well, like I said, Maria is my first lesbian relationship. I've sort of been out all along, but there have been various stages of out. The last 4 years, I have been very out, like I have been out at work. I make it just a natural part of my conversation that I talk about Maria as my partner and I feel in doing so people come to accept this as kind of a "normal" state of affairs, you know, meaning that this is an everyday thing just like a heterosexual relationship and that there is nothing crazy about it.

That seems like it is pretty much it except I would like to say that we have a lot of friends through our local lesbian organization. A lot of our friends tell us, and a lot of acquaintances tell us, that they think that we have the ideal relationship, and that is interesting. I think we have a good relationship and I am happy with the relationship. I believe we could work on it, and I believe we are working on it some, but people see what they want to see. They see that we have the ideal relationship. I don't think there is such a thing as the ideal relationship. Relationships are individual and individuals have relationships according to themselves. And that's it.

Discussants

Is sex a natural function:
Implications for sex therapy

Ellen Cole

I BEGAN READING *Boston Marriages* with considerable skepticism. I had talked enough with some of the contributors to know they viewed romantic but asexual relationships between lesbians as a reasonable option. I, on the other hand, secretly thought (very secretly, not wanting to offend) they were merely justifying their own past (shhh — dysfunctional) relationships. As a sex therapist, trained by Masters and Johnson and still working more or less with their original model, I believed that "sex is a natural function," and that when a regular and satisfying sex life has "gone off the tracks," it's the sex therapist's job to discover the roadblocks and remove them. The couple, then, can resume on the natural course of regular, satisfying genital sexual involvement. Any other resolution would be unnatural and pathological, and would be considered a "treatment failure." What follows is, first, my initial reaction to the book in light of this background; second, responses from the 14 students in my undergraduate Psychology of Women course who read *Boston Marriages* in manuscript form and wrote brief reaction papers; and third, my conclusions about relationships that are Boston marriages and my thoughts about the implications for sex therapy.

NOTE: I would like to thank the members of my psychology of women class for their thoughtful papers and comments that informed my thinking as I wrote this chapter: Victoria Abel, Dana Blythe, Melissa Boer, Denise Cavitt, Mary Kate Fitzpatrick, Jim Galvin, Crin Hout, Kimberly Joyce, Melissa Lanier, Jessie Seif, Sharon Sweeney, Sarah Swope, Cheryl Walters, and Hillary Weinberg.

My initial reaction

First, I like the format of this book: the theoretical papers preceding the great variety, in both format and content, of personal stories. Second, the content shocked, disturbed, challenged, and ultimately engaged me.

Some of the concepts that are widely accepted by sex therapists include the following: sex is a natural function; when sex is not going well there is a reason, usually psychogenic in origin, pathological in nature; a primary goal of the sex therapist is to make an accurate diagnosis of the sexual dysfunction and develop a treatment plan accordingly; regular sexual activity is recommended for both physical and emotional health (a sign in the reception area at the Masters and Johnson Institute says "Use It or Lose It"); and the average couple in the United States has sex (almost always defined as heterosexual intercourse) 2.5 times a week. Each of these concepts was challenged by *Boston Marriages*.

A number of months ago, in another state, a lesbian couple came to see me because one partner, I'll call her Susan, no longer wanted to have sex, and the other, Janine, was hurt, confused, and angry. Susan and Janine had purchased a home together, owned a recreational vehicle which they enjoyed on weekends, had combined their finances, and were clearly a devoted couple. In fact, they had participated in a marriage ceremony and referred to each other as "my spouse." My initial assessment, confirmed through an extensive sexual history, was that Susan was "sexually aversive" and her aversion was rooted in childhood sexual abuse. I devised a treatment plan that consisted of desensitization exercises to relieve Susan of her fears and allow her to enjoy sex with Janine. Janine's job, I expected, would be to back off while Susan got past her fears and discovered her innate and natural love of sex. In other words: Susan had a diagnosible condition; Janine was part of the treatment, but only in a passive role; and in the end Susan would become more like Janine. I imagined the day that Susan and Janine would indeed have satisfying, comfortable, fun-loving, erotic genital sex on a regular basis.

A sine qua non of good sex therapy is that the therapist's goals must be that of the clients. I saw no discrepancy here between my expectations of a satisfactory therapy outcome and the expressed goals of my clients. Janine wanted sex, Susan felt guilty, inadequate, and "sick," and she was terrified of losing Janine. She agreed she was supposed to want to have sex. Therefore, the two of them had a mutual goal, and that goal made perfect sense to me. I saw no need to challenge it.

I now see that what I was confronted with was a Boston marriage. And I see that I had been assuming that sexuality between Susan and Janine was absolutely primary and necessary to the survival of the relationship. I now question these assumptions and imagine how I might have proceeded differently.

Were Susan and Janine to walk into my office today, I would encourage them to explore their common ground and their individual definitions of relationship. I don't think I would assume that Susan needed to be more like Janine. Perhaps the development of an active sexuality would emerge as a mutual goal, but perhaps it wouldn't. And I would want to know much more about what Susan might do that could be fun and sensual and sexual for her, without entering into distasteful or unacceptable territory. Might they masturbate in each other's company, for instance? Might touching of breasts be stimulating and fun, as long as it didn't lead to genital involvement? I would encourage this couple to consider a range of valid options.

In fact, after about three months of weekly sessions with Susan and Janine, Susan was no longer afraid to have sex and reported sexual experiences that were comfortable and sometimes mildly pleasurable. She was genuinely willing to have sex on a regular basis (approximately weekly, in her case), but without enthusiasm. If it were not for Janine, she would still prefer not to have sex at all. Improved communication about sex was probably the biggest gain from therapy for each woman. Sex was no longer a taboo or scary topic for either of them, and they were each extremely relieved to be able to candidly discuss their desires, hopes, and preferences. By traditional sex therapy standards, this would probably be considered a treatment success because the couple, at therapy's end, was engaging in weekly sex, without fear or pressure. However, through *Boston Marriages'* lens, what I did not do with this couple was challenge their assumptions early on. And of course I couldn't, because I had not yet challenged my own.

Responses from undergraduates

My psychology of women class consists of 14 undergraduates enrolled at a small progressive liberal arts college in Arizona. Thirteen are

women, one is a man; eleven of the women identify themselves primarily
as heterosexual, one woman is a lesbian currently in a relationship that
she describes as "definitely sexual." All of the students in my class are
white. Each student read a prepublication copy of *Boston Marriages* and
wrote a brief reaction paper.

I was surprised by their positive responses. I had expected that asexuality would seem foreign and weird to these college students and that
they might be starting out with homophobic attitudes about all lesbian
relationships. I was worried that the book would give the wrong message, would perpetuate the ancient stereotype that lesbians are mentally
ill, or that all lesbians don't have sex. I had many second thoughts about
assigning the book and the paper.

Instead, the overwhelming majority loved the book and strongly identified with it. One woman ended her paper by stating, "I am really glad to
have been able to read this book and to have learned about a new issue.
The stories were touching and absorbing. I feel privileged to have been
able to read about these women's lives."

There were only two critical voices. One woman, the lesbian in the
class, detests labels. She says, "All of my life I have been terrified of
labels. At 6 I was afraid to be called "Four-Eyes" when I got my glasses,
and at 13 I was horrified to label myself a Lesbian. I thought everyone
would hate me if I admitted my attraction to women. Today, I still shy
away from that label as it limits me, it stamps me, it's too hard to erase."
She sees the term "Boston marriage" as yet another label that classifies
and separates. The other dissenter was "disheartened" by the personal
stories. She says that after reading the theoretical papers she was looking
forward to "lovely chapters describing healthy, loving lesbian relationships," but found instead "manipulation, control, denial, distorted attitudes, dysfunctional perceptions — a morass of sad and sick stories."

These, however, were the exceptions. Many students noted with dis-
may that it is more acceptable in our society to be lesbian or gay than
nonsexual. Many experienced validation and a deeper understanding of
their own asexual but romantic relationships with women. One student
put it this way: "I can relate well to the concept of the Boston marriage. I
relish my friendships with womyn. I find myself sexually attracted to
many womyn, but something inside me holds me back from the physical
intimacy." And another: "Over and over, I develop highly intimate, very
sensual relationships with women. Many people have asked if we're

'involved,' and I haven't known what to say. Now I know there are more ways to define committed relationships than just sexual activity."

The story of Iris and Ruth, "bliss-mates," rang a special note with my students. One woman explained that their relationship gave her

a model of a functional commitment that helps me to understand both my deeply woman-focused life and my sexual attraction to men. My primary relationships have always been with women, even when I'm involved with and committed to a particular man. Rather than sexual desire, I think I have a soulful desire for women. My two closest friends and I are talking about a lifelong commitment to each other and are trying to figure out how to actualize it. I've sent them quotes from *Boston Marriages*.

And, finally, the main themes that emerged from the student papers and the discussion that ensued were the distinct and strong affirmation of choice that the book provided, and the recognition that sexuality and relationships need to be redefined. As one student said, echoed in similar words by just about the entire class:

We don't need any more "shoulds." I want choices about my relationships. I want the freedom to define for myself how to manifest my devotion to the company of women. Though my sexual expression is very important to me, and though I'm not convinced that all the relationships I read about in *Boston Marriages* are healthy or happy ones, I honor these women's relationships as attempts to create their own lives as they want them, with few models and little support, validation, or community.

Another student, also reflecting the majority, calls for *redefinition*. She urges us — therapists, lesbians, college students, and human beings — to keep defining what sexuality is and what intimate relationships are. She says, "Instead of focusing on sexlessness in a negative way, let's rejoice in the love and honesty these women, in Boston marriages, are finding."

Implications for sex therapy

A popular bumper sticker among students at my college is still, "Question Authority." Their *Boston Marriages* papers reminded me, once again, that truth and wisdom are relative concepts, not absolute. My students have reminded me that freedom of choice is the highest order of societal organization, and that loving and committed relationships are grounded in more than mutual stimulation of breasts and genitals.

I would now augment any list of sex therapy concepts with the following: Periods of celibacy, or even indefinite celibacy, may be perfectly appropriate for an individual or a couple. It may be appropriate for a sex therapist to validate a consensual Boston marriage. If one partner wants sex and the other does not, the therapist should not automatically assume that the latter partner has a deep-seated pathological condition that needs to be fixed, or that the outcome of a successful course of therapy would be for that partner to change. The goal of sex therapy should always be to accommodate the couple, and in some cases this may mean accepting asexuality. It is not necessarily a treatment failure if a couple comes into therapy and leaves therapy without having regular sex. Sex therapy should not have any absolute standard of sexual behavior as its unexamined goal.

Sex therapy currently assumes that the goal is to be sexual. *Boston Marriages* has made a subtle shift in my thinking about this assumption. There are wide paths to explore in the land of relationships, and we make a mistake by automatically pathologizing those paths which may not include sex.

In fact, it has occurred to me, since reading *Boston Marriages*, that there may even be advantages for some women, for some couples, who do not have sex. In other words, asexuality is not necessarily pathological; it also may represent something more positive than merely avoidance of an unpleasant or undesirable activity. It may represent a higher state for some. I think, for instance, of the unparalleled intensity of early teenage romance. For me, at least, this was a time of strong, pure, positive feelings of lust and love without sex. I think, too, of the monastic tradition, where celibacy allows a certain kind of undivergent attention to communion with one's deepest self and with the realm of the spiritual. A friend of mine, a professor of religious studies, has said, "Passion for the ultimate is channeled in a different way when there isn't a physical relationship in one's life."

What happens when one partner wants sex and the other does not, as was the case with Janine and Susan, and many of the couples in this book? The role of the sex therapist, then, is to be very careful about helping both women stay clear about expressing and representing themselves. It is all too easy for women to acquiesce and sacrifice at the expense of their own integrity. The key here is not to assume that the partner who wants to have sex is "right," while at the same time being very careful to challenge deference and abdication. If sex therapy's goal is, as I believe it should be, to accommodate the couple, that means that the wishes of each must be honored equally. It may be just as possible that the sexual partner could find a good way to abridge or compromise her needs in service to the relationship as it would be for the nonsexual partner to compromise hers. Traditional sex therapy always considers the second possibility, never the first.

Is sex a natural function? After reading *Boston Marriages*, my answer is yes . . . and no. As I was taught by William Masters and Virginia Johnson, I believe that sex is a natural biological function, much like sleeping, eating, and breathing. I was also taught by Masters and Johnson that natural functions are subject to voluntary control. I can hold my breath; there is enormous variety between people's sleeping and eating patterns. Masters and Johnson would conclude, therefore, that the sex therapist's role is to discover why and how the natural function of sex has been voluntarily controlled and to set things straight. After reading *Boston Marriages*, my thoughts are a little different. Just as there is enormous variety in eating and sleeping patterns, there is also, and especially, enormous variety in sexual preferences. In fact, given that bad and abusive sex is almost the cultural norm for women, one might wonder how women could actually end up wanting sex with their partners, ever. And so, yes, sex is a natural biological function. But it may very well not be psychologically and emotionally and spiritually natural for some women. There may be, and clearly *Boston Marriages* tells us there are, times when the "natural function" is asexuality.

A matter of language

Marcia Hill

WHITE, middle-class America, the guardian of the cultural norms, confers legitimacy on relationships under very carefully circumscribed conditions. In other times and places, expectations for relationships have differed from those we now hold. Assumptions about what is "natural" or "instinctive" change with the times. In another time, another place, commitment to family members or to tribe might be expected to take precedence over commitment to one's sexual partner, for example. Or, as Lillian Faderman has described, intimacy between some pairs of women might be understood to be greater than the intimacy either of those women has with her husband. It is no accident that the editors of this book have looked to models in American history to find a way to talk about a relationship pattern that is not currently in the popular discourse.

The patterns may vary with time and location, but the fact of an externalized locus of definition and endorsement for relationship patterns seems to stay constant. Perhaps cultural control over what kinds of intimacy or commitment were sanctioned was more necessary at times when one's survival was predicated on belonging to a particular group. Then, ways of determining whether an individual belonged — to a clan, to a religion — were paramount. The requirements for group membership were rigid, but they were also carefully articulated: a certain network of family relationships, a particular kind of responsibility to tribe, another commitment to one's religious community. As Western society has become less focused on clan identity, those markers have faded in importance. But the paradigm of externalized definition has not changed; we have simply changed the focus of validation from group membership to sexual partnership. We have found ourselves with fewer cultural expectations for commitment, but the expectations we retain are just as rigid. And those expectations are even less articulated, less overt, than they have been historically.

Members of oppressed groups, of course, have also had to retain or create group identity as a way of surviving in a culture that does not automatically confer belonging on them. Lesbians, Jews, Asian Americans and other ethnic groups, the disabled, women in general, and others all look to group identity as a buffer to oppression and a source of pride. Yet, on the interpersonal level within each group, there are sets of rules and expectations about what constitutes a "real" relationship, what is considered a legitimate arena for commitment. I wish to focus on this, the interpersonal level, and to look at the matter of the rules themselves.

Perhaps we are coming to a time when we can afford to change the paradigm of how we understand relationships. This would entail a change not just in the ways we have of grouping relationships, but in the fact of using groupings at all. To group and define relationships based on commitment rather than sexual intimacy, for example, changes only the basis for our differential valuing of relationships, not the fact of that valuing. Changing the method of determining what is legitimate does not subvert the concept of defining legitimacy externally. A real paradigm change would entail using an individual or internal way of defining relationships, rather than a group or external definition. Of course, there's a lot to lose if we make such a change. Heterosexual privilege, for example, would go down the drain. If there is not a way to group relationships and classify them as more or less worthy of endorsement based on external standards, then there is not a way for any person or couple to claim status based on the nature of that relationship. But wait, before you start cheering, consider that we would also lose lesbian group identity, at least as it currently exists. Lesbian identity is, after all, a function of the current paradigm which delineates relationships on the basis of sex.

What *is* all this obsession about sex anyway, about naming our sexual relationships and behaviors and deciding how legitimate each one is? It even seems that the English language describes relationships primarily on the basis of sexuality. We have "mate," "spouse," "consort," and the like (usually with an implied meaning of heterosexual), and then a collection of words for nonsexual relationships: "friend," "comrade," "chum," and so forth. A few of the latter imply a relationship within a work

setting ("colleague," "partner"). Aside from the work/nonwork distinction, however, the words for nonsexual relationships generally give almost no information about intimacy or commitment. It would seem that
what matters in a relationship is whether there is sexual intimacy. In the
context of sexual intimacy, we note commitment. But if there is not
sexual intimacy, we don't seem to be interested in commitment or even
any kind or depth of intimacy. Doesn't this seem a bit odd?

What's going on here? The whole matter of sex is completely befud-
dled by the overlay of patriarchy. Sex is used systematically and consistently against women as a weapon of control: rape, incest, harassment —
and the threat of all of those. Many of us are specifically damaged
sexually, and those of us who aren't still feel the impact of always living in
a war zone. What woman fully owns her body and her sexuality? How
can we even begin, under these circumstances, to know what desire
means to us? To know how playfully or passionately, how quietly or
wildly, how often or infrequently we might shape our expressions of
sexual closeness?

There is a poignant quality to many of the passages in this book. We
hear the women who are telling their stories groping toward some way
of describing a relationship that is central in their lives, and yet is mini-
mized or distorted. Is this relationship real? Am I normal? Angie says, "I
think that if I'm in a partnership with someone and we're not sexual, that
I have a sexual dysfunction." And there is a kind of wistfulness as these
women imagine another way of thinking about relationships, a way that
does not make sex a central definer. Esther Rothblum, in the introduction, misses the "absolute acceptability" of childhood best friends,
friends that, as Laura Moxie puts it, one is "totally bonded with." Laura
later considers one way that kind of commitment might be enacted: "I'd
like to say, 'I'm moving to this city. Who would like to move with me?'"
This is, in fact, a radical proposal in a cultural context that considers
sexual relationships the only relationships committed enough to move
for. Ruth says, "Imagine saying 'just lovers' like some people say 'just
friends.'" Imagine.

And that's only the beginning. Any unwarranted focus on what's considered appropriate pathologizes most people — human beings are just
too diverse. So, as American culture continues to devalue and attempt to
control women's bodies, we see obsessive concern about weight, increasing numbers of women with eating disorders, overwhelming percent-

ages of women who think that simply eating what they wish is impossible, an almost universal sense among women that our bodies are wrong. Our cultural obsession with sex has similar consequences. Are we having sex too often or not often enough? Does this or that activity "count" as sex anyway? Are our fantasies, our level of passion, our sexual habits normal? Are our relationships, with their particular form of sexual expression, or lack of sexual expression, or feelings without expression — are these okay?

The term "Boston marriage" is revolutionary in that it gives us language for one more form of relationship. As Ruth puts it, "It would be good to have a name for this for only one reason, and that would be to expand people's consciousness." A name gives this particular relationship legitimacy, makes it "real." To have a name for these relationships expands the boundaries of what a relationship is. Further, it is a particular act of courage to define a relationship that challenges the given order by not falling neatly into our usual pattern, which says that either it's sexual and therefore important or not sexual and therefore "just friends."

But the use of the term "Boston marriage" is also, ultimately, self-defeating. If we want to move toward, as Marny Hall puts it, demoting genital access as the index of relational significance, then we find ourselves with one more term that defines relationships in terms of genital access. In a society obsessed with sexual definition and with hierarchy, we might create a way to describe our reality, only to have it inevitably ranked in the patriarchal list of relational importance. I imagine "Boston marriage" finding itself somewhere between "lover" or "life partner" and "friend" or "roommate." We are trapped. If we lack language, we are lost in our oppression, not even having a way to talk to one another about what we experience. Yet if we create new language, it cannot be used other than in the context in which we live and shape its meaning. As Marny Hall points out, it is "impossible to define lesbian sex independently of the discourses of any period." I would add that it is impossible to define *any* relationship independently of the discourses of the time.

Further, as the stories of the couples in this book vividly show, there is still wide variation in what constitutes a Boston marriage. These relationships run an enormous gamut in terms of emotional intimacy, other kinds of intimacy, commitment, and expectations. Some strike me as satisfying and whole; others seem painful to one degree or another. Perhaps the degree of mutuality in the relationship is the best indicator of the relationship's well-being. Leslie Raymer's story, for example, of mutual goals and affection, or Ruth and Iris's description of "bliss" stand in stark contrast to Pat's pain and confusion at her partner's expectation — so different from her own — that sex be a central factor in commitment. The risk of using a single descriptive term — "Boston marriage" — to include this range of experiences is that the richness and reality of each particular relationship is lost.

Having made those criticisms, I would still welcome the addition of one more way of talking about relationships. It seems to me that the term "Boston marriage" is one of those in-between steps on the road to radical change. Perhaps ultimately we need either language that refuses to make assumptions about any relationships, or language to describe relationships in all their richness, with no more focus on sex than on any other aspect of intimacy. But we will not get there without challenging the limitations of our language for describing relationships as it exists now. And that means finding ways to talk about what is *really* going on in our relationships. As with the feminist consciousness-raising groups of 20 years ago, when we can tell one another the truth about our lives, we discover that we are not as alone or as different as we thought we were. And, more profoundly, we discover that much of what we thought was "true" or "real" or "normal" was simply a figment of the patriarchy's pathological imagination.

Essentially, this is a book about language. It succeeds to the extent that it assists the reader in thinking and talking about relationships in new ways. If we carry that premise further, how else might we describe relationships outside of a context that is focused on sex and possession? A relationship implies some level of intimacy, from the simple recognition of the other that marks acquaintanceship, to the deepest levels of mutual knowing. We need ways to describe depth of intimacy. It is shocking that the aspect of our connection with others that affects us most forcefully, that counters our isolation and mirrors for us who we are, is one that we cannot describe very accurately. Further, there is the matter of kinds of intimacy. Physical intimacy is one kind, and that would include affection, sexuality, and the kind of physical familiarity that one feels with a housemate or with someone (such as a child) whose physical needs one takes care of. Emotional intimacy is another: the intimacy of shared history, of shared vulnerability and feeling. Intellectual or cognitive closeness might be shared by partners in a work project who know well the workings of the other's mind but little of her life outside the workplace. Perhaps spiritual intimacy is a way to describe a bond that transcends all of these.

Commitment is another major factor in a relationship. At present, we only recognize commitment between some sexual partners. One of the gifts of this book is its implicit endorsement of commitment outside of a sexual relationship. What, then, about the commitment in the relationship of a caretaker (day-care worker, attendant for the disabled, therapist, teacher) to her charge: a willingness to take responsibility for some aspect of the other's welfare? This is a commitment to be dependable in a particular way, an agreement about what one can ask of the other, and there are many variations. Practically speaking, think about who you would ask for a ride to the car mechanic. Who would help you move or buy your groceries if you were sick? Emotionally, whom can you ask for support and a sympathetic ear when you feel most hurt? What about the commitment we experience in friendships when both parties consciously choose to do the difficult sorting through that is necessary to maintain intimacy in spite of misunderstandings or disappointments? There is an unspoken commitment made in many relationships to devote a certain amount of time and effort to one another. There is the commitment to take the other into account when making important decisions, which is a way of letting our relationships shape our lives. Perhaps we would hurt one another less if we could think about the level of commitment we actually experience and want in a particular relationship, separate from our habitual assumptions about what kind of commitment is "allowed." We might even find ways to mark and celebrate those other commitments, those other intimacies.

The possibilities can seem overwhelming at first. And yet, there's something freeing about that, too, a kind of excitement that comes with the richness that opens up as the alternatives multiply. Marny Hall envisions a variety of intimacy patterns emerging as we become less attached to formulaic ways of ranking and defining relationships. In talking with a colleague about this, she noted that there is a body of sociological literature devoted to describing relationships. How is it that this information, these descriptions, have not found their way into the popular discourse? The language available to describe reality, particularly such a fundamental aspect of reality as relationships, serves as a method of social control. If we can't say it, it's hard to think it, and even harder to enact it. That standard question of all political analysis, Who benefits? serves us well here. The beneficiary of the status quo is the relationship that is considered most legitimate: the heterosexual marriage. And, within that relationship, as much research shows, the person who generally benefits is the male. Consider further: who benefits from our not making commitments outside of a sexual context? Who benefits from our limited ability to value nonsexual intimacy? From the poverty of our language for describing intimacy? What kinds of intimacy would we describe and value, what kind of commitments would we make and honor, if we based our definitions of relationship in the reality of our experience?

Think for a moment about what you truly experience in your relationships. In which relationships do you experience commitment? Your most committed relationship may not be with your sexual partner. Are your sexual feelings really limited to your sexual partner only? What kind and degree of intimacy do you experience in your relationships? Your most intimate relationship may or may not be with the person who shares your bed. Do you have friendships with an element of sensuality? Friendships with a clear feeling of commitment? Former lovers that you are occasionally sexual with? A relationship that is physically intimate but not emotionally intimate? One that is physically intimate but not sexually intimate? Let the reality of each relationship, rather than its name, speak to you.

What language do you want that is still unavailable to you? I wish I had a way to describe the closeness that I feel with some family members, but not others, that contains an element of friendship and a level of commitment that is more than a blood tie. I want a way to talk about the tender intimacy of taking care of another person, and a way to make a distinction between the closeness of physical caretaking and the closeness of emotional caretaking. I want to be able to say something about the body comfort, the familiarity, that develops in some friendships, in some relationships with housemates, but not in others. I wish I had language for the slight sexual buzz that I often feel with friends, a correlate of safety and emotional closeness, that does not necessarily imply a wish to develop a sexual relationship. I'd like language for commitment in friendship and for the variety of ways that I can depend on the people closest to me. I want to be able to speak about levels of emotional intimacy, about knowing and being known in relationship.

What do you want in relationship patterns? In your own life, you can probably already identify several patterns, one or two of which may already not quite fit the accepted definitions. What would you want to say about your relationships if you had the language to do so? Imagine what relationship patterns you might develop if you did not even think in terms of definitions. Imagine what you might say about your relationships if your language was generated from your own experience. Then make a relational commitment that is not socially endorsed. Tell someone else the truth about your experience of intimacy. Take a step toward a relationship revolution.

So, what is a "Boston marriage" anyway

Oliva M. Espin

I HAVE READ the manuscript of this book several times before sitting down to write about my own thoughts on the topic. As I read and re-read the theoretical articles, the personal narratives, and the reactions to the manuscript, I had a range of responses that focus on different points that the manuscript addresses. What follows is my attempt to make some sense out of my varied and sometimes contradictory thoughts on the personal narratives contained in this book and on the concept of the Boston marriage itself.

First of all, I am delighted that the issue of romantic nonsexual relationships among lesbians is coming to light in a positive way. The lesbian experience is as varied as the lesbian population, and this book addresses one aspect of this experience that is seldom discussed except in negative terms such as "bed death." I think the ideas and stories contained in this book will provide relief and peace of mind to some couples who may be wondering why they are so happy with each other when supposedly their lack of sex is proof that something is wrong between them.

It is true that lesbians are presented with the need to create "markers" that define "lesbian relationships" as different from "just friendships." It is also true that society is so imbued with male-defined concepts of sexuality, that the importance and significance of genital/sexual contact in lesbian relationships may be inflated. On the one hand, I believe that it is perfectly possible for human beings to live happy lives without being sexually active. On the other hand, I do not want to lose sight of the fact that the active genital/sexual contact that two women engage in for each other, not for a man's benefit, is a powerful statement that only active lesbian sexuality can make. Aside from whatever pleasure these women may derive from their sexual activity, their pleasuring each other is a powerful political statement. Lesbian sex is a statement about the value of women's bodies and sexual feelings in spite of and against prescriptions about women's bodies and their sexual feelings created by patriarchal notions of what sexuality should be. It is in being sexual without a man that lesbians actively state that men are not needed, that "women need men as much as fish need bicycles." Lesbian sexuality is a statement that women's sexuality is valuable in itself, without patriarchal definitions.

Having said that, I quickly want to add that I have experienced and believe in the possibility of intense, meaningful, nonsexual relationships between women that are much more than "just friendships." By this I do not mean that friendships are not valuable or even essential. All I am trying to do is differentiate between friendships, no matter how essential for survival, and a deep life commitment or long-term partnership in which the participants recognize themselves and are recognized by others as "more than friends."

When I read the personal narratives contained in this book, I have a sense that the stories presented reflect two fundamentally different types of relationships. There are stories in which the narrator or narrators describe a willing partnership in which genital sex does not seem to be an essential component and in which participants describe themselves as being fairly satisfied with such an arrangement. There are other stories, however, in which it seems clear that one partner is suffering a great deal, feels rejected and abandoned — in other words, is not a willing participant in a nonsexual partnership. I hesitate to call this latter experience a Boston marriage.

Perhaps it is hard to define a Boston marriage beyond the self-definition provided by people who tell their story in this book. However, I have some difficulty assuming that any lesbian who has been rejected by a woman who defines herself as heterosexual, or by a partner who chooses to become involved with some other woman, is in a relationship that can be considered a Boston marriage. I understand that historically a Boston marriage implied some form of partnership, not just an instance of unrequited love. This distinction between a willing nonsexual partnership versus individual feelings not shared by the other person seems to fit what I believe to be the definition of a 19th-century Boston marriage. But we must keep in mind that we do not know what "really happened" between the women in 19th-century Boston marriages.

In the last years of the 20th century, I believe that not having sex can be fine and perfectly healthy for a lesbian couple, but I also believe that it can indeed be a sign of a troubled relationship or of no relationship at all.

I know that because many women have been so hurt sexually as children, it is possible for them to love deeply while not being able or willing to engage in genital sex. If both women understand the weight of the past, or the need to focus on other aspects of their relationship, I believe this is a valid and healthy alternative for a lesbian couple. On the other hand, if one of the partners is feeling rejected, and moreover, the rejecting partner may be involved in a sexual relationship with somebody else, it is hard for me to see how this could be a Boston marriage as opposed to just another relationship in trouble. Are we not stretching the concept by assuming that these two people are involved in a Boston marriage?

To complicate matters further, in a culture characterized by rampant homophobia, it is unclear whether the women refusing to be sexual are just responding to the negative impact of homophobia or to their own needs and desires. Although it is extremely difficult for most women to be fully in touch with their own sexual needs and desires, whatever they might be, women who cannot even acknowledge being in love with another woman are often even less in touch with those needs and desires. It may be that, for some of the women described in these narratives, it is less threatening to believe that because they are not having genital sex with a woman, they are not lesbian. But can they be considered to have a Boston marriage? Some of the women who tell us their stories in these pages speak of the pain of rejection and the pain of not having been acknowledged as partners. Were not the 19th-century partners in the original Boston marriages willing to acknowledge their love for each other even if not expressed genitally?

The difficulty in recognizing a healthy relationship between women, regardless of how much sex takes place between them, is compounded by the fact that "true" female sexuality, lesbian or not, is an elusive concept in a patriarchal context. However, and precisely because of that, it is all too easy for women to believe themselves to be on high moral ground when they are not being actively sexual. Ironically, the myth about the moral superiority of women based on their supposed asexuality, so prevalent in the 19th century, is still alive among women who are trying to rescue female sexuality from patriarchal myths. The danger of seeing the absence of genital sex as unhealthy with the concomitant questioning of the health of a relationship, could be too easily substituted by not exploring the possibility that the lack of sex could be an indicator of conflict either individual or relational. We may too often have seen the lack of genital sex among partners as unhealthy, as some of the chapter authors tell us. Perhaps we have focused too much on genital sex as the defining factor in lesbian relationships. And yet, I believe that questioning why two women in a committed relationship choose not to have sex continues to be appropriate in some cases. I believe that we need to strike a healthy balance between our acceptance or rejection of the validity of a decision to have or not have sex because women choose to have or not to have sexual contact for both healthy and unhealthy reasons.

After all, how do we know that all the women involved in the original Boston marriages of the last century were indeed nonsexual. To the contrary, I have difficulty believing there were no women sexually attracted and sexually involved with each other in the 19th century. Indeed, I suspect that Victorian morality did not exist unchanged before Victoria and her era. Then, as now, I am sure some women who loved each other deeply expressed that love sexually and some did not, regardless of what they called themselves and their relationships.

I would be curious to know if the partners of the women whose narratives are included in this book would consider themselves to be in a partnership with the narrator, regardless of the term used to describe it. If one of the women thinks she is in a partnership, and the other one denies it, are they? Is the one denying it a victim of her own homophobia or other personal issues? Is she refusing to acknowledge the true nature of their relationship? Or is the woman who believes she is in a partnership just living an illusion? How can we acknowledge the silencing and the concomitant pain experienced by some of the narrators who felt rejected and unacknowledged as partners by women they deeply loved? How do we accept the reality and the experience of the women who would not or could not see themselves in a relationship with another woman?

To continue my struggle with terms and definitions, I want to focus on the concept of celibacy. I was struck by the idea of equating celibacy with aloneness. Perhaps because I have lived most of my life in places where this idea does not hold true, I suspect there is something related to cultural values in this equation. The perception of aloneness and of "the capacity to be alone" as virtues always impresses me as culturally centered. In a cultural context in which nuclear families and couples are seen as the most important connections and relationships, it is possible to equate celibacy with being alone. In most of the world, however, celibate individuals are not alone. They live their lives surrounded by extended family, communities, and lifelong friends. These people constitute a warm, protective network that provides the celibate person with relief from the pressure to engage in sexual relationships. In these cultural contexts, the absence of sexual relationships throughout adult life, except in the context of heterosexual marriage, may be perceived as a proof of virtue rather than abnormality.

Because of this network of relatives and friends, the need to seek a sexual partner, or to engage in a sexual partnership in order to have some companionship, is less pronounced. Heterosexual marriage in these contexts has more to do with reproduction than with companionship. However, this warm, protective network tends to be rather intrusive, and it interferes with any sort of sexual relationship not officially sanctioned by society. In this context, it is both easier and more necessary for women to be part of lifelong nonsexual relationships. Like the Victorian women of the proverbial Boston marriage, these women and their network do not understand their deep connection as sexual. Their partnership, in fact, is seen as a proof that they are "decent" women, not engaged in sex outside of marriage (which, of course, is understood to mean heterosexual sex).

Even though in modern-day Latin America, for example, there are women who live as lesbians and are indeed sexual with each other, some of these women's partnerships are looked upon by their network of family and friends as nothing but friendship (i.e., "*amigas intimas*"), and accepted without question. On the other hand, were their sexual contact known, they would be the subject of prejudice and pressure by these networks of friends and relatives. At the other end of the spectrum are women who, although sharing "intimacy" all their lives, have not been sexual with each other, and find themselves in Boston marriages.

As I read this manuscript and wrote these remarks, I remembered innumerable examples of these partnerships that I witnessed while growing up. I remembered, for example, a nun in a school in which I taught about 25 years ago in Latin America who was visited daily by a woman friend. This nun and her friend spoke for hours every day in the visiting parlor of the convent. Since all doors to the parlor were open wide and since her friend was not allowed in the cloister and nuns could not leave the convent unaccompanied, I am quite sure that these two women were never sexual with each other. However, it was very clear that for many years, these two women were each other's most important relationship. They spent endless hours together and would constantly refer to each other when talking to other people. Even then, it was very clear to me (and, I should add, to some of the other nuns who were rather jealous of this relationship) that this was not mere "friendship." Eventually, this nun was transferred to another country. Rumor had it that this relationship had played a major part in her superior's decision to transfer her. Since then, I have had several opportunities to observe this kind of Boston marriage between nuns and lay women in several other Latin American countries.

Another example I witnessed is that of single aunts so common in Latin American families, whose "intimate" women friends were always invited to family gatherings. These women were usually active in religious organizations, and I can assert with reasonable assurance that they were never sexual with each other. They would not have forgiven themselves and would have avoided each other as objects of temptation (or "occasions of sin") if that were the case. Yet, they saw each other every day and also spent endless hours talking to each other in front of relatives, yet distant enough from them so their conversation could not be overheard. These women were indeed celibate, but rarely alone.

To summarize, what I am trying to say is that although there are women who consider themselves lesbians and are actively sexual with each other everywhere in the world, there are also some cultures and societies that are more accepting and encouraging of Boston marriages than others. I am also trying to say that the experience of a loving partnership with or without genital sex can be a positive one for women. But too many contradictions and pains, both individual and relational, might be glossed over by idealizing the relationship as a Boston marriage.

I realize that there are many possible responses to my comments, and furthermore, I realize that I do not have answers to my own questions. I do not think this book intends to give answers, so I do not feel obliged to create my own. Both the authors of the commentaries and the narrators of personal experience leave me with thoughts and questions. I feel privileged to have had the opportunity to engage in this conversation about a topic seldom addressed in positive terms in the lesbian community in this country.

Notes on contributors

The authors not included here preferred to remain anonymous.

KATHLEEN A. BREHONY, PH.D., is a clinical psychologist in private practice in Virginia Beach, Virginia, where she focuses on issues relevant to women. She served for seven years on the editorial board of *Women and Therapy*.

LAURA S. BROWN, PH.D., is a clinical psychologist in private practice in Seattle, Washington, and clinical professor of psychology at the University of Washington. She has written extensively on lesbian psychology, feminist therapy theory and ethics, and assessment and diagnosis from a feminist perspective. She was a 1987 winner of the Association for Women in Psychology Distinguished Publication Award.

MARIE A. CINI, M.S., is completing her doctorate in social psychology at the University of Pittsburgh. Her research interests include lesbian courtship and relationship development and small group processes. She has presented her critique of heterosexual bias in relationship theory at the Association for Women in Psychology conferences.

ELLEN COLE, PH.D., is certified as a sex educator and sex therapist by the American Association of Sex Educators, Counselors, and Therapists. She is a psychologist and director of the Master of Arts Program at Prescott College, Prescott, Arizona.

OLIVA M. ESPIN, PH.D., is professor of women's studies at San Diego State University, where she teaches and researches the psychology of women from a variety of cultural backgrounds.

LILLIAN FADERMAN, PH.D., is author of *Surpassing the Love of Men* and *Odd Girls and Twilight Lovers: A History of Lesbian Life in Twentieth Century America.* She is professor of English at California State University-Fresno and general editor of the book series *Between Men/Between Women* for Columbia University Press.

As a lover, friend, and therapist of lesbians, MARNY HALL, PH.D., has been traveling among worlds of intimacy for twenty-five years. Lesbian relationships have been the subject of her professional work, her research (both formal and informal), and her writing. She has contributed articles to several anthologies and is currently working on a book entitled *Why Limit Me to Ecstasy? A New Map of Lesbian Intimacies.* Marny is also the author of *The Lavender Couch: A Consumer Guide to Psychotherapy for Lesbians and Gay Men.*

MARCIA HILL, ED.D., is a psychologist and feminist therapist in private practice in Montpelier, Vermont. She is the current chair of the Feminist Therapy Institute and is on the editorial board of *Women and Therapy.* She is in at least one nontraditional relationship and has been annoyed for years at people's assumptions about her relationships.

JOANN LOULAN is a lesbian mother, psychotherapist, writer, and public speaker in Portola Valley, California.

LESLIE RAYMER is a regular ol' lesbian gal of European American descent. She lives happily in Indiana. ("Yes, it's conservative, but I bought a big, nice house on 3 acres for $45,000 . . . orchard, barns, the whole bit!") She enjoys her work at a lesbian-managed sports complex; her current passions are teaching women's studies, writing, activism, and the romance of being with her family every day.

SUZANNA ROSE, PH.D., is associate professor of psychology and women's studies at the University of Missouri-St. Louis. She also is founder and director of the St. Louis Lesbian and Gay Research Project, which conducts research on lesbian and gay relationships and sexuality, hate crimes and victimization, and AIDS.

ESTHER D. ROTHBLUM, PH.D., is a professor in the Department of Psychology at the University of Vermont, where she is currently University Scholar. She received the Distinguished Publication Award of the Association for Women in Psychology in 1987 and the Distinguished Scientific Contribution Award, Division 44 of the American Psychological Association, in 1992.

DEBRA H. ZAND, M.A., is completing her doctorate in clinical psychology at the University of Missouri-St. Louis and is an instructor in the women's studies program. She also is a member of the St. Louis Lesbian and Gay Research Project team. Her research focuses on lesbian relationship development and therapist sexual misconduct.